Roma Migrants in the European Union

This book situates Roma mobility as a critical vantage point for migration studies in Europe, focusing on questions about Europe, 'European-ness', and 'EU-ropean' citizenship through the critical lens of Roma racialisation, marginalisation, securitisation, and criminalisation, and the dynamics of Roma mobility within and across the space of 'Europe'.

Enabled primarily through ethnographic research with diverse Roma communities across the heterogeneous geography of 'Europe', the contributions to this collection are concerned with the larger politics of mobility as a constitutive feature of the socio-political formation of the EU. Foregrounding the experiences and perspectives of Roma living and working outside of their nation-states of 'origin' or ostensible citizenship, the book seeks to elucidate wider inequalities and hierarchies at stake in the ongoing (re-)racialisation of both Roma migrants and migrants in general.

Showcasing political, economic, legal, and socio-historical criticism, this book will be of interest to those studying race and racialisation in Europe, mobility and migration into and within Europe, and those studying the mobility of the Roma people in particular. This book was originally published as a special issue of the *Social Identities* journal.

Can Yıldız is a Ph.D. student in the Department of Geography at King's College London, UK. Her current doctoral research, provisionally titled "The Roma Spectacle: Foreignness, Racialisation, and Mobility among Roma Women in and out of a London Prison," examines the British criminal justice system from the vantage point of eastern European Roma women who serve time in prison for committing petty offences such as pickpocketing and shoplifting.

Nicholas De Genova is a scholar of migration, borders, race, citizenship, and labor. He holds an appointment as Professor and Chair of the Department of Comparative Cultural Studies at the University of Houston, USA. He is the author or editor of several books, including *The Borders of "Europe": Autonomy of Migration, Tactics of Bordering* (2017).

Roma Migrants in the European Union
Un/Free Mobility

Edited by
Can Yıldız and Nicholas De Genova

LONDON AND NEW YORK

First published 2020
by Routledge
2 Park Square, Milton Park, Abingdon, Oxon, OX14 4RN

and by Routledge
605 Third Avenue, New York, NY 10017

First issued in paperback 2020

Routledge is an imprint of the Taylor & Francis Group, an informa business

Introduction, Chapters 3–5 © 2020 Taylor & Francis
Chapter 1 © 2018 Huub van Baar. Originally published as Open Access.
Chapter 2 © 2017 Angéla Kóczé. Originally published as Open Access.
Chapter 6 © 2017 Ioana Vrăbiescu and Barak Kalir. Originally published as Open Access.

With the exception of Chapters 1, 2 and 6, no part of this book may be reprinted or reproduced or utilised in any form or by any electronic, mechanical, or other means, now known or hereafter invented, including photocopying and recording, or in any information storage or retrieval system, without permission in writing from the publishers. For details on the rights for Chapters 1, 2 and 6, please see the chapters' Open Access footnotes.

All rights reserved. No part of this book may be reprinted or reproduced or utilised in any form or by any electronic, mechanical, or other means, now known or hereafter invented, including photocopying and recording, or in any information storage or retrieval system, without permission in writing from the publishers.

Trademark notice: Product or corporate names may be trademarks or registered trademarks, and are used only for identification and explanation without intent to infringe.

British Library Cataloguing in Publication Data
A catalogue record for this book is available from the British Library

Typeset in Myriad Pro
by Newgen Publishing UK

Publisher's Note
The publisher accepts responsibility for any inconsistencies that may have arisen during the conversion of this book from journal articles to book chapters, namely the inclusion of journal terminology.

Disclaimer
Every effort has been made to contact copyright holders for their permission to reprint material in this book. The publishers would be grateful to hear from any copyright holder who is not here acknowledged and will undertake to rectify any errors or omissions in future editions of this book.

ISBN 13: 978-0-367-72736-9 (pbk)
ISBN 13: 978-0-367-33487-1 (hbk)

Printed in the United Kingdom
by Henry Ling Limited

Contents

Citation Information	vi
Notes on Contributors	viii
Introduction – Un/Free mobility: Roma migrants in the European Union *Can Yıldız and Nicholas De Genova*	1
1 Contained mobility and the racialization of poverty in Europe: the Roma at the development–security nexus *Huub van Baar*	18
2 Race, migration and neoliberalism: distorted notions of Romani migration in European public discourses *Angéla Kóczé*	35
3 Challenging Europe's external borders and internal boundaries: Bosnian *Xoraxané Xomá* on the move in Roman peripheries and the contemporary European Union *Marco Solimene*	50
4 In and out from the European margins: reshuffling mobilities and legal statuses of Romani minorities between the Post-Yugoslav space and the European Union *Julija Sardelić*	65
5 On the threshold: becoming Romanian Roma, everyday racism and residency rights in transition *Rachel Humphris*	81
6 Care-full failure: how auxiliary assistance to poor Roma migrant women in Spain compounds marginalization *Ioana Vrăbiescu and Barak Kalir*	96
Index	109

Citation Information

The chapters in this book were originally published in the journal *Social Identities*, volume 24, issue 4 (July 2018). When citing this material, please use the original page numbering for each article, as follows:

Introduction
Un/Free mobility: Roma migrants in the European Union
Can Yıldız and Nicholas De Genova
Social Identities, volume 24, issue 4 (July 2018) pp. 425–441

Chapter 1
Contained mobility and the racialization of poverty in Europe: the Roma at the development–security nexus
Huub van Baar
Social Identities, volume 24, issue 4 (July 2018) pp. 442–458

Chapter 2
Race, migration and neoliberalism: distorted notions of Romani migration in European public discourses
Angéla Kóczé
Social Identities, volume 24, issue 4 (July 2018) pp. 459–473

Chapter 3
Challenging Europe's external borders and internal boundaries. Bosnian Xoraxané Xomá on the move in Roman peripheries and the contemporary European Union
Marco Solimene
Social Identities, volume 24, issue 4 (July 2018) pp. 474–488

Chapter 4
In and out from the European margins: reshuffling mobilities and legal statuses of Romani minorities between the Post-Yugoslav space and the European Union
Julija Sardelić
Social Identities, volume 24, issue 4 (July 2018) pp. 489–504

Chapter 5
On the threshold: becoming Romanian Roma, everyday racism and residency rights in transition
Rachel Humphris
Social Identities, volume 24, issue 4 (July 2018) pp. 505–519

Chapter 6
Care-full failure: how auxiliary assistance to poor Roma migrant women in Spain compounds marginalization
Ioana Vrăbiescu and Barak Kalir
Social Identities, volume 24, issue 4 (July 2018) pp. 520–532

For any permission-related enquiries please visit:
  www.tandfonline.com/page/help/permissions

Notes on Contributors

Nicholas De Genova is a scholar of migration, borders, race, citizenship, and labor. He holds an appointment as Professor and Chair of the Department of Comparative Cultural Studies at the University of Houston, USA. He is the author or editor of several books, including *The Borders of "Europe": Autonomy of Migration, Tactics of Bordering* (2017).

Rachel Humphris is a Lecturer in Sociology and Politics at Queen Mary University of London, UK. Her research interests include migration, urbanization, globalization, citizenship, race/ethnicity, gender, and qualitative methods.

Barak Kalir is an Associate Professor in the Department of Anthropology, and the Co-Director of the Institute for Migration and Ethnic Studies (IMES), in the Faculty of Social and Behavioral Sciences at the University of Amsterdam, the Netherlands. His research interests include deportation, national belonging, and the interface between legality and illegality in the social dynamics that shape human mobility across (state) borders.

Angéla Kóczé is Assistant Professor of Romani Studies and Academic Director of the Roma Graduate Preparation Program at the Central European University, Hungary. Her research focuses on the intersections between gender, ethnicity, and class, as well as the social and legal inequalities faced by the Roma in various European counties.

Julija Sardelić is a Marie Skłodowska-Curie Postdoctoral Fellow at the KU Leuven International and European Studies Institute (LINES), Belgium. Her research encompasses broader themes of citizenship and migration, but she particularly focuses on the position of marginalized minorities and migrants in Europe (such as Romani minorities, refugees and other forced migrants, and legally invisible and stateless persons). From July 2019, Julija will be a Lecturer at the Political Science and International Relations Department, Victoria University of Wellington.

Marco Solimene is a Postdoctoral Researcher and Lecturer in the Department of Anthropology at the University of Iceland. He investigates conceptualizations and practices of mobility among Roma families in Rome.

Huub van Baar is an Assistant Professor of Political Theory at the Institute of Political Science at Justus Liebig University Giessen, Germany; a Senior Research Fellow at the Amsterdam Centre for Globalisation Studies at the University of Amsterdam, the

Netherlands; and an affiliated researcher of the Amsterdam Centre for European Studies, the Netherlands.

Ioana Vrăbiescu is a Postdoctoral Researcher in the Department of Anthropology at the University of Amsterdam, the Netherlands. She holds a PhD in Political Science and has an academic background in gender studies and international relations. Her research focuses on the workings of state, policing mobility and borders, as well as on the intersectional analyses applied to citizenship dynamics.

Can Yıldız is a Ph.D. student in the Department of Geography at King's College London, UK. Her current doctoral research, provisionally titled "The Roma Spectacle: Foreignness, Racialisation, and Mobility among Roma Women in and out of a London Prison," examines the British criminal justice system from the vantage point of eastern European Roma women who serve time in prison for committing petty offences such as pickpocketing and shoplifting.

Introduction – Un/Free mobility
Roma migrants in the European Union

Can Yıldız and Nicholas De Genova

ABSTRACT
This special issue showcases work that theorises and critiques the political, economic, legal, and socio-historical ('ethnic' or 'cultural') subordination of the European Roma (so-called 'Gypsies'), from the specific critical vantage point of Roma migrants living and working within and across the space of the European Union (EU). Enabled primarily through ethnographic research with diverse Roma communities across the heterogeneous geography of 'Europe', the contributions to this collection are likewise concerned with the larger *politics of mobility* as a constitutive feature of the sociopolitical formation of the EU. Foregrounding the experiences and perspectives of Roma living and working outside of their nation-states of 'origin' or ostensible citizenship, we seek to elucidate wider inequalities and hierarchies at stake in the ongoing (re-)racialisation of Roma migrants, in particular, and imposed upon migrants, generally. Thus, this special issue situates Roma mobility as a critical vantage point for migration studies in Europe. Furthermore, this volume shifts the focus conventionally directed at the academic objectification of 'the Roma' as such, and instead seeks to foreground and underscore questions about 'Europe', 'European'-ness, and EU-ropean citizenship that come into sharper focus through the critical lens of Roma racialisation, marginalisation, securitisation, and criminalisation, and the dynamics of Roma mobility within and across the space of 'Europe'. In this way, this collection contributes new research and expands critical interdisciplinary dialogue at the intersections of Romani studies, ethnic and racial studies, migration studies, political and urban geography, social anthropology, development studies, postcolonial studies, and European studies.

Central to our approach in this special issue is a desire to re-situate questions of Roma mobility, and the consequently fluid and contradictory sociopolitical dynamics of Roma racial subordination, at the heart of any critical enquiry regarding 'Europe'. Roma mobility is particularly central to questions concerning EU-ropean citizenship, the borders of EU-rope, the so-called 'migrant crisis' in Europe, and the rise of far-right, anti-immigrant racist populism across the space of Europe. That is to say, rather than fetishise research about 'the Roma' as such, as an essentialised 'ethnic group' to be studied in isolation, we insist that there can be literally no adequate investigation into the very meanings of 'Europeanness' or the politics of 'European' identity in the presumably wider field of

European studies that does not situate these questions of Roma racialisation and subjugation at its centre. In this regard, we also intend for our collective intervention to unsettle the regrettable scholarly status quo within Romani studies, which has long been so woefully polarised between rigid orthodoxies preoccupied, on the one hand, with verifying or validating the presumed 'objectivity', 'authenticity', and essentialised integrity of Romani 'culture' and 'ethnicity' or, alternately, with more sociological or political-economic approaches that emphasise the socio-economic subordination of the Roma in stubborn disregard for the cultural politics of racism. As a result, there has been an ossified binary opposition between essentialist and positivistic accounts that fetishise Roma identity, 'culture', and 'ethnicity', on the one hand, and those that deny outright the importance of race/ethnicity and the salience of Roma 'ethnic' identity on the other. The contributions to this special issue advance the existing debates in the field of Romani studies by aspiring to supersede this analytical double-bind. Thus, while we are not interested in disputing the empirical reality of Roma 'culture', we focus instead on the historically specific processes implicated in the production, reproduction, and transformation of these enduring coordinates of Roma identity and foreground processes of minoritisation – and more precisely, racialisation, securitisation, and criminalisation – to directly underscore the processes that reify 'the Roma'. Such processes of reification inform both the affirmative recognition as well as the derogatory stereotyping or derisive disregard of the 'group' identity/ies of various Roma communities across Europe. By foregrounding more synthetic, constructivist, critical approaches to Roma racialisation, in ethnographically sensitive relation to the historical specificities of contemporary trans-European dynamics of Roma mobilities across an uneven sociopolitical geography, this volume hopes to make a productive intervention into what has been a rather stalled debate.

How does it feel to be a (European) problem?

The pioneering African American intellectual W.E.B. Du Bois famously articulated the ever-unasked question posed implicitly to Black Americans: 'How does it feel to be a problem?' (1903/2007, p. 7). Surely, from centuries of enslavement in premodern Romania (Achim, 2004; Beck 1989) through their genocidal extermination in the Nazi Holocaust (Zimmermann, 1996), the diverse groups of people variously denigrated as 'Gypsies' have long been comparably sociopolitically produced as a racial 'problem' of and for Europe. Yet, the post-Cold War integration of Europe and the consolidation of the European Union (EU) have fundamentally reconfigured the juridico-political institutional framework in which 'European' political questions and 'problems' are formulated. Consequently, Huub van Baar (2011a), among other scholars, has incisively discerned a political and juridical process of *Europeanisation* with regard to the social condition of minoritised Roma communities, particularly in the wake of (eastward) EU enlargement and the extension of EU citizenship. Indeed, even the ever more established normativity and ubiquity of the very label 'Roma' – as a generic name for heterogeneous (multilingual, pluri-national, multi-cultural) minoritised communities variously calling themselves Rom, Roma, Vlach Roma, Romany, Xomá, Sinti, Ashkali, Bayash, Kalé, Manouches, Gitanos, 'Egyptian', Gypsies, etc. – is an effect of this larger process of EU institutionalisation (cf. Guild & Carrera, 2013; Sigona & Trehan, 2009; Simhandl, 2006; van Baar, 2011a; Vrăbiescu, 2014).

In a memorable turn of phrase, which strikingly recalls to mind the DuBoisian analogy, Nando Sigona and Peter Vermeersch declare, '[The Roma's] problems have become "European problems"' (2012, p. 1190). Sigona and Vermeersch underscore the extent to which 'many Roma still belong to the poorest, most segregated, most discriminated against and least "integrated" populations in Europe, and their chances for socio-economic mobility continue to be extremely low' (2012, p. 1189). Consequently, alluding to what van Baar (this volume; cf. 2011a) has designated to be 'the security-development nexus', Sigona and Vermeersch note that European policy debates regarding the government of the Roma have been endemically polarised between appeals for 'social inclusion', the improvement of 'minority rights', and measures to counteract discrimination, at one end of the spectrum, and calls for 'security' and the control of Roma mobility and migration, on the other. Thus, violent histories of racist discrimination and 'exclusion' have long been interwoven, in fact, with various formations of (subordinate) 'inclusion' (Sigona, 2011; van Baar, 2011b). Little surprise, then, that despite the fact that various European nation-states and EU authorities have devoted significant resources in recent years to eradicating the persistence of anti-Roma discrimination with campaigns to 'integrate' their Roma 'minorities' and 'improve' their material living conditions, Roma people (as minoritised communities) remain among the 'least integrated' and most persecuted (racialised) 'populations' in Europe! (cf. Jocanovic, 2015; also see van Baar, 2017; Vrăbiescu & Kalir, 2017). That 'the Roma' should be deemed the object of one or another policy intervention aimed at either the presumed 'improvement' of their sociopolitical status and condition or, alternately, the object of various securitarian measures designed to enhance their subjection to governmental authority and policing, however, merely reveals anew the extent to which 'the Roma' as such have been produced as a premier 'problem' for state power in Europe. To the extent that 'their problems have become "European problems"', therefore, it seems incontrovertible that Roma people themselves – as members of a racialised (and racially subordinate) social category or ostensible 'group' (no matter how heterogeneous and amorphous) – have merely been re-fashioned as the 'problem'; indeed, they have acceded to the status of a truly 'European' – which is to say, EU-ropean – 'problem'.

We must ask, however, are not the Roma's problems precisely the problems intrinsic to the sociopolitical racial order of Europe itself? Hence, we may go further and also posit that 'Europe' as such similarly emerges as a new kind of problem – first and foremost, for Roma people themselves, but also for critical inquiry and politically engaged theoretical reflection (see also De Genova, 2016).

One predictable strategy among diverse Roma communities for remedying the pernicious and enduring obstacles to their (upward) socio-economic mobility has been recourse to spatial (geographical) mobility, notably facilitated by EU citizenship, particularly the ostensible 'freedom of movement' and the putative 'right to residence' in other EU member states (cf. Aradau, Huysmans, Macioti, & Squire, 2013; Çağlar & Mehling, 2009; Guild & Carrera, 2013), which have been celebrated as distinguishing features of this citizenship. Of course, these migratory dynamics have never been contained exclusively within the parameters of the EU as such, but rather exceed the space and boundaries of the EU to encompass the uneven 'postsocialist' geography of an extended (eastern) 'Europe', where Roma people (as minoritised communities) quite consistently came out the 'losers' of the various tumultuous neoliberal capitalist and neo-nationalist transitions (Bhabha, 1999; Fekete, 2016; Sardelić, 2015; Stewart, 2012; see also Sardelić, 2017;

Solimene, 2017). Hence, the contemporary re-racialisation of 'the Roma' across Europe is inseparable from their emergence over the last two decades as a premier, if often neglected, exemplar of new formations of trans-European cross-border mobility – which is to say, the contemporary configuration of their racialisation is increasingly inextricable form their status as 'migrants'.

Étienne Balibar suggests importantly that the (re-)racialisation of 'the Roma' at the European scale can only be adequately understood alongside the experiences of non-European migrants within 'the general framework of ... the emerging *European apartheid*, the dark side of the emergence of a "European citizenship"'. Consequently, in Balibar's reflections, Roma have emerged as a crucial 'test case' for the hypothesis regarding a new '"European" racism' that has accompanied EU-ropean unification (Balibar, 2009, pp. 2–3; emphasis in original). The stakes of this ongoing process of re-racialisation of the European Roma, of course, concern their prospective disqualification from the very equation of 'European'-ness itself, in a larger process of re-stabilising 'European' identity – as a (postcolonial) formation of racial whiteness (De Genova, 2016; see also Vajda, 2015; Vrăbiescu, 2014). Balibar notes that the scapegoating of minoritised Roma communities reflects the incomplete and 'suspended' Europeanisation of the EU member states themselves, which remain mutually distrustful and resentful; for them, therefore:

> The Roma are like a *nation in excess* in Europe, which is singled out for hate not only because it is spread across borders, but because it incarnates the archetype of a *stateless people*, resisting the norms of territorialisation and cultural normalisation (all the more ironic given that, in many respects, this singularity is itself the result of persecutions). (2009, p. 4; emphases in original)

What Balibar seems to imply but does not say explicitly, however, is that – for these very reasons – Roma may arguably be characterised as *more* 'European' than any of the ostensibly 'official' (normative) 'national' identities. In effect, minoritised Roma communities – so consistently repudiated by and disqualified from each nation-state's nationalist project (cf. Agarin, 2014; Bancroft, 2001; Fekete, 2014; Rövid, 2011; Surdu & Kovats, 2015; Vermeersch, 2012), and so systematically deprived of the most elementary entitlements of their putative citizenship (Sigona, 2009; Tóth, 2013; Bhabha, 2017) – inhabit a virtually stateless condition that epitomises one kind of (potentially) supra-national formation that can be understood to approximate the EU-ropean ideal itself (De Genova, n.d.-b). In any case, the very substantial pan-European transnationality of the Roma directly challenges the conceits and destabilises the presuppositions of any nationalism.

In this respect, the notion of Roma as a 'nation in excess' seems counter-productive, as it would appear to merely recapitulate and expose the conceptual poverty of any normative lexicon trapped within methodologically nationalist premises. Such methodological nationalism is operative whether a 'people' is exalted as a 'nation' or, alternately, disqualified from 'nationhood' and reductively relegated to the status of a (sub-national) 'ethnic group'. After all, it is only in a 'Europe' imagined as a community of 'nations' that the ever-repudiated Roma are pressed to approximate the status of a 'nation' which could potentially be recognised as an equal alongside the rest. This of course is not to deny the validity of an insurgent Roma nationalist project as one sort of oppositional politics within the EU-ropean framework, but only to underscore that such a project would be predictably beleaguered, both intellectually and pragmatically, by all of the territorial fetishism and cultural essentialism that has distinguished every other nationalism. While critically aligned with various Roma projects of self-determination, therefore, we must nevertheless remain sceptical about the plausibility of any nationalism for a genuinely radical emancipatory politics.

We must nonetheless be cautious as well about liberal gestures upholding the 'European' identity or status of Roma people, inasmuch as the official designation of 'the Roma' as Europe's 'largest ethnic minority' (see, e.g. European Commission, 2010, 2011, 2012; cf. Guglielmo & Waters, 2005; McGarry, 2011) already confirms a kind of reluctant Europeanisation. Whereas every European 'national' identity could only ever represent a numerical minority within the larger formation of a unified and singular 'Europe' – such that EU-rope itself might otherwise be best imagined as a kind of league of minorities – 'the Roma', who actually *outnumber* several presumable 'nationalities' (such as 'the Danes' or 'the Portuguese'), are depicted as one of Europe's 'minorities', while those who can uphold and enforce their 'national' status with state power are presumed to be part of the legitimate (genuinely 'European') 'majority'. Indeed, by way of comparison, it would be unthinkable to propose the absurdity of Asia's or Africa's 'largest ethnic minority'. Leaving unstated but implicit the normative racial presumption of who exactly can be counted as Europe's 'ethnic majority', then, this (re-)minoritising gesture (now, on the scale of 'Europe') enfolds Roma communities within 'Europe', but re-inscribes them as a singular (homogenised, monolithic) 'ethnic' alterity that is finally 'European' only inasmuch as it is constructed as effectively *non*-European: they are figured as inextricably *in* Europe, but never truly *of* 'Europe', and thus, always vexingly 'out of place'. Indeed, we are never informed of which groups are supposed to be the second or third largest in this debased category of European 'minorities', and in this sense, it is specifically (and perhaps exclusively) 'the Roma' who are branded with this special status of 'European minority'. Our contention, therefore, is that a critical interrogation of Roma experiences of, and perspectives on, how it feels to be socially and politically *produced* as a 'problem' within the context of the contemporary EU will provide a vital critical resource for problematising 'Europe' itself.

Furthermore, the invocation of the 'European minority' category implicitly raises the concomitant spectre of 'non-European' minorities, and subtly aligns 'the Roma' with their 'non-European' counterparts, thereby implicitly disqualifying Roma people from their proper place within Europe. Such correlations both recapitulate the fundamental ideological equation of racial difference with foreignness, and hence with migration (De Genova, 2010), on the one hand, while also rendering 'the Roma' anew as presumed 'nomads', such that the contemporary migration or refugee movements of Roma are made to appear to be but the latest iteration of a perpetual and intrinsic nomadism (De Genova, n.d.-b; Drakakis-Smith, 2007; Hepworth, 2012, 2014, 2015; van Baar, 2011b). Assertions within Romani studies that 'despite a long history of settlement and co-existence, Roma remain the quintessential migrant group' (Guglielmo & Waters, 2005, p. 763) tend to recapitulate long-entrenched habits of presumptively treating Roma as the ever-unassimilated progeny of 'non-European' ancestors, and thus risk uncritically re-inscribing the perpetual (racialised) 'foreignness' of minoritised Roma communities that they may otherwise seek to critique. Moreover, it is noteworthy that racist anti-immigrant discourse in Europe increasingly affiliates the Roma with various other racialised figures of 'alien' menace. Take, for instance, the contention of prominent French right-wing television and radio commentator and columnist Éric Zemmour that the barbarian pillage of

Europe following the fall of the Roman Empire is being re-enacted today by 'thieving violent gangs of Chechens, Romas, Kosovars, North Africans, and Africans' (Lichfield, 2014). There is evidently an ideological nexus of 'non-European'-ness that increasingly conjoins the figures of 'Roma' with 'migrant' with 'Muslim' with 'terrorist' with 'criminal' with racialised Blackness (De Genova, 2016, n.d.-a).

Particularly amidst the proliferating discourses of 'migrant crisis' and refugee 'emergencies' that have wracked European public culture and political debate since 2015 (De Genova, n.d.-a; New Keywords Collective, 2016), we must be attuned to the persistent circulation of multifarious insinuations equating a more generic 'migration problem' in EUrope with the racialised phantasm of veritable invasions of destitute Roma – transposed as the criminalising spectacle of Roma beggars and thieves – across the wealthier precincts of the EU (Yıldız & Humphris, n.d). This was indeed a major (albeit euphemised) sub-text in the political discourse that culminated in the campaign for Britain to leave the EU, known as Brexit (see, e.g. Mintchev, 2014; Richardson, 2014). The channelling of hostility toward 'migration' (in general) against EU-citizen 'migrants', and those originating from (postsocialist) 'Eastern European' EU member states in particular, into a politically focused antagonism toward Britain's membership in the EU was the defining political signature of the UK Independence Party (UKIP), and became the hallmark of the pro-Brexit campaign. Not only did this involve an insidious elision of working-class 'Eastern European' migrants with the more specific abjection of (often homeless) Roma migrants, it has actually entailed a very calculated and manifold degradation of the EU citizenship of both British and non-British alike. EU nationals who understood their juridical status not as that of 'migrants' but rather as that of EU-ropean citizens enacting their rights to 'mobility' are now exposed to the uncertainty and precarity of migranthood: they do not know how long they may be permitted to stay and work or what their entitlements will be. Analogously, British EU citizens who have hitherto been able to travel, work, and reside across the EU will come under new restrictions, as yet unknown. In effect, all have been newly 'migrant'-ised (Bhambra, 2016). Without flattening the substantial differences and inequalities among these variegated shades of migranthood, Brexit has forced a wide cross-section of British residents to contemplate how it feels to be a (European) problem. These recent developments again remind us that anti-Roma racism, far from a residual artefact of times gone by or merely an involuted 'local' peculiarity of the eastern European countries, is a potent and viral fermenting agent in the toxic cocktail of anti-immigrant nativism and racism throughout Europe today.

The Roma as a racial formation

To adequately theorise anti-Roma racism, however, and in the interests of advancing an adequately anti-racist scholarship, we need recourse to the analytic category of *race*. More precisely, for present purposes, we must be able to account for the specific historical and sociopolitical circumstances by which 'the Roma' come to be produced (and reproduced) as a distinctly racialised 'group'. Confronted with the pervasive post-Holocaust/ postcolonial evasion of any frank engagement with race that David Theo Goldberg (2006, 2009, pp. 151–198) has aptly characterised as 'racial Europeanism', we are consequently left to contend with the peculiarly European paradox of an ostensible anti-racism without race, whereby the very category of 'race' is repudiated and presumptively disallowed as *race-ist*. In other words, by failing to uphold a critical analytical category of race, and thus, a theory of racism as the historically specific sociopolitical production of historically mutable racial distinctions and meanings, any purported anti-racist politics will tend to amount to a merely liberal politics of anti-discrimination. In its very refusal to interrogate these processes and struggles of racialisation, such an anaemic anti-racism re-stabilizes the notion that racism is little more than prejudice and a discriminatory hostility toward phenotypic and anatomical differences, and thus re-naturalizes the anachronistic notion of race as 'biology'. This peril is not averted, however, through the simple disavowal of biological racism in favour of an explanation of sociopolitical inequalities and hierarchies on the basis of 'cultural' difference.

Seemingly endemic tendencies toward essentialising and homogenising 'Roma' identities have been debated in the field of Romani studies during much of the last 20 years or more (Tremlett, 2009), and have been effectively inseparable from the ambivalent politics of labelling that inevitably entangle the designation of 'the Roma' as a culturally distinct 'ethnic group' with the dominant and pervasive sociopolitical identification of that 'group' with a 'problem' (Tremlett & McGarry, 2013). In this special issue, we are concerned to contribute toward the vital task of accounting for the historical specificity of contemporary sociopolitical dynamics of Roma subjugation, marginalisation, securitisation, and criminalisation within the EU, while nonetheless resisting the common temptation to reinscribe these processes of producing and reproducing the subordination of 'the Roma' within a culturalist narrative of Roma particularity. In short, we seek to conceptualise Roma conditions, experiences, and perspectives in a manner that refuses to reproduce what Wim Willems has memorably depicted as 'splendid isolation' (1997, pp. 305–306). Dominant representations have produced 'the Roma' as an isolated and reified 'object of study', whereby Roma people (as reified minoritised 'communities') appear to be self-contained, hermetically sealed, and so radically different from everyone else that it becomes virtually impossible to recognise them as participants within wider social formations of migration or migrant networks, racialised 'minority' social formations, class formations of labour or precarity, urban neighbourhoods or trans-local socio-spatial formations, or any other modes of meaningful social belonging (Durst, 2010; Kaneva & Popescu, 2014; Ladányi & Szelényi, 2001; Simhandl, 2006). Roma seem to be always exquisitely alone, irreducibly separate and distinct, and by implication, their sociopolitical marginalisation comes to appear as the inevitable effect of their own intrinsic ('ethnic') singularity, if not their putative ('cultural') 'incorrigibility' (Fekete, 2014; van Baar, 2012; see also Kóczé, 2017; Solimene, 2017). Hence, the fetishisation of Roma 'difference' seems as intractable as ever (Pusca, 2010, 2016, pp. 113–115).

From the critical standpoint of interrogating the historical and ongoing sociopolitical *production* and reproduction of the Roma as a fetishised figure of European alterity, however, we must recognise that such *culturalist* discourses of Roma 'difference' – whether such difference is construed to be 'cultural' or 'ethnic' – have always been inextricable from the larger forces of their *racial* subordination. The persistent and pervasive construction of a monolithic and homogenised 'Roma' identity has conventionally been predicated upon a muddled notion of 'cultural' particularity, apparently transmitted through the ages, within a presumed context of shared ancestry and common kinship. In this manner, the notion of 'ethnicity' – grounded always in the putative existence of an 'ethnic group', such as 'the Roma' – appears to conjoin cultural particularity with genealogy, thereby re-stabilising the pseudo-biological foundations for the very 'group'-ness of the ostensible group. As a result, we are left with the essentialist notion of a discrete, enduringly well-defined, bounded group that perpetually reproduces itself, rather than a historically specific account of the sociopolitical conditions and forces contributing to the production of that group as such. Thus, the sociopolitical subjugation of the Roma that has systematically reinforced the segregation and exclusion of various minoritised Roma communities routinely serves to reinscribe their ostensible distinctness, and thus appears to verify the persistence of some sort of 'cultural' essence. Consequently, one fundamentally misguided strategy for combatting anti-Roma racism has been a repeated commitment to the detection of precisely such an identifiable Roma 'essence', the recognition of such a unique Roma identity, and the affirmation of such a bounded and distinct Roma 'culture'. Yet, while particular Roma communities of course inevitably and indisputably have their own customs and cultural practices, and may indeed feel a genuine affinity for one another despite their differences, these sorts of culturalist obsessions about Roma specificity and distinction tend to divert our intellectual focus and critical scrutiny away from the sociopolitical and legal orders in which that 'difference' has been enduringly inscribed as a figure of pathologised otherness, and historically castigated as an object of alternating strategies of more or less brutal marginalisation or coercive assimilation.

Here, we seek to emphasise the fundamental conceptual incoherence and political disutility of the very concept of 'ethnicity', in favour of a forthright and critical focus on race and racialisation. By pretending to somehow bridge the conventional divide between 'culture' – what people *do* – and 'race' (understood uncritically as 'biology' or 'natural' inheritance) – what people *are* – the concept of 'ethnicity' effectively reinstates precisely that defining binary and thereby re-stabilizes the naturalisation of 'race'. Given minoritised Roma communities' tremendous diversity, itself produced historically in a variety of specific and discrepant relations to divergent imperial and national formations, 'the Roma' notoriously cannot satisfy any rigid schematic definition of what is presumed to 'objectively' constitute an 'ethnic group'. Of course, the Roma are not alone in this predicament, as this would likewise be true for virtually every other ostensible 'ethnicity'. There is inevitably substantial heterogeneity within any and all sociopolitical formations of 'race', 'ethnicity', 'culture', or 'nation'. We do not propose to undermine the integrity of Roma identity through this critique but only to expose the utter insufficiency of the very notion of 'ethnicity' as an interpretive and analytical rubric for adequately theorising the Roma condition and formulating a rigorously anti-racist intellectual position. Indeed, the customarily positivistic (pseudo-objective) and essentialist sorts of criteria for 'ethnic group' membership – much like those for 'nationhood' or 'Europeanness' – have always tended to contribute only increased incoherence to the task of stipulating what exactly constitutes the integrity of 'Roma' as a *sociopolitical* category, and thereby has served to undermine the prospect of adequately identifying and naming the Roma condition. Here, it is instructive to contemplate the remark of one of the ethnographic interlocutors in the research of Ioana Vrăbiescu (2016, p. 199): 'Only after I was evicted, thrown out into the street with my baby, did I realize that I am Roma.'

What finally constitutes 'Roma' (or its numerous equivalents) as a relatively durable and enduring sociopolitical category – in short, as the label for a kind of identifiable 'group' that can now be routinely designated as 'the Roma' (despite what has often been a radical instability of Roma ascription and self-identification) – is precisely the shared

(*European*) historicity of anti-'Gypsy' *racial* subjugation and the manifold and discrepant forms of Roma anti-racist resistance and self-determination. In other words, much as the people who have come to be known as 'Roma' in fact comprise a great multiplicity of distinct communities, with discrepant histories as well as multiple and complex linguistic and cultural characteristics – indeed, whether they themselves do or do not identify as 'Roma' – it is only possible to analyse and theorise the substantive shared features of their sociopolitical condition in Europe with recourse to a conceptual framework that can name their historical production and reproduction *as a racial formation*. It ought to be clear but deserves to be explicitly and emphatically re-affirmed that this proposition in no way upholds any anachronistic notion of 'race' as a 'natural' (quasi-biological, pseudo-objective) fact of genealogy. The pernicious power of racial distinction operates precisely through the *naturalisation* of social and political inequalities as putatively 'natural' (quasi-biological) differences derived from common kinship and shared ancestry, but 'race' is no fact of nature. Rather, race is a fact of sociopolitical domination – particularly the historically specific hierarchies of social power, wealth, and prestige enforced on a global scale through the violent and oppressive regimes of white supremacy that originated in 'European' projects of conquest, dispossession, enslavement, and colonial rule – as well as histories of insubordination, anti-racist resistance, and self-determination. Hence, rather than any simplistic and inevitably over-generalised homogeneity based on either shared 'culture' or 'biology', what truly constitutes 'the Roma' as such – as a distinct and enduring *sociopolitically* constituted 'group' – is a shared (European) historicity, which is never exclusively reducible to racialised (anti-'Gypsy') subjugation and the anti-racist struggles of minoritised Roma communities, but neither is it ever separable from these. Beyond shared historical experiences, however, the ongoing contemporary sociopolitical processes and struggles of Roma racialisation can only be adequately comprehended by investigating the practices of abjection, marginalisation, and criminalisation to which these particular racialised bodies, persons, and collectivities are subjected within and across the variegated and contradictory space of EU-rope in the twenty-first century, including the variety of forms of government deployed to discipline and subdue Roma mobilities.

Mobility, free, and unfree

If the Roma have long been subjected to various apparatuses for their production as one or another variety of European 'problem', the contemporary sociopolitical and juridical institutionalisation of the EU nevertheless supplies a substantially new framework for the government of 'the Roma' as a specifically EU-ropean 'problem' (Riedner, Álvarez-Velasco, De Genova, Tazzioli, & van Baar, 2016; Simhandl, 2006; van Baar, 2011a). This is true for minoritised Roma communities across the space of EU-rope. Nonetheless, the production of the Roma as a EU-ropean 'problem' has manifested itself with particular force with respect to the cross-border mobilities of Roma *as migrants*.

After all, 'mobility' itself has been promoted as a defining feature and a signature achievement of European integration. The 'free movement' of people is upheld as one of the EU's fundamental principles. European Commission directive 2004/38 outlines the principle of a putative 'right' of all EU citizens to reside and work in any EU member state for up to three months without any restrictive conditions. As Claudia Aradau and her colleagues explain:

> Mobility is here no longer simply an economic opportunity and a vehicle of economic integration between states. Neither is it limited to individuals enacting rights of free movement. Rather, it creates the conditions for demanding a European polity that is defined by European citizens with a common status and identity. Thus, the individual freedom of movement of different EU citizens is scaled up to a collective conception of mobility as fostering European identity. Claiming European citizenship through free movement integrates the claimant into a project of creating a political Europe. (Aradau et al., 2013, p. 141)

Thus, whether or not one invests the notion of 'European citizenship' with any emancipatory hopes, 'European'-ness is posited as a supranational identity that is literally created through transnational mobility, and a citizenship that purports to be genuinely 'European' truly requires cross-border movement as a condition for its very possibility. In this regard, 'mobility' has become an equivocal figure inseparable from the sociopolitical project of EU-ropean integration itself (Riedner et al., 2016).

Through the criminalising and securitising lens (Nacu, 2012; Project on Ethnic Relations, 1999; Simoni, 2011; van Baar, 2014) of welfare protectionism and ghettoisation (Picker, Greenfields, & Smith, 2015; van Baar, 2012; see also Humphris, 2017; Vrăbiescu & Kalir, 2017), however, 'free movement' is configured as a distinctly neoliberal project (see Kóczé, 2017; van Baar, 2017). Following an initial three-month period of unregulated residence, mobile EU citizens are subject to the following conditions: (1) Registration with the relevant (nation-state) authorities; and (2) Whereas those who are formally employed or self-employed are not required to meet any other conditions, individuals not continuously working for wages or a regular salary, (including students and retirees) 'must have sufficient resources for themselves and their family, so as not to be a burden on the host country's social assistance system, and comprehensive sickness insurance cover' (EUR-lex, 2015). Despite the requirement to not be an economic 'burden' to the host state, however, the directive specifies that 'under no circumstances may an expulsion decision be taken on economic grounds' (European Parliament, 2009; cited in Hepworth, 2015, p. 103). Nonetheless, as Kate Hepworth (2015, pp. 104–105) highlights in her study of the predicaments of Roma migrants in Italy, Roma migrants often cross nation-state borders by informal means, such as private minibus services, and therefore are unable to produce any official record of their arrival. This 'irregular' status as mobile EU citizens, coupled with their lack of access to 'acceptable' housing, consequently exposes them to expulsion from their chosen destination countries (see Humphris, 2017; Kóczé, 2017; Solimene, 2017; Vrăbiescu & Kalir, 2017). Similarly, in many western European countries, Roma migrants are often only offered jobs informally as day-labour in construction, cleaning, and care work, whether contracted independently or through labour recruitment agencies, and are customarily paid well below the legal minimum wage and supplied no official record of employment (Craig, 2011; Grill, 2015; Oates, 2009; Ryder & Cemlyn, 2014). Thus, in Europe's most glamorous globalised cities, such as London, Paris, Berlin, and Milan, Roma migrants are routinely engaged in onerous, low-paid, often unsafe jobs during the day, while not uncommonly finding themselves homeless by night, often sleeping outdoors or in makeshift camps (Clough-Marinaro & Daniele, 2011; Çağlar & Mehling, 2009; FRA, 2014; Vermeersch, 2011; see also Solimene, 2017).

The hegemonic EU-ropean political ideal of 'free movement' thus becomes riddled with 'a free movement across countries that is defined by social and security excesses and an imperative to contain them ... [reconfiguring] free movement from an opportunity into a series of dangers' (Aradau et al., 2013, p. 138). The mobility of Europe's working poor, and particularly of Roma, transmutes the 'free movement' of presumably self-governing and 'responsible' *individuals* into a 'problem' perceived to be always a matter of unruly *collectivities* – (racial) formations of 'group' mobility – and thus, is presented as 'a question of categorising those who can be legitimately mobile and those whose mobility needs to be restricted on grounds of security' (Aradau et al., 2013, p. 138; see also Solimene, 2017; van Baar, 2017). Hence, the abjection of the 'undesirable' mobility of Roma 'citizens' reveals a constitutive contradiction within the larger EU-ropean project. Repeatedly and persistently, 'the Roma' paradoxically emerge as a 'problem' precisely *because* of their EU citizenship and the consequent requirement for EU member states to circumvent or subvert EU law in order to render Roma migrants 'irregular' and deportable (Çağlar & Mehling, 2013, p. 173).

Indeed, it is fair to say that Roma people have been perennially (and inordinately) burdened by the pernicious ascription of racialising and criminalising stigma to their mobility. Here, we are reminded of all the notorious constructions of 'Gypsies' as 'nomads', and the well-worn apparatus of suspicion and derision that has conventionally shadowed this allegedly unsettled condition that seems to ensue from the unsettling but purportedly intrinsic mobility of the Roma themselves. However, contemporary EU-ropean (statist) constructions of Roma 'nomadism' not only signal the most entrenched expressions of methodological and political sedentarism (Malkki, 1995), but also have routinely served as the desultory alibis for campaigns of evictions and deportations, and thus, a protracted strategy of state-enforced mobility for the Roma (Clough-Marinaro & Daniele, 2011; De Genova, n.d.-b; Fekete, 2014; Hepworth, 2012; Nacu, 2012; see also Humphris, 2017; Kóczé, 2017; Solimene, 2017). Here, of course, it is imperative to also note the productivity of both sporadic pogroms and systematic violence perpetrated by racist mobs or neo-fascist gangs that complement and exacerbate the handiwork of the police (Clark & Rice, 2012; Fekete, 2016; Mirga, 2009). Hence, Roma communities have been widely subjected to statist as well as extra-state strategies of both coercive immobilisation (through segregated ghettoisation and encampment) (see Sardelić, 2017) and forced mobilisation (through various forms of expulsion and displacement) (see Solimene, 2017; van Baar, 2017).

The deportation of EU-national Roma migrants across the internal borders of the EU exposes the operations of hierarchical sociopolitical orders of race, class, and gender within an ostensibly egalitarian and universalistic citizenship regime (see Humphris, 2017; Kóczé, 2017; Vrăbiescu & Kalir, 2017). Roma deportability and *evictability* (van Baar, 2016) have consequently been premier features of what Hepworth has incisively characterised as precisely their *abject* (EU-ropean) *citizenship* (2012, 2014, 2015). Moreover, as Liz Fekete incisively argues, in the face of the newly reanimated 'pan-European racism' against them, minoritised Roma communities can only encounter 'Europe' as something approximating 'a huge open prison' (2014, p. 68). Thus, from the vantage point of Roma and other poor migrants, EU-rope is a contradictory space in and across which their putative 'right' to 'free movement' as ostensible EU-ropean citizens is inextricably ensnared with the disciplinary enforcement of their more fundamental sociopolitical *un*-freedom, even as their autonomous subjectivities and their free mobility remain genuinely constitutive of a more basic dialectic of Roma/migrant struggle for space and freedom within and across 'Europe'.

In the context of official ideologies dedicated to reaffirming the spectral figure of Roma nomadism (Hepworth, 2015; Sigona, 2010; van Baar, 2011b; see also Kóczé, 2017; Solimene, 2017) and subjecting Roma mobilities to various strategies of securitisation (see van Baar, 2017), it is therefore all the more crucial to nonetheless discern and foreground the autonomous subjective dynamics of Roma mobility as practices of collective self-determination and even resistance to the sociopolitical orders that they desert by migrating (see Solimene, 2017), in some instances even formally seeking asylum as refugees fleeing these regimes of discrimination and violence (see Sardelić, 2017). It is indeed the renewed problematisation of the Roma *as migrants* – their production and representation as a precisely 'European problem' of indisciplined and disruptive mobility – that has emerged in recent years as the premier manifestation of their (re-)racialisation. In the securitising EU-ropean framework of Roma migrants' emphatically unwelcome mobility, we are concerned therefore to inquire into how indeed their migratory trajectories may be apprehensible nonetheless as veritable *appropriations* of mobility, and thus as autonomous enactments of their elementary freedom of movement.

The combination of requirements and restrictions on 'free movement' imposed by the EU and member states, replete with their specific dynamics of racialisation and abject citizenship for Roma people, taken together with the autonomy of Roma migration, epitomises a kind of cross-border movement within and across the space of 'Europe' that we designate here to be *un/free mobility*. Importantly, the un/free mobility of Roma migrants is neither purely free nor strictly unfree, but rather emerges through the contradictions of autonomy and control as these operate in tandem in a more expansive process of re-bordering EU-rope and re-racialising what may be apprehensible as 'citizenship', 'belonging', or 'membership' within the distinct 'national' welfare regimes of the EU's member states (see Humphris, 2017; Vrăbiescu & Kalir, 2017). EU citizenship offers neither a perfect free-for-all of rights to mobility nor a completely restrictive regime of controlled movement. Rather, through the complex modulations of un/free mobility, 'free' and 'unfree' signal the co-existence and co-constitution of discrepant sociopolitical and legal statuses upheld simultaneously within a single but variegated citizenship regime. Hence, the complicity between a EU-ropean 'right' of free movement with multiple securitised apparatuses dedicated to undermining the freedom of Roma migrants reveals a toxic symbiosis by which 'migrant' workers, including mobile EU citizens, are systematically stripped of employment 'rights' and social welfare entitlements achieved historically through centuries of labour struggle.

The abject sociopolitical condition of Roma migrants, so exquisitely shaped by this delicate balance of free/unfree movement, has been evidently produced through their racialisation as 'Europeans' with a difference. In this respect, however, the Roma predicament – and above all, their differential (subordinate) *inclusion* as un/free labour within the larger neoliberal sociopolitical regime of the EU – signals a more fundamental and far-reaching erosion of citizenship in Europe, more generally. The social formations of un/free mobility epitomised by Roma migrants instructively elucidate analogous mobilities among other 'groups' or categories of migrants within and across the space of 'Europe', and the criminalisation and policing of Roma comes to serve as an experimental laboratory for the policing of other subordinate racial 'minorities' and other impoverished citizens (as well as non-citizen migrants). Traversing the nested and contradictory regimes of citizenship and migrant legality and illegality, these formations of un/free mobility are differentially subjected to the invidious juridical frameworks which produce the unstable grounds for unequal living and working conditions, and thus substantiate and sustain differences and divisions through which various categories of migrants may be manipulated against one another as well as non-migrant ('native') citizens (Fox, 2013; Fox, Moroşanu, & Szilassy, 2012; Grill, 2012a, 2012b). The fragmentations of un/free mobility and differential citizenship, then, supply some of the decisive conditions of possibility for labour subordination, precarity, and social marginalisation as well as the often fragmentary forms of resistance. Yet, within and across these agonistic differences and antagonistic divisions, there nonetheless arise new possibilities for unforeseen formations of affinity, affect, identification, coalescence, and community.

This special issue reflects the cutting-edge work of scholars whose research on Roma mobilities in the space of the EU makes an important contribution toward placing the marginalisation of the Roma at the veritable centre not only of 'minority' questions in racial and ethnic studies, in general, but also at the very heart of migration and mobility studies in the European context. Research related to the historical and sociopolitical particularities of minoritised Roma communities is indispensable for migration and border studies in the European context as well as for the critical study of race and ethnicity in any context, yet there can be no adequate Roma-focused research that is not also thoroughly engaged in the debates in these other fields. The persistent and counter-productive re-entrenchment of the 'splendid isolation' of Roma studies is plainly an intellectual and, more importantly, a political dead-end. Together with other prominent examples of racially subordinate identities, such as Black, Muslim, 'refugee', 'migrant', 'asylum-seeker', 'foreign', and 'of migrant background', among others, the Roma are politically imagined as a permanent figure of alterity for 'Europe' – an iconic European Other – and thus charged with carrying the ideological and social burden of sustaining and re-stabilising a hegemonic 'European' identity that can remain meaningful, relevant, and valuable to its presumptive (self-)authorised bearers. Furthermore, to the extent that the question of 'Europe' has itself become inextricable from the always tacitly racialised questions of migration, this special issue situates the experiences and perspectives of 'the Roma' – as migrants – as a decisive critical lever with which to pry open what we may call the 'European' Question (De Genova, 2016). In short, there can be no truly critical inquiry under the titular heading of 'European studies' that does not recognise the historical predicament and enduring sociopolitical condition of minoritised Roma communities to be central and constitutive of any and all things 'European'.

Disclosure statement

No potential conflict of interest was reported by the authors.

References

Achim, V. (2004). *Roma in Romanian history*. Budapest: CEU Press.
Agarin, T. (2014). Travelling without moving? Limits of European governance for Roma inclusion. *Ethnicities*, *14*(6), 737–755.

Aradau, C., Huysmans, J., Macioti, P. G., & Squire, V. (2013). Mobility interrogating free movement? Roma acts of European citizenship. In E. Isin & M. Saward (Eds.), *Enacting European citizenship* (pp. 132–154). Cambridge: Cambridge University Press.

Balibar, É. (2009). Foreword. In N. Sigona & N. Trehan (Eds.), *Roma politics in contemporary Europe: Poverty, ethnic mobilisation and the neoliberal order* (pp. viii–xiii). London: Palgrave MacMillan.

Bancroft, A. (2001). Closed spaces, restricted places: Marginalisation of Roma in Europe. *Space and Polity, 5*(2), 145–157.

Beck, S. (1989). Origins of gypsy slavery in Romania. *Dialectical Anthropology, 14*, 53–61.

Bhabha, J. (1999). Belonging in Europe, citizenship and post-national rights. *International Social Science Journal, Blackwell Publishing, 51*(159), 11–23.

Bhabha, J. (2017). The politics of evidence: Roma citizenship deficits in Europe. In B. N. Lawrance & J. Stevens (Eds.), *Citizenship in question: Evidentiary birthright and statelessness* (pp. 43–59). Durham: Duke University Press.

Bhambra, G. K. (2016, December 8). Brexit, the commonwealth, and exclusionary citizenship. *OpenDemocracy*. Retrieved from https://www.opendemocracy.net/gurminder-k-bhambra/brexit-commonwealth-and-exclusionary-citizenship

Çağlar, A., & Mehling, S. (2009). *The Roma and the Third Country Nationals enacting EU Citizenship in Berlin: Desiring the undesirable and the politicisation of the judical sites*. Enacting European Citizenship (ENACT), European Union's Seventh Framework Programme. Retrieved from http://www.enacting-citizenship.eu/index.php/global/download/deliverables/WP5D53.pdf/

Çağlar, A., & Mehling, S. (2013). Sites and scales of the Law: Third-country nationals and EU Roma citizens. In E. Isin & M. Saward (Eds.), *Enacting European citizenship* (pp. 155–177). Cambridge: Cambridge University Press.

Clark, C., & Rice, G. (2012). Spaces of hate, places of hope: The Roman Roma in Belfast. In M. Stewart (Ed.), *The gypsy 'menace': populism and the New anti-gypsy politics* (pp. 167–190). London: Hurst.

Clough-Marinaro, I., & Daniele, U. (2011). Roma and humanitarianism in the eternal city. *Journal of Modern Italian Studies, 16*(5), 621–636.

Craig, G. (2011). *United Kingdom – Promoting social inclusion of Roma: A study of National Policies*. European Commission DG Employment, Social Affairs and Inclusion. Retrieved from http://www.york.ac.uk/inst/spru/research/pdf/Roma2011.pdf

De Genova, N. (2010). Migration and race in Europe: The trans-Atlantic metastases of a post-colonial cancer. *European Journal of Social Theory, 13*(3), 405–419.

De Genova, N. (2016). The European question: Migration, race, and postcoloniality in Europe. *Social Text, 128*, 75–102.

De Genova, N. (n.d.-a). The 'Migrant Crisis' as racial crisis: Do 'Black Lives Matter' in Europe? In *Ethnic and Racial Studies*.

De Genova, N. (n.d.-b). The securitisation of Roma mobilities and the re-bordering of Europe. In H. van Baar, A. Ivasiuc & R. Kreide (Eds.), *The politics of security: Understanding and challenging the securitization of Europe's Roma* (under review). London: Palgrave Macmillan.

Drakakis-Smith, A. (2007). Nomadism a moving myth? Policies of exclusion and the gypsy/traveller response. *Mobilities, 2*(3), 463–487.

Du Bois, W. E. B. (1903/2007). *The souls of black folk*. New York: Oxford University Press.

Durst, J. (2010). 'What makes us gypsies, who knows … ?!': Ethnicity and reproduction. In M. Stewart & M. Rövid (Eds.), *Multi-disciplinary approaches to Romany studies* (pp. 13–34). Budapest: Central European University Press.

Eurlex. (2015). *EU freedom of movement and residence*. Retrieved from http://eur-lex.europa.eu/legal-content/EN/TXT/?uri=URISERV%3Al33152

European Commission. (2010). *The social and economic integration of the Roma. (online)*. Brussels: European Union. Retrieved from http://eur-lex.europa.eu/legal-content/en/ALL/?uri=CELEX:52010DC0133

European Commission. (2011). *An EU framework for national Roma integration strategies up to 2020*. (Online). Brussels: European Union. Retrieved from http://ec.europa.eu/justice/policies/discrimination/docs/com_2011_173_en.pdf

European Commission. (2012). *What works for Roma inclusion in the EU. Policies and model approaches*. (Online). Brussels: European Union. Retrieved from http://ec.europa.eu/justice/discrimination/files/whatworksfor_romainclusion_en.pdf
European Parliament. (2009). *Right of Union citizens and their family members to move and reside freely within the territory of the Member States*. (online). Retrieved from http://europa.eu/legislation_summaries/education_training_youth/lifelong_learning/133152_en.htm
Fekete, L. (2014). Europe against the Roma. *Race & Class, 55*(3), 60–70.
Fekete, L. (2016). Hungary: Power, punishment and the 'Christian-national idea'. *Race &Class, 57*(4), 39–53.
Fox, J. E. (2013). The uses of racism: Whitewashing new Europeans in the UK. *Ethnic and Racial Studies, 36*(11), 1871–1889.
Fox, J. E., Moroşanu, L., & Szilassy, E. (2012). The racialisation of the new European migration to the UK. *Sociology, 46*(4), 680–695.
FRA. (2014). *Poverty and employment: The situation of Roma in 11 EU member states*. Luxemburg: Publications Office of the European Union. Retrieved from http://fra.europa.eu/sites/default/files/fra-2014-roma-survey-employment_en.pdf
Goldberg, D. T. (2006). Racial Europeanization. *Ethnic and Racial Studies, 29*(2), 331–364.
Goldberg, D. T. (2009). *The threat of race: Reflections on racial neoliberalism*. Malden, MA: Wiley-Blackwell.
Grill, J. (2012a). "'It's building up to something and it won't Be nice when it erupts': Making of Roma migrants in a 'multicultural' Scottish neighborhood". *Focaal: Journal of Global and Historical Anthropology, 62*, 42–54.
Grill, J. (2012b). 'Going up to England': Exploring mobilities among Roma from Eastern Slovakia. *Journal of Ethnic and Migration Studies, 38*(8), 1269–1287.
Grill, J. (2015). 'Endured labour' and 'fixing up' money: The economic strategies of Roma migrants in Slovakia and the UK. In M. Brazzabeni, M. I. Cunha, & M. Fotta (Eds.), *Gypsy economy* (pp. 88–106). New York, NY: Beghahn.
Guglielmo, R., & Waters, T. W. (2005). Migrating towards minority status: Shifting European policy towards Roma. *Journal of Common Market Studies, 43*(4), 763–785.
Guild, E., & Carrera, S. (2013). Introduction: International relations, citizenship and minority discrimination: Setting the scene. In D. Bigo, S. Carrera, & E. Guild (Eds.), *Foreigners, refugees or minorities? Rethinking people in the context of border controls and visas* (pp. 1–29). Farnham: Ashgate.
Hepworth, K. (2012). Abject citizens: Italian 'nomad emergencies' and the deportability of Romaan Roma. *Citizenship Studies, 16*(3-4), 431–449.
Hepworth, K. (2014). Encounters with the clandestino/a and the nomad: The emplaced and embodied constitution of (Non-)citizenship. *Citizenship Studies, 18*(1), 1–14.
Hepworth, K. (2015). *At the edges of citizenship: Security and the constitution of Non-citizen subjects*. Surrey: Ashgate.
Humphris, R. (2017). On the threshold: Becoming Romanian Roma, everyday racism and residency rights in transition. *Social Identities*. doi:10.1080/13504630.2017.1335831
Jocanovic, Z. (2015). *Why Europe's 'Roma Decade' didn't lead to inclusion*. Open Society Foundation. Retrieved from https://www.opensocietyfoundations.org/voices/why-europe-s-roma-decade-didn-t-lead-inclusion
Kaneva, N., & Popescu, D. (2014). "We are Romanian, not Roma": Nation branding and postsocialist discourses of alterity. *Communication, Culture & Critique, 7*(4), 506–523.
Kóczé, A. (2017). Race, migration and neoliberalism: Distorted notions of Romani migration in European public discourses. *Social Identities*. doi:10.1080/13504630.2017.1335827
Ladányi, J., & Szelényi, I. (2001). The social construction of Roma ethnicity in Bulgaria, Romania and Hungary during market transition. *Review of Sociology, 7*(2), 79–89.
Lichfield, J. (2014, December 21). Sacking of Islamophobic television presenter provokes free-speech row in France. *The Independent*. Retrieved from http://www.independent.co.uk/news/world/europe/sacking-of-islamophobic-television-presenter-provokes-freespeech-row-in-france-9939085.html

Malkki, L. (1995). Refugees and exile: From 'refugees studies' to the national order of things. *Annual Review of Anthropology, 24*, 495–523.

McGarry, A. (2011). The Roma voice in the European union: Between national belonging and transnational identity. *Social Movement Studies, 10*(3), 283–297.

Mintchev, N. (2014). *Logics of exclusion: Culture, economy and community in British anti-immigration discourses*. Retrieved from http://repository.essex.ac.uk/15356/1/Logics_of_Exclusion_Culture_Economy_and.pdf

Mirga, A. (2009). The extreme right and Roma and Sinti in Europe: A new phase in the use of hate speech and violence? *Roma Rights Journal, 1*, 5–9.

Nacu, A. (2012). From silent marginality to spotlight scapegoating? A brief case study of France's policy towards the Roma. *Journal of Ethnic and Migration Studies, 38*(8), 1323–1328.

New Keywords Collective. (2016). Europe/crisis: New keywords of 'the crisis' in and of 'Europe'. In N. De Genova & M. Tazzioli (Eds.), *Near futures online* (pp. 1–45). New York, NY: Zone Books. Retrieved from http://nearfuturesonline.org/europecrisis-new-keywords-of-crisis-in-and-of-europe/

Oates, A. (2009). *Gangmasters: A day in gangland*. Health and Safety at Work. Retrieved from http://www.healthandsafetyatwork.com/hsw/content/gangmasters-day-gangland

Picker, G., Greenfields, M., & Smith, D. (2015). 'Colonial reflections: The "gypsy camp" as a spatio-racial political technology'. *City, 19*(5), 741–752.

Project on Ethnic Relations. (1999, October 7–8). *Roma and the Law: Demythologizing the Gypsy Criminality Stereotype*. Report of a meeting held in Paris. Retrieved from http://www.per-usa.org/Reports/RomaandtheLaw00.pdf

Pusca, A. (2010). The 'Roma problem' in the EU. *Borderlands e-Journal, 9*(2), 1–17.

Pusca, A. (2016). *Post-Communist aesthetics: Revolutions, capitalism, violence*. Oxon: Routledge.

Richardson, J. (2014). Roma in the news: An examination of media and political discourse and what needs to change. *People, Place and Policy, 8*(1), 51–64.

Riedner, L., Álvarez-Velasco, S., De Genova, N., Tazzioli, M & van Baar, H. (2016). Mobility. In De Genova & M. Tazzioli (Eds.), *New keywords of 'the crisis' in and of 'Europe'. Near Futures Online* #1 (pp. 28–34). New York: Zone Books. Retrieved from http://nearfuturesonline.org/europecrisis-new-keywords-of-crisis-in-and-of-europe-part-6/

Rövid, M. (2011). One-size-fits all Roma? On the normative dilemma of the emerging European Roma policy. *Romani Studies, 21*(1), 1–22.

Ryder, A., & Cemlyn, S. (2014). *Civil society monitoring on the implementation of the national Roma integration strategy in the United Kingdom*. Budapest: Decade of Roma Inclusion Secretariat Foundation. Retrieved from http://www.birmingham.ac.uk/Documents/college-social-sciences/social-policy/iris/2014/UK-civil-society-monitoring-report-en-1.pdf

Sardelić, J. (2015). Roma minorities and uneven citizenship access in the post-Yugoslav space. *Ethnopolitics, 14*(2), 159–179.

Sardelić, J. (2017). In and out from the European margins: Reshuffling mobilities and legal statuses of Romani minorities between the Post-Yugoslav space and the European Union. *Social Identities*. doi:10.1080/13504630.2017.1335829

Sigona, N. (2009). "The 'Problema Nomadi' vis-à-vis the political participation of Roma and Sinti at the local level in Italy". In N. Sigona & N. Trehan (Eds.), *Roma politics in contemporary Europe: Poverty, ethnic mobilisation and the neoliberal order* (pp. 272–292). London: Palgrave MacMillan.

Sigona, N. (2010). 'Gypsies out of Italy!' social exclusion and racial discrimination of Roma and Sinti. In A. Mamone & G. A. Veltri (Eds.), *Italy today: The sick man of Europe* (pp. 143–157). Abington: Routledge, Taylor & Francis Group.

Sigona, N. (2011). Governance of Roma people in Italy: Discourse, policy and practice. *Journal of Modern Italian Studies, 16*(5), 590–606.

Sigona, N., & Trehan, N. (2009). Introduction: Roma politics in neoliberal Europe. In N. Sigona & N. Trehan (Eds.), *Roma politics in contemporary Europe: Poverty, ethnic mobilisation and the neoliberal order* (pp. 1–20). London: Palgrave MacMillan.

Sigona, N., & Vermeersch, P. (2012). Editors' introduction: The Roma in the New EU: Policies, frames and everyday experiences. *Journal of Ethnic and Migration Studies, 38*(8), 1189–1193.

Simhandl, K. (2006). 'Western gypsies and travellers' – 'Eastern Roma': The creation of political objects by the institutions of the European Union. *Nations and Nationalism*, *12*(1), 97–115.

Simoni, A. (2011). Roma and legal culture: Roots and Old and New faces of a complex equality issue. *European Anti-Discrimination Law Review*, (13), 11–19.

Solimene, M. (2017). Challenging Europe's external borders and internal boundaries. Bosnian *Xoraxané Xomá* on the move in Roman peripheries and the contemporary European Union. *Social Identities*. doi:10.1080/13504630.2017.1335828

Stewart, M. (2012). Populism, Roma and The European politics of cultural difference. In M. Stewart (Eds.), *The gypsy 'menace': Popularism and the new anti-gypsy politics* (pp. 3–23). London: Hurst.

Surdu, M., & Kovats, M. (2015). Roma identity as an expert-political construction. *Social Inclusion*, *3*(5), 5–18.

Tóth, J. (2013). Czech and Hungarian Roma exodus to Canada: How to distinguish between unbearable destitution and unbearable persecution. In D. Bigo, S. Carrera, & E. Guild (Eds.), *Foreigners, refugees or minorities? Rethinking people in the context of border controls and visas* (pp. 39–54). Farnham: Ashgate.

Tremlett, A. (2009). Bringing hybridity to heterogeneity in Roma studies. *Romani Studies*, *19*(2), 147–168.

Tremlett, A., & McGarry, A. (2013, January). *Challenges facing Researchers on Roma Minorities in contemporary Europe: Notes towards a Research Programme* (ECNI Working Paper, No. 62). Flensburg: European Centre for Minority Issues. Retrieved from http://www.ecmi.de/publications/detail/62-challenges-facing-researchers-on-roma-minorities-in-contemporary-europe-notes-towards-a-research-program-259/

Vajda, V. (2015, December 7). Towards 'Critical Whiteness' in Romani studies. *Roma Rights Journal #2*. Retrieved from http://www.errc.org/article/roma-rights-2-2015-nothing-about-us-without-us-roma-participation-in-policy-making-and-knowledge-production/4433/7

van Baar, H. (2011a). *The European Roma: Minority representation, memory, and the limits of transnational governmentality* (Ph.D. diss.). University of Amsterdam, Amsterdam.

van Baar, H. (2011b). Europe's Romaphobia: Problematization, securitization, nomadization. *Environment and Planning D: Society and Space*, *29*(2), 203–212.

van Baar, H. (2012). Socio-economic mobility and neo-liberal govermentality in post-socialist Europe: Activation and the dehumanisation of the Roma. *Journal of Ethnic and Migration Studies*, *38*(8), 1289–1304.

van Baar, H. (2014, December 3). The securitisation of gypsies, travellers and Roma in Europe: Context, critique, challenges. Keynote lecture delivered at New Scotland Yard, London, UK.

van Baar, H. (2016). Evictability and the biopolitical bordering of Europe. *Antipode*. doi:10.1111/anti.12260.

van Baar, H. (2017). Contained mobility and the racialization of poverty in Europe: The Roma at the development-security nexus. *Social Identities*. doi:10.1080/13504630.2017.1335826

Vermeersch, P. (2011). Roma and mobility in the European Union. In K. Pietarinen (Ed.), *Roma and traveller inclusion in Europe: Green questions and answers* (pp. 91–97). Brussels: Green European Foundation and Finnish Green Cultural and Educational Centre.

Vermeersch, P. (2012). Reframing the Roma: EU initiatives and the politics of reinterpretation. *Journal of Ethnic and Migration Studies*, *38*(8), 1195–1212.

Vrăbiescu, I. (2014). The subtlety of racism: From antiziganism to Romaphobia. In T. Agarin (Ed.), *When stereotype meets prejudice: Antiziganism in European societies* (pp. 143–170). Stuttgart: ibidem-Verlag.

Vrăbiescu, I. (2016). Evictions and voluntary returns in Barcelona and Bucharest: Practices of metropolitan governance. *Intersections: East European Journal of Society and Politics*, *2*(1), 199–218.

Vrăbiescu, I., & Kalir, B. (2017). Care-full failure: How auxiliary assistance to poor Roma migrant women in Spain compounds marginalization. *Social Identities*. doi:10.1080/13504630.2017.1335833

Willems, W. (1997). *In search of the true gypsy*. London: Frank Cass.

Yıldız, C., & Humphris, R. (n.d.). *De-valuable, disposable, deportable: Spatio-racial formations of homeless Roma migrants in Central London*. Unpublished manuscript.

Zimmermann, M. (1996). *Rassenutopie und Genozid: Die nationalsozialistische Losung der Zigeunerfrage*. Hamburg: Christians Verlag.

1 Contained mobility and the racialization of poverty in Europe
The Roma at the development–security nexus

Huub van Baar

ə OPEN ACCESS

ABSTRACT
This paper starts from the observation that, since the collapse of eastern European state socialism, the Roma have become the subject and target of Europe-wide development programs and discourses, while, at the same time, they have been problematized in terms of social, public and national security. Due to the ways in which development and security have ambiguously come together in Europe's recent history, I will argue that the living conditions of the poorest among the Roma have not only worsened, but also, and more fundamentally, the divide between Europe's rich and poor has become seriously racialized and almost unbridgeable. I explain how the *bio-* and *geo*political conditions under which development and security have merged in Europe's engagement with the Roma have led to a situation in which the official aim of Roma-related development programs – the improvement of their living conditions and life chances – tends to result in a deadlock.

Various scholars have argued that, when it comes to poverty and the conditions under which it can occur and be maintained, the boundaries between the Global South and the Global North have been radically blurred (Ferguson, 2006; Mezzadra, Reid, & Sammadar, 2013; Ong, 2006). Indeed, poverty and the conditions under which precarious life and labor are produced, maintained and reinforced have become an integral part of the Global North and the dynamics between the Global North and South. At the same time, others have argued that, due to the ways in which Western authorities, donors and international governing organizations (IGOs) approach the combatting of poverty through development, the situation of the global poor is not substantially changing, even worsening, particularly along the lines of an increasing division between the Global North and South that is partially based on discriminatory border regimes developed in the West (for the latter, see De Genova & Peutz, 2010; Jansen, de Bloois, & Celikates, 2015; New Keywords Collective, 2016; van Houtum, 2010).

Escobar (1995), for instance, has argued that postcolonial discourses and practices of development have contributed to the constructing of the 'Third World' and to the

---

CONTACT Huub van Baar ✉ huub.van.baar@uva.nl
© 2018 The Author(s). Published by Informa UK Limited, trading as Taylor & Francis Group
This is an Open Access article distributed under the terms of the Creative Commons Attribution-NonCommercial-NoDerivatives License (http://creativecommons.org/licenses/by-nc-nd/4.0/), which permits non-commercial re-use, distribution, and reproduction in any medium, provided the original work is properly cited, and is not altered, transformed, or built upon in any way.

maintaining of the conditions of its dependency on the 'First World'. Pogge (2010) has claimed that affluent states in the Global North have knowingly contributed to the maintenance of poverty, oppression and political and economic inequalities on a massive scale. Duffield (2010) has explored how the merging of security and development in governmentalizing approaches to poverty in and migration from the Global South has led to a radical life chances divide between the Global North and South.

Much less attention has been paid, though, to the ways in which practices of development and security articulated within the contested borders of post-1989 Europe have impacted on those who have become the target of 'intra-European' development programs, on Romani minorities particularly. I will argue that, due to the ways in which they have become the targets of discourses and practices of development and security, the viability of development programs has been seriously endangered, and poverty in Europe has been considerably racialized, resulting in a state of affairs that dramatically impacts on the prospects for Roma to escape poverty and societal isolation.

I will explain how, since the 1990s, the Roma have become the target of development and security practices and discourses, and how development and security have increasingly been merged in national and international governmental commitments to Europe's Roma. I will clarify that we cannot consider 'development' and 'security' as a-historical terms, because practices thereof and their interrelationships have significantly changed over time. Partially as a consequence of neoliberal practices of governing and how they are assembled with other governmental practices, we have seen a 'biopolitical turn' in the ways in which Roma-related development programs are articulated in Europe. Increasingly, policy discourses conceive and perceive development 'in terms of how life is to be supported and maintained, and how people are expected to live, rather than according to economic and state-based models' (Duffield, 2010, p. 53). Consequently, 'developmentalities' regarding the Roma tend to socially isolate particularly the poorest among them and contribute more to governing their poverty than to improving their living circumstances.

I will connect my reflections on development with the often-degrading ways in which Romani minorities have been treated domestically in Europe and with how central and eastern European Romani migrants have been approached in western Europe. Due to the Roma's securitization and the ways in which they are faced with states of 'deportability' (De Genova, 2002) and 'evictability' (van Baar, 2017a), they are subjected to regimes of forced mobility and immobility. While practices of deportation and deportability have led to their forced mobility and contained circulation at the European level, practices of racialized ghettoization due to eviction and durable segregation have resulted in situations that come close to forced immobility.

I will argue that the combination of practices of biopolitical development with the Roma's geopolitical separation tends to result in a racialization of poverty in Europe. This tendency implies neither that Europe's poor are always Roma, nor that all Roma are poor, but that they have become structurally overrepresented among the poor. The biopolitical and geopolitical conditions under which development and security have merged have led to a situation in which the official aim of Roma-related development programs – improving their living conditions and life chances – tends to result in its opposite and exacerbates a significantly racialized divide between Europe's rich and poor.

Institutional developmentalism and Europe's post-1989 security agenda

In an early human rights report written about the Roma's postsocialist situation, a Bulgarian Rom told a reporter: 'Your visit here was the first time someone showed an interest in our problems' (Helsinki Watch, 1991, p. 1). These first post-1989 years would become formative of how the Roma would become problematized in the Foucauldian sense and of how the interest in them would take shape at the international level.[1] After 1989, human rights organizations and transnational activist networks played a vital role in representing the situation of the Roma as a 'human emergency' and in bringing them onto Europe's agendas (Ram, 2010; van Baar, 2011b). One of the cornerstones of the Maastricht Treaty of the European Union (EU) would be 'respect for and protection of minorities' (European Council, 1993, p. 13). In its annual reports on the progress made toward accession of the central and eastern European candidate countries, as well as in its 2004 report on the Roma's situation in the then enlarged EU, the European Commission (2002, 2004) concluded that the situation of these states' Roma was alarming; that their rights continued to be violated; that discrimination against them remained widespread and that the policy attempts at the Roma's 'inclusion' had largely 'failed'.

The arrangement of nationally and internationally organized non-governmental and governmental attention to the Roma has led to a historically novel kind of 'institutional developmentalism' within Europe's contested borders. The Roma would become the focus of an endeavor in which the development of generic political, social and economic institutions and infrastructures – from parliamentary democracy, rule of law, human rights and minority protection to accessible public services and a market economy – had to lead to the protection of the Roma's rights and to their inclusion in Europe's societies.

This institutional developmentalism is integral part of what I have called 'the Europeanization of Roma representation' (van Baar, 2011a, pp. 1–19, 153–189), that is, firstly, the post-1989 problematization of the Roma in terms of their 'Europeanness'; secondly, the classification of heterogeneous groups scattered over Europe under the umbrella term 'Roma' and, thirdly, the devising of Europe-wide programs dedicated to their inclusion, integration, development, rights, empowerment and participation. Historically, those who are called, or call themselves, 'Roma' have often been considered a 'non-European' minority, with origins outside of Europe, 'dangerous' for 'progress' and 'civilization' in Europe. Yet, since the 1990s, the Roma have been reclassified as a 'European minority' to be respected and included as 'true Europeans'.

These emerging development interests in Roma issues have intermingled with the ways in which Europe has redefined itself politically, both 'internally' and globally, after the collapse of socialism. I have shown (van Baar, 2011a, pp. 174–184) that the initial post-1989 optimism regarding the prospects for reunifying Europe's eastern and western parts quickly made place for deep concerns. One of these was westward migration from postsocialist states. These concerns had two dimensions. Firstly, the ways in which central and eastern Europe's transitions have reinvigorated migration have resulted in the merging of novel European security and development discourses and programs, and in problematizing postsocialist states as 'migration-producing countries' that endanger Europe's security. The High Commissioner on National Minorities, in 1993 a newly installed body within the forerunner of the Organization for Security and

Cooperation in Europe (OSCE), formulated this merging, and its impact on Roma-related issues, as follows:

> The aim ... should be to improve the 'quality of life' in migration-producing countries [sic] ... for the sake of such improvements, but also for the reduction in pressures on international migration. In addition to commerce, investment and development assistance leading to economic opportunity, efforts at addressing the *specific* problems of the Roma, including discrimination and violence against them, will contribute considerably to improving their 'quality of life.' Such efforts are likely *to encourage people to continue their lives where they already are.* (van der Stoel, 1993, p. 11, emphasis added)

As Guglielmo and Waters (2005, p. 768) observe, the rationale behind this approach was not primarily *conflict* prevention – which is the OSCE's official main aim – but, rather, *migration* prevention. They also explain that

> there were competing visions within European institutions as to whether the problems of Roma were a security issue, a social issue or a rights issue, or indeed what the proper relationship between security, socioeconomic reform and rights is for policy addressing marginalized groups. (2005, p. 769)

Yet, even while there has been dissensus among the various actors about the way in which the Roma are to be problematized, in these actors' commitment to Roma-related issues, security and development have increasingly been merged.

This merging strongly relates to a second dimension of the concerns regarding migration of Roma. While the EC reports on the progress of candidate states toward EU accession were in agreement about their classification of the Roma's situation in central and eastern Europe as deeply worrying, when Roma migrated to Western Europe to ask for asylum, their claims were nevertheless and almost unconditionally rejected. The securitization of the Roma prior to the 2004 EU enlargement was not incidental, but, increasingly, *central* to how the 'old' EU states dealt with Roma since the beginning of Yugoslavia's dissolution and since the intensifying securitization of EU migration and border policies more generally (van Baar, 2011a, 2015a). Yet, to comprehend the impact of the merging of development and security on the Roma, we need to write the history of the present from the angle of how discourses and practices of security and development have considerably changed since 1989.

Reproblematizing security and development in Europe

The changing policy approaches to both security and development, and the reflection upon them in simultaneously reshaping security and development studies, have had much to do with shifting understandings of conflicts and the causes behind them (Buzan, Wæver, & de Wilde, 1998, Escobar, 1995). Duffield (2001, 2007) suggests that we need to historicize our understandings of security, development and their nexus, and to interrogate the rationales behind the post-Cold War emergence of discourses and practices of, most notably, 'human security', 'sustainability' and 'human development'. He observes that, while conflicts in the Global South between the 1950s and 1980s were primarily explained in terms of conflicts between different national (mostly postcolonial) states, since the 1980s, they have increasingly been portrayed as conflicts between ethnicized, religionized, culturalized or otherwise minoritized and majoritized groups. A shift has taken place according to which security has no longer only, or primarily, been related to 'national', state-related security, but also, and increasingly, to a people-centered kind of security, often conceptualized as 'human security'. In development studies and correlated literatures, the advent of 'human security' is frequently considered as the consequence of a blossoming humanism within international relations and organizations that would increasingly take into account internationally recognized human rights norms, acknowledge the role of individuals and communities in safeguarding their own security, and include threats to human life such as poverty, displacement and diseases.

This shift of the central focus related to prioritizing the security of people, rather than states, and, thus, to a broadening of security to incorporate society, has led to a similar change in approaches to development:

> [In this domain, we have seen] a move away from an earlier dominance of state-led modernization strategies based on the primacy of economic growth and assumptions that the underdeveloped world would, after passing through various stages, eventually resemble the developed. Rather than economic growth per se, a broader approach to development emerged based on aggregate improvements in health, education, employment and social inclusion as an essential precursor for the realization of market opportunity. (Duffield & Waddell, 2006, p. 44)

The postcolonial idea of the 1960s and 1970s that the development of the 'Third World' had to be based on the improvement of individual national economies that would be gradually incorporated into the 'developed' world economy has largely made place for the neoliberal idea that societies must be developed and 'defended' and that, accordingly, 'dangerous underdevelopment', based on inter-ethnic, inter-cultural or inter-religious group conflicts, has to be combatted.

The logic behind this change of approach to concentrating on the relationships between conflict, security and development, argues Duffield (2007, pp. 4–8), has also been key to the emergence of 'liberal interventionism', that is the legitimization of intervention in areas and populations qualified as 'underdeveloped' on the basis of the alleged necessity to improve life and living circumstances; to develop and empower communities; to create and improve 'capacities' and social capital; to reduce the risk that poverty will result into 'destabilizing' conflict and migration; and to govern through ethnicized, religionized or culturalized communities, and through civil societies generally. These approaches to security and development, and the justification of various interventions aimed at 'getting the social relations right' can also be traced within EU development approaches that have emerged since the mid-1990s:

> [Development instruments now need to take into account] their potential for balancing the interests and opportunities of different identity groups within a state, for encouraging democratic governments that enjoy widespread legitimacy among the population, for fostering consensus on key national issues ... and for building mechanisms for the peaceful conciliation of group interest. (European Commission, 1996, p. 4)

The intermingling of security and development, and the legitimization of humanitarian, military and developmental interventions, have been debated in the contexts of development and the 'new wars' in the Global South or in those of '(post-)conflict resolution' in, for instance, successor states of Yugoslavia and the Soviet Union (Duffield, 2001, 2007; Fassin & Pandolfi, 2010). Yet, these changes have been underresearched in the case of Europe's

Roma, which could be considered as Europe's largest post-1989 development project carried out within its territorialized borders and enacted by diverse actors.

Here, we have seen a double movement that epitomizes the blurred boundaries between the Global North and South. While institutions such as the EU have internalized formerly largely externalized development programs, IGOs such as the World Bank and the United Nations, which traditionally focused on the Global South, have 'discovered' the 'developing world segments of ... European societies [that] are predominantly made up of Roma' (UNDP, 2002, p. 21). What is at stake here can be conceived as a contemporary, postcolonial form of what Foucault (2004, p. 103) called the 'boomerang effect'. This designates the process in which 'a whole series of colonial models [of governing] was brought back to the West, and the result was that the West could practice something resembling colonization, or an internal colonialism, on itself' (Foucault, 2004). Similarly, in the Roma case, a series of postcolonial models, discourses, technologies and practices of development that have been ambiguously enacted in postcolonial settings in the Global South – ranging from social capital building to governing through communities, civil societies and participation – have been 'brought back' to Europe to be articulated transnationally to deal with the Roma (van Baar, 2011a).

After 1989, the Roma came not only into view of IGOs because, from then on, they were considered 'as representing a security issue' (Kovats, 2001, p. 95) or, for that matter, a development issue, but also because new notions and practices of development and security, and of their intersections, have emerged (van Baar, 2011a, pp. 153–189, 233–269). Newly developed discourses and practices of 'human security' and 'human development' represent a *biopolitical* fusion of development and security by perceiving human beings – who are considered as 'not well able' to guarantee their own 'basic needs' – in terms of underdevelopment, and hence, a security concern (Chandler, 2013; Duffield, 2007). Governmental interventions are portrayed as necessary to secure their well-being and to reduce the possibly negative effects on the wider human and political communities to which the poor belong, but also to enable them to adapt and become resilient to external pressures and threats. If we view 'human security' less from the quasi-positivist humanistic angle that still dominates in development studies and the social inclusion agenda for Europe's Roma, and rather from the standpoint of how it embodies a governmentalizing technology, we can interrogate it more critically:

> Similar to sustainable development, with which it is related, as a concept human security is able to bridge divisions, blur established interests and bring together erstwhile separate sectors and actors. Being able to enmesh, order and coordinate different loci of power, human security is an important governmentalizing technology ... While security and development have always been interconnected, human security reflects the contemporary reworking of this relationship. In particular, it unites these terms on an international terrain of non-insured groups, communities and peoples. (Duffield, 2007, pp. 113–114)

The various elements discussed here – the focus on intra-state conflicts between ethnicized, religionized or culturalized groups; the adoption of human security or human development notions guaranteeing 'basic needs' and 'capacities'; and the legitimization of development interventions – have coalesced in the approaches to the Roma of numerous intergovernmental and non-governmental organizations, including the EU, the OSCE, the Council of Europe (COE), the Open Society Institute (OSI), the World Bank and UN agencies.

For two decades now, the discourses of these transnational agencies have articulated a will to turn the tide for Europe's Roma (van Baar, 2011a). In the reports of IGOs, the mentioning of attempts at 'improving' the Roma's living circumstances is omnipresent, even though the notion of 'improving' rarely refers to concrete 'improvements' in the present, but rather to that which is desired and anticipated in the future. The stated aim is 'to close the gap between Roma and non-Roma in access to education, employment, healthcare and housing' (European Commission, 2014, p. 1) or to mobilize programs 'aimed at improving the situation of Roma and at closing any gaps between Roma and the general population' (FRA, 2014, p. 7).

The metaphors of gaps, traps, vicious circles and bridges have become integral parts of the development discourses of these IGOs. The first large regional reports about the Roma of the UNDP (2002) and the World Bank (2005), for instance, were respectively called *Avoiding the dependency trap* and *Breaking the poverty circle*, and the ways in which such traps should be avoided and circles broken have often been symbolized through the metaphor of bridges and the institutionalization of bridging 'mediators' in the domains of health care, schooling, policing and community or labor market interventions (epitomized by the 2011 launched and EU/COE-funded ROMED initiative, which is dedicated to 'Roma mediation' in each of these domains).

The rationale of these discourses is that, through the development programs and techniques that have been, or have to be, devised – whether focusing on social inclusion, capacity building, human security, participation, empowerment, community development or policing – the Roma will become less dependent, less vulnerable, less poor, less isolated and more 'capable' to become full members of the societies in which they live and to exercise their citizenship better than is presently the case.

I refer to this institutionalized will to improve the Roma's situation as a post-socialist 'institutional developmentalism' because, technically similar to the modernist (postcolonial) developmentalism spanning the 1950s to the 1970s, these discourses suggest that, after passing through various stages that are put on a continuum, the currently 'underdeveloped' Roma will gradually join in with 'developed' majorities. Several of the main development programs of the EU, the World Bank and OSI – such as the 'Decade of Roma Inclusion 2005–2015' and the 'EU Framework for National Roma Integration Strategies up to 2020' (European Commission, 2011) – are based on this developmentalist logic and 'enlightened' way of thinking that, in a foreseeable future, imagines the 'inclusion' of the Roma in Europe.

Yet, this rationale contrasts with the ways in which many Roma-related development programs have been articulated on the ground. The neoliberalization of development has resulted in a strong biopoliticization of development (van Baar, 2011a). Consistent with the biopolitical dimensions of development discourses and programs, a people-centred, human development and human security approach to the situation of the Roma concentrates, most notably, on material as well as spiritual self-reliance at individual and communal levels; local, community-based forms of development; 'active' citizenship including socioeconomic and sociopsychic activation; community and capacity building; awareness raising; human and social capital formation; stimulating 'desired' ways of living; and guaranteeing 'basic needs' such as sanctuary and rudimentary infrastructures. These diverse programs center on the *bio*political conditions that would have to be fulfilled to improve the Roma's circumstances and increase their 'capabilities'. The bio-politicization of Roma-related development programs does not necessarily mean that, 'on paper', these programs have always been problematized along these lines, but, rather, that this biopolitics has been articulated through and in the concrete everyday ways in which these programs have been assembled with 'local' cultures, conditions and traditions of governance (van Baar, 2011a, 2012).

However, these biopolitical practices of neoliberal development, and how they have been merged with security, are no longer based on practicing development along the lines of a developmental continuum according to which the 'underdeveloped' Roma can gradually join in with their 'developed' fellow citizens. Rather, the biopolitics of development has largely departed from the diagram of a *gradual scale* between 'us' and 'them' and introduced that of a *fault line* between 'their' lives and 'ours'.[2] The manifestation of this discontinuity relies not only on a biopolitical *view* of development, but also on how present-day *bio*political *practices* of development have been coupled with *geo*political barriers put up for Roma at the local and transnational European level.

Contained mobility and the geopolitics of Europe's securitized borders

As I have suggested above, the securitization of Roma prior to the EU enlargements of 2004 and 2007 was central to how they, and particularly the migrants among them, were treated in EU member states. I have also explained how the rationale of the 'developmentalities' toward the central and eastern European Roma has been considerably based on migration prevention. These securitizing moves regarding migration, though, have not been limited to discursive framings and rationalities of European minority governance. Rather, and contrary to the EU's prevailing self-image, they have been fully incorporated in the EU's architecture and its technologies of supranational governance. The Europeanization and securitization of migration and border policies in post-1992 Europe can be considered as a spillover effect of European economic integration, and particularly of the development of the EU's internal market (Huysmans, 2006). The largely economically inspired incorporation of the Schengen Treaty into the EU system in the 1990s and the 'removal' of the EU's internal borders have engendered a cycle of transformations in which policies of migration, transnational crime, trafficking and terrorism have been *conjointly* communitarized, that is brought under the EU's supranational 'Community method'.

At this institutionalized nexus of freedom and security, desired forms of the circulation of persons, capital, goods and services, such as those that are usually associated with business, tourism, student exchanges and high-skilled migration, are ambiguously distinguished from unwelcome and undesirable forms of circulation that would endanger the proper functioning of the EU's internal market and its interdependent freedom of movement. Not only transnational crime, terrorism and trafficking have been classified among these 'dangerous' forms of circulation, but also irregularized migration including that of the global poor (Duffield, 2007; Jansen et al., 2015; New Keywords Collective, 2016). This distinction has been articulated 'ambiguously', because, through these policy transformations, the EU has brought its approach to migration together with the combatting of transnational crime, shadow economies, trafficking and terrorism.[3] Migration policies have been directly linked with the EU's reshaped security policies and, thus, with a strong trend to irregularize migration as a (potentially) destabilizing phenomenon – a tendency that has only become more explicit with the deepening of Europe's 'migration/refugee crisis' (New Keywords Collective, 2016). We can consider this problematization of migration in terms of security as a *direct* form of securitization, institutionally propagated at the EU level, and emerging next to several indirect, mostly social and cultural forms of securitization (see Huysmans, 2006; van Baar, 2017a). These types of securitization have strongly intermingled with national and subnational ones in which various actors have been involved, ranging from state-related actors such as politicians, policy-makers, the police and other security experts to the media, 'vigilant' citizen groups, populists and extremists.

Particularly since 2010, when the expulsion of Romani migrants from France was widely mediatized, scholars have discussed the treatment of Roma from the angle of securitization and noted how they have been problematized in terms of alleged threats to public order, public health, social security systems and national security (Aradau, 2015; Parker, 2012; van Baar, 2011b). The securitizing trends toward the Roma – toward both migrants and domestic minorities – are part of a wider trend to irregularize their statuses as citizen, migrant, asylum seeker or refugee. Through traversing practices and strategies of orientalization, securitization and nomadization, the Roma have been problematized as 'backward' and 'inferior', as 'criminal', 'dangerous' and 'treacherous', as 'drifting parasites' and 'willful wanderers' and, thus, as irregular in the diverse meanings associated with deviating from what has been rendered 'normal', 'natural' and 'regular' (van Baar, 2015b). These problematizations have normalized rigid and racializing measures against the Roma, ranging from eviction, ethnic profiling and heightened surveillance to confiscation and demolition of their properties, deportation and school and residential segregation.

Since the collapse of state socialism, and largely due to these racializing processes of irregularization, we have seen increased and radical efforts to control and steer the ability of both poor domestic Roma and Romani migrants to circulate at local, regional, national and transnational levels in Europe (see also Kóczé, 2017). Processes of irregularization have become an integral part of the current movement to legitimize treating Roma differently to other EU citizens; to relegate them to substandard, segregated or provisional housing, education, health care and, in the most extreme, increasingly normalized cases, to evict them from their houses or sites and expel them from countries (van Baar, 2011b, 2015a).

The formation of conditions of deportability (De Genova, 2002) and evictability (van Baar, 2017a) – the lived experiences and predicaments under which the forcible removal of persons from the state, or from a sheltering place more generally, can materialize in the first place – have become vital to the political economy of international migration management and its intersections with the development–security nexus. While practices of deportation have led to the forced mobility of Roma and to their contained circulation at European level, those of racialized ghettoization due to eviction and enduring segregation have resulted in situations that come close to their forced immobility and restricted 'production of locality' (Appadurai, 1996). The fact that many European citizens have begun considering these rigid, often illegal measures as 'normal' (FRA, 2009) demonstrates the 'successfulness' of securitization and the depoliticization of how socio-economic and migrant mobilities of Roma are approached. Their displacement tends to be considered to be apolitical and technocratic in nature, and as a 'reasonable' prerequisite for enforcing social and public order (van Baar, 2014).

Several migration and border scholars have argued that contemporary border regimes have notably contributed to the blurring of the boundaries between 'inside' and 'outside', a development that has gone together with processes of selective and racializing filtering of labor mobilities (De Genova, 2002; Mezzadra & Neilson, 2012). Rather than assuming that a society can only claim its totality through exclusion, Sandro Mezzadra and Brett Neilson have argued that the position of irregularized migrants could be more adequately discussed in terms of 'differential inclusion'. Indeed, at the contested boundaries between the Global North and South we have seen:

> a legal production of illegality and a corresponding process of migrant inclusion through illegalization that creates the conditions under which a racial divide is inscribed within the composition of labor and citizenship. From this perspective, the devices and practices of border reinforcing shape the conditions under which border crossing is possible and actually practiced and experienced ... [T]he concept of differential inclusion points to a substitution of the binary distinction between inclusion and exclusion with continuous parametric modulations – that is, processes of filtering and selecting that refer to multiple and shifting scales, ratings and evaluations. (Mezzadra & Neilson, 2012, pp. 67–68)

The logic of differential inclusion corresponds to the one that I attribute to the Europeanization of Roma representation: we have seen an ambiguous shift from considering the Roma as the externalized outsiders against which Europe defined itself to representing them, since 1989, as the *internalized* outsiders to be included as productive, participating and 'true' Europeans (van Baar, 2011a). Mechanisms of differential inclusion have not been at odds with socialist or welfarist approaches to the Roma and their labor market position. Yet, while pre-1989 regimes of differential inclusion – for instance, the nomadization of the Roma – were used to regulate East and West European Romani minorities *domestically*, since 1989 they have been mobilized to manage newly emerged, transnational forms of labor and migration of Roma within Europe's contested borders (van Baar, 2011b).

In the context of development programs in the Global South, Duffield (2010) has argued that, due to these programs' focus on self-reliance and biopolitical forms of development that do not substantially contribute to durable ways out of poverty but to the maintenance of a precarious status quo, development at its nexus with security tends to result in the ambiguous containment of underdevelopment and in the permanent emergency of self-reliance. Indeed, since the self-reliance that these programs promote tends to lead to various types of delicate, temporary repair networks, they constantly need to be propelled again and legitimized as such. What I have called 'the perpetual mobile machine of forced mobility' (van Baar, 2015a) – regarding both migrant and socio-economic mobility – points to a similar mechanism in relation to the present-day position of (particularly eastern and central European) Roma. This machine 'drains' labor from Roma and the ways, in and through this machine, in which development and security have been merged tend to perpetuate the Roma's precarious situation and to depoliticize the currently reinforced states of evictability, deportability and precarity. Seen from the angle of differential inclusion, both eviction and deportation, as well as their spatial counterparts of encampment and ghettoization, are 'technologies of citizenship' (Walters, 2010) which, in the Roma's case, tend to regulate their mobility, societal belonging and difference racially and spatially.

Roma-related development programs, seen as technologies of security in the sense of containing underdevelopment, unceasingly intersect with mechanisms of expulsion and marginalization, understood as technologies of citizenship in the sense of regulating mobility, belonging and difference differentially. As remarked, this intermingling is not something that is automatically or intentionally inherent in how development and human security-oriented programs have been devised, but, usually, becomes manifest only at the moments of assembling them with 'local' cultures, conditions and traditions of governance. I would like to delineate how this process of merging works in practice by exploring the case of Roma in Eastern Slovakia.

Many Slovak Roma live in radically segregated rural enclaves and urban ghettoes. Most have been involved in development programs, which focus on community development through social work and community centers, which are indirectly, through NGOs and national governments, funded by IGOs. One of the largest, long-term involved development NGOs is ETP, which describes its work as follows:

> ETP Slovakia engages the most motivated Roma in the construction of new homes, thereby improving their work habits, teaching construction skills and, as a result, helping them secure and retain full time jobs. In addition to this livelihood development, ETP Slovakia operates a network of family support community centers ... which involves the entire Roma family in accessing savings and micro-loan programs, legal, and social services. In addition, we provide pre-school clubs, dropout prevention programs, parental courses, and mentoring for teenagers as well as a wide variety of social and cultural activities for the entire community through the community centers.[4]

As this profile illustrates, Roma-related development takes families, communities, livelihood systems and social networks and, thus, life or population, as its main points of reference, and not the state. To a considerable extent, these human security and development projects aim at strengthening community-based self-reliance through helping to meet 'basic needs',[5] even while these programs support Roma to find their ways vis-à-vis public services (see also van Baar, 2011a, pp. 249–253).

These practices take place in a societal environment of severe civil and institutional hostility, Romaphobia and 'reasonable anti-Gypsyism' (van Baar, 2014), in which the Roma's securitization is omnipresent. In Slovakia, as elsewhere in Central and Eastern Europe, the Roma are allegedly involved in a constant conflict with their non-Roma fellows, for the shadow economies in which several Roma are engaged, the benefits on which many of them rely, and the demographic boom that they would cause, are often considered as proofs that they *are* threats to the overall functioning of the state. Moreover, the ways in which nationally and internationally supported programs to 'activate' the Roma (e.g. through active labor market policies) have been enacted locally in Eastern Slovakia have led to serious forms of their exploitation and dehumanization. In the presence of societal hostility and in the absence of both jobs and adequate training programs, the public works and other activation activities in which many Roma have been involved in order to get conditional access to social benefits, have been used by private and public employers to organize cheap labor forces. While some companies have first fired Roma and then reemployed them through activation arrangements that offer them 60% of the minimum wage, municipalities have frequently mobilized activation schemes to let Roma do largely superfluous work and, therefore, perform well-known Gypsy stereotypes publicly (van Baar, 2012). One mayor whom I met in 2015 and who was aware of the drawbacks of activation work, nevertheless mobilized it because he considered it as a tool to demonstrate to non-Roma that, at least, the Roma show their *willingness* to work.

The persistent logic of this, what Barker (1981) once called, 'new racism' is 'for *ordinary people* to held *genuine fears* that their sense of identity, security or welfare is threatened for social order to be at risk' (Duffield, 2007, p. 200, his emphasis). This racial discourse has turned out to be 'reasonable' and, thus, acceptable for 'you do not even need to dislike or blame those who are so different from you in order to say that the presence of these aliens constitutes a threat to your way of life' (Barker, 1981, p. 18).

In this context, in which development has been considerably biopoliticized and the Roma's marginalization legitimized through securitization and 'reasonable' anti-Gypsyism, development has become the equivalent of 'repair packages' that, because they can hardly become sustainable, involve 'a regime of international social protection of last resort' (Duffield, 2007, p. 18) that requires its permanent reenactment.

My local and more general observations do not imply that the role of activism within the heterogeneous Romani movement and that of social and community work are of no value or have only negligible impact. Social and community workers, including those associated with non-governmental and faith-based organizations, often make a difference at the local level, as intermediaries between individuals, families and communities and within areas such as health care, education, faith, rights and access to social services, justice and relief (Škobla, Grill, & Hurrle, 2016). Furthermore, movement actors have played a key role in attempts at contesting present-day security, development, migration and citizenship regimes (van Baar, 2011a, 2015b, 2017b). Through 'travelling activism' (van Baar, 2011a), they try to re-politicize those Roma problematizations and societal mechanisms that seriously hinder the improvement of the Roma's situation or maintain anti-Roma racisms. These actors have mobilized the Europeanization of Roma representation to claim, for instance, (the right to) rights; seats in diverse political bodies; decision-making power more generally; a place in national and European histories and memories, and also their incorporation into the study of exclusion from which they have usually been excluded. Often, these actors and networks mobilize newly developed initiatives of participatory governance to try to turn 'problem spaces' – in which the Roma are one-sidedly considered as 'problem groups' or depoliticized subjects of development – into what Honig (1996) calls 'dilemmatic spaces'. These spaces offer no ready-made solutions to problems of securitization, development and differential inclusion, but make conflict, contradiction and the impact of processes such as securitization visible and audible, and, thus, public and open to dispute and deliberation (van Baar, 2011a, pp. 248–267).

My reflections do not suggest that the complex infrastructures of current migration, citizenship, security or development regimes, and those developed by Roma themselves, have not been mobilized to challenge, dispute or reverse the objectives for which these regimes and their mechanisms have 'officially' been launched (Solimene, 2017). I have extensively argued that 'counter-conducts' – practices that challenge dominant power relations – appear *within*, rather than outside, the horizon of prevailing governmentalities (van Baar, 2011a). Practices of contestation become manifest during, rather than only after or external to, articulations of all kinds of governmentalizing interventions: 'Relations of contest or struggle … are constitutive of government, rather than simply a source of programmatic failure and (later) redesign' (O'Malley, Weir, & Shearing, 1997, p. 505).

At the same time, the diverse struggles of the actors within, across and outside more formal Romani social, civil and religious movements have taken place within, rather than outside, the context of far-reaching processes of neoliberalization and the ways in which these have been assembled with local and national cultures, conditions and legacies of governance. Consequently, even though Roma have found ways to challenge, negotiate and circumvent the ways in which they have become the targets of ambiguous security and development regimes, they and their allies have simultaneously been faced with immense difficulties to dispute the persistent trend toward racializing poverty in Europe (van Baar, 2011a, pp. 233–269).

Bridging contained mobility and biopoliticized development

Several bilateral and European agreements have made developmental aid and programs for countries in the Global South conditional on their willingness to support the 'repatriation' of irregularized persons that migrated from these countries to Europe. Through this outsourcing of migration and border policies to countries in the EU's vicinity, the EU and its members have managed to include new technologies of intervention in these countries (Duffield, 2007; Jansen et al., 2015; van Houtum, 2010).

This mechanism has not remained limited to the Global South, but has been extended to states at Europe's contested borders, such as Romania, Bulgaria and the successor states of Yugoslavia. In 2012, for instance, the French and Romanian governments signed a deal that has facilitated the 'implementation ... of 80 concrete projects aimed at the reintegration of returnees from France' (quoted in ERRC, 2012a), particularly Romanian Roma. Another example relates to the 2010 deal between the German and Kosovo governments in which they agreed upon the 'repatriation' of 14,000 persons to Kosovo, among whom some 10,000 were Kosovo Roma and their children, most of whom have grown up in Germany. The majority of these Roma asked for asylum in Germany in the 1990s during the Yugoslav wars. They were 'tolerated' on the basis of a questionable legal act, the so-called Duldung arrangement, that temporarily suspends their deportation and legally enacts a permanent state of deportability (van Baar, 2017b).

Simultaneously, several German states have started the 'Kosovo Return Project URA 2' or, shortly, 'URA', which means 'bridge' in Albanian:

> In order to support ... the reintegration of people returning home, German authorities ... have got together in the 'URA 2' project to make their specific contribution towards a successful and sustainable return management in the Republic of Kosovo. (BAMF, 2015, p. 2)

The addition of the word 'management' to 'return' seems to indicate that the management of the deportation policies, rather than the return itself, has to become 'successful and sustainable'. URA's rationale is to create the conditions to 'encourage voluntary return' and to focus on the returnees' 'real needs' (Roma Center, 2014, p. 38), which include support for reintegration; social counseling; psychological care; psycho-therapeutic advice; help with administrative formalities, medical care, and school attendance of children; grants for promising business plans, and 'costs for furnishings of up to €600 for voluntary returnees and of up to €300 for forced returnees' (BAMF, 2015, p. 2). Yet, several organizations have documented that the reality of how URA 2 has been mobilized on the ground has been grim, particularly regarding Romani 'returnees' (ERRC, 2012b; Roma Center, 2014; UNICEF, 2012). Not only has the situation of Roma in postwar Kosovo been dramatic; the care for the deported Roma has also been minimal.

If we compare the illegal, yet officially sentenced deportation of Roma from Belgium in 1999,[6] firstly, with the post-2007 illegal, though tolerated and still ongoing deportation of Roma from France and, secondly, with the fully legalized expulsion of Roma from Germany of the present decade, we can observe a non-linear, disturbing trend in which the 'legal production of illegality' (De Genova, 2002) has been strikingly normalized and incorporated in the present-day nexus of security and development regarding Europe's Roma.

Here as in the general situation that I have described, we deal no longer with 'modernizing or industrializing state[s] concerned with reducing the wealth gap between the developed and underdeveloped worlds' but, rather, with human security states 'tasked with containing population and reducing global circulation of non-insured peoples through promoting the developmental technologies of self-reliance' (Duffield, 2007, p. 123). The official philosophy of Roma-related development projects starts from the premise that 'they' can gradually become like 'us' and, thus, that 'they' are primarily on the same socioeconomic ladder as 'we' are; 'they' simply require the support of development projects in order to climb higher. Nonetheless, the ways in which the biopolitics of development intersects with the intra-European geopolitical conditions of contained mobility have resulted in a situation in which, for the poorest among the Roma, it has become increasingly more difficult to escape poverty and societal isolation. Thus, despite the metaphors of bridges and bridgeable gaps, the ways in which the Roma have become the subject of both institutionalized development and security have led to a largely unbridgeable, significantly racialized divide between Europe's rich and poor.

Notes

1. A Foucauldian (1997) analysis of problematization does not focus on the construction of a phenomenon or group as a 'problem' that has a more or less clear (policy) solution. Instead, problematization can be described as 'the set of discursive and non-discursive tools and practices through which something has been shaped in a thinkable and pliable form and actively constituted as an object of expertise and knowledge' (van Baar, 2011a, p. 12).
2. Elsewhere, I have discussed the Foucauldian notion of diagram (van Baar, 2011a, p. 36–39).
3. For an elaborated discussion of this theme, see Bigo (2008), Huysmans (2006) and van Baar (2015a, 2017a).
4. See http://wbi.worldbank.org/developmentmarketplace/ready-to-scale/etp-slovakia?destination=&page=6&viewall=all& (accessed 12 October 2015).
5. The definition of these 'basic needs' might differ from case to case. For a discussion of the problems related to defining basic needs, see van Baar (2011a, p. 244–247).
6. The notorious case of illegally deported Slovak Roma from Belgium and the subsequent trial against the Belgian state have been well documented (Cahn & Vermeersch, 2000).

Acknowledgements

I would like to thank Can Yıldız, Nicholas De Genova and two anonymous reviewers for their encouragements and helpful comments.

Disclosure statement

No potential conflict of interest was reported by the author.

Funding

The research from which this paper is drawn was funded by the German Research Foundation (DFG) [grant number SFB/TRR 138], entitled 'Dynamics of Security: Forms of Securitization in Historical Perspective'.

References

Appadurai, A. (1996). *Modernity at large*. Minneapolis, MN: University of Minnesota Press.
Aradau, C. (2015). Security as universality? In T. Balzacq (Ed.), *Contesting security* (pp. 89–103). London: Routledge.
BAMF. (2015). *Kosovo return project URA2*. Nürnberg: Author.
Barker, M. (1981). *The new racism*. London: Junction Books.
Bigo, D. (2008). Globalized (in)security. In D. Bigo & A. Tsoukala (Eds.), *Terror, insecurity and liberty* (pp. 10–48). London: Routledge.
Buzan, B., Wæver, O., & de Wilde, J. (1998). *Security: A new framework of analysis*. London: Lynne Rienner Publishers.
Cahn, C., & Vermeersch, P. (2000). The group expulsion of Slovak Roma by the Belgian government. *Cambridge Review of International Affairs, 13*(2), 97–114.
Chandler, D. (2013). Where is the human in human-centred approaches to development? In S. Mezzadra, J. Reid, & R. Sammadar (Eds.), *The biopolitics of development* (pp. 67–86). New Delhi: Springer.
De Genova, N. (2002). Migrant 'illegality' and deportability in everyday life. *Annual Review of Anthropology, 31*, 419–447.
De Genova, N. & Peutz, N. (Eds.). (2010). *The deportation regime*. Durham: Duke University Press.
Duffield, M. (2001). *Global governance and the new wars*. London: Zed Books.
Duffield, M. (2007). *Development, security and unending war*. Cambridge: Polity.
Duffield, M. (2010). The liberal way of development and the security-development impasse. *Security Dialogue, 41*, 53–76.
Duffield, M., & Waddell, N. (2006). Securing humans in a dangerous world. *International Politics, 43*, 1–23.
ERRC. (2012a). *New deal between France and Romania on Roma returns must not breach rights to free movement*. Budapest: ERRC.
ERRC. (2012b). *Abandoned minority*. Budapest: ERRC.
Escobar, A. (1995). *Encountering development*. Princeton, NJ: Princeton University Press.
European Commission. (1996). *Linking relief, rehabilitation and development*. Brussels: Author.
European Commission. (2002). *EU support for Roma communities in central and Eastern Europe*. Brussels: Author.
European Commission. (2004). *The situation of Roma in an enlarged European Union*. Brussels: Author.
European Commission. (2011). *An EU framework for national Roma integration strategies up to 2020*. Brussels: Author.
European Commission. (2014). *Report on the implementation of the EU framework for national Roma integration strategies*. Brussels: Author.
European Council. (1993). *European council in Copenhagen*. Brussels: European Council.
Fassin, D. & Pandolfi, M. (Eds.). (2010). *Contemporary states of emergency*. London: Zone Books.
Ferguson, J. (2006). *Global shadows*. Durham: Duke University Press.
Foucault, M. (1997). Polemics, politics and problematizations. In P. Rabinow (Ed.), *Ethics* (pp. 111–119). New York, NY: The New Press.
Foucault, M. (2004). *Society must be defended: Lectures at the Collège de France 1975–1976*. London: Penguin.
FRA. (2009). *Data in focus report: The Roma*. Vienna: European Union Agency for Fundamental Rights.
FRA. (2014). *Poverty and employment: The situation of Roma in 11 EU member states*. Vienna: European Union Agency for Fundamental Rights.

Guglielmo, R., & Waters, T. (2005). Migrating towards minority status. *JCMS: Journal of Common Market Studies, 43,* 763–786.
Helsinki Watch (1991). *Destroying ethnic identity.* New York, NY: Author.
Honig, B. (1996). Difference, dilemmas and the politics of home. In S. Benhabib (Ed.), *Democracy and difference* (pp. 257–277). Princeton: Princeton University Press.
Huysmans, J. (2006). *The politics of insecurity.* London: Routledge.
Jansen, Y., de Bloois, J., & Celikates, R. (Eds.). (2015). *The irregularization of migration in contemporary Europe.* Lanham, MD: Rowman & Littlefield.
Kóczé, A. (2017). Race, migration and neoliberalism: Distorted notions of Romani migration in European public discourses. *Social Identities.* doi:10.1080/13504630.2017.1335827
Kovats, M. (2001). The emergence of European Roma policy. In W. Guy (Ed.), *Between past and future* (pp. 93–116). Hatfield: University of Hertfordshire Press.
Mezzadra, S., & Neilson, B. (2012). Between inclusion and exclusion. *Theory, Culture & Society, 29*(4/5), 58–75.
Mezzadra, S., Reid, J., & Sammadar, R. (Eds.). (2013). *The biopolitics of development.* New Delhi: Springer.
New Keywords Collective. (2016). Europe/Crisis: New keywords of the 'crisis' in and of 'Europe'. *Near Futures Online* 1. Retrieved from http://nearfuturesonline.org/europecrisis-new-keywords-of-crisis-in-and-of-europe/
O'Malley, P., Weir, L., & Shearing, C. (1997). Governmentality, criticism, politics. *Economy and Society, 26,* 501–517.
Ong, A. (2006). *Neoliberalism as exception.* Durham: Duke University Press.
Parker, O. (2012). Roma and the politics of EU citizenship in France. *JCMS: Journal of Common Market Studies, 50,* 475–491.
Pogge, T. (2010). *Politics as usual.* Cambridge: Polity.
Ram, M. (2010). Interests, norms and advocacy. *Ethnopolitics, 9,* 197–217.
Roma Center. (2014). *Abgeschobene Roma im Kosovo.* Göttingen: Roma Center.
Škobla, D., Grill, J., & Hurrle, J. (2016). *Exploring field social work in Slovakia.* Bratislava: Inštitút pre výskum práce a rodiny.
Solimene, M. (2017). Challenging Europe's external borders and internal boundaries. Bosnian *Xoraxané Xomá* on the move in Roman peripheries and the contemporary European Union. *Social Identities.* doi:10.1080/13504630.2017.1335828
UNDP. (2002). *The Roma in central and Eastern Europe: Avoiding the dependency trap.* Bratislava: Author.
UNICEF. (2012). *Silent harm.* Prishtina: UNICEF.
van Baar, H. (2011a). *The European Roma: Minority representation, memory and the limits of transnational governmentality.* Amsterdam: F&N.
van Baar, H. (2011b). Europe's Romaphobia: Problematization, securitization, nomadization. *Environment and Planning D: Society and Space, 29,* 203–212.
van Baar, H. (2012). Socioeconomic mobility and neoliberal governmentality in post-socialist Europe. *Journal of Ethnic and Migration Studies, 38,* 1289–1304.
van Baar, H. (2014). The emergence of a reasonable anti-gypsyism in Europe. In T. Agarin (Ed.), *When stereotype meets prejudice: Antiziganism in European societies* (pp. 27–44). Stuttgart: Ibidem.
van Baar, H. (2015a). The perpetual mobile machine of forced mobility. In Y. Jansen, J. de Bloois, & R. Celikates (Eds.), *The irregularization of migration in contemporary Europe* (pp. 71–86). Lanham, MD: Rowman & Littlefield.
van Baar, H. (2015b). Enacting memory and the hard labor of identity formation. In A. McGarry & J. Jasper (Eds.), *The identity dilemma* (pp. 150–169). Philadelphia: Temple University Press.
van Baar, H. (2017a). Evictability and the biopolitical bordering of Europe. *Antipode, 49,* 212–230.
van Baar, H. (2017b). Boundary practices of citizenship. In R. Gonzales & N. Sigona (Eds.), *Within and beyond citizenship* (pp. 143–158). Stanford, CA: Stanford University Press.
van der Stoel, M. (1993). *Report on the situation of Roma and Sinti in the CSCE area.* The Hague: Conference on Security and Cooperation in Europe.

van Houtum, H. (2010). Human blacklisting. *Environment and Planning D: Society and Space, 28*, 957–976.

Walters, W. (2010). Imagined migration world. In M. Geiger & A. Pécoud (Eds.), *The politics of international migration management* (pp. 73–95). Houdmills: Palgrave Macmillan.

World Bank (2005). *Roma in an expanding Europe: Breaking the poverty circle*. Washington, DC: Author.

2 Race, migration and neoliberalism

Distorted notions of Romani migration in European public discourses

Angéla Kóczé

🔓 OPEN ACCESS

ABSTRACT
This article analyzes the migration of Roma based on recent public, academic, policy and political debates in connection with two specific case studies in France and Italy. Moreover, it aims to understand how contemporary racialized discourses and neoliberal social and political forces (re)create Roma as a racialized internal 'other' to legitimize subtle anti-Romani politics in Europe. By doing that, it argues that the current migration of Roma cannot be understood apart from the proliferation of the hegemonic neoliberal ideology that facilitates the racialization of Roma and normalizes their social exclusion in Europe. Moreover, it explores the role of neoliberalism in the racialization and subjugation of Roma in Europe.

Introduction

This article will review and engage, primarily in sociological debates, on the migration of Roma, particularly from Romania and Bulgaria to France and Italy (Fassin, 2010; Hepworth, 2012; McGarry & Drake, 2013; Nacu, 2012; Picker, 2012; Sigona, 2011). Furthermore, it will situate the analysis within this well-developed literature in order to identify mechanisms, which link the processes of migration, racialization and neoliberalism. This theoretical connection between migration and racialization, coupled with neoliberalism, does not appear in a standard Romani migration related analysis.

Accordingly, this paper discusses the fact that the European Union (EU) cannot promise the social inclusion of Roma without social and economic mobility and spatial integration. Furthermore, it cannot promote minority rights and anti-discrimination without addressing the patterns of historical, structural and institutional racial discrimination that paralyze the social, economic and political integration of the racialized Romani migrants in Europe. For the purpose of this article, neoliberalism should not be confused with political liberalism. Traditional political liberalism is based on various democratic values, such as freedom, human rights and active citizenship. Conversely, neoliberalism privileges economic freedom at the expense of political freedom, democratic citizenship and human rights (Brown, 2006). The current debates on the migration of Central and Eastern European Roma within the EU neoliberal framework has created rhetorical and, as a result, material borders between racialized Romani migrants (many of whom are EU citizens) and non-

---

CONTACT Angéla Kóczé ✉ koczea@wfu.edu

© 2017 The Author(s). Published by Informa UK Limited, trading as Taylor & Francis Group

This is an Open Access article distributed under the terms of the Creative Commons Attribution-NonCommercial-NoDerivatives License (http://creativecommons.org/licenses/by-nc-nd/4.0/), which permits non-commercial re-use, distribution, and reproduction in any medium, provided the original work is properly cited, and is not altered, transformed, or built upon in any way.

Romani citizens. The latter enjoy 'freedom of movement' as a fundamental principle of the EU, whereas the former are excluded from the realm of 'freedom of movement'.

Scholarly discussions regarding the migration of Roma from Eastern to Western European countries tend to neglect the importance of neoliberal forms of governance. At the same time, scholarship on neoliberalism tends to disregard the role that racial neoliberalism has played in the displacement and marginalization of Romani migrants. Migration studies tend to focus either on the irregularization and securitization of Romani or on the impact of right-wing exclusionary discourse that has been internalized by people across the political spectrum on the position of Romani migrants. Huub van Baar argues (2014, p. 29), in the case of Romani expulsion in France, the left-right distinction between political parties does not matter much, since both sides are treating Romani migrants in the same way. Meanwhile, studies principally informed by critiques of neoliberalism tend to underestimate Eurocentric racialization and non-discursive practices that intersect with neoliberalism as forms of governance (Roberts & Mahtani, 2010). In the last few years, scholars have produced comprehensive and novel scholarship on the migration of Roma (see e.g. Hepworth, 2012; Sigona, 2014; Stewart, 2012b; van Baar, 2012, 2014, 2015) without explicit connection between race/racialization and neoliberal governance that shapes the migration, displacement, irregularization, *deportability* (De Genova, 2002) and *evictability* (van Baar, 2015) of Roma. This theoretical connection exposes the combination of neoliberal policies and racist discourse that continues to depict Romani people as racialized subordinated Europeans.

Critical junction of race, migration and neoliberalism

Migration of Roma is often referenced in public discourse as a cultural characteristic, which subsequently essentializes 'nomadism' as an internal feature of Romani culture (Kóczé & Trehan, 2009). Even today, textual and visual representations of Roma are racialized and take center stage in influencing everyday social practices and policies. Representation is a very complex meaning making process, particularly when we are dealing with European racialized 'others', such as Roma. Their differences are clustered around several main themes, including their subordinated status signified by skin color and bodily differences (Junghaus, 2015). Besides that, Roma are also represented in European cultural discourse as a group with an 'innate laziness' or 'musical talent' (Kóczé & Trehan, 2009). So, this racialized regime of representation essentializes, naturalizes and fixes the subjugated position of Roma in Europe while whiteness remains invisible and unmarked (Imre, 2005).

The emerging trend, regarding the migration of Roma shows similar discursive practices, which are repeated with some variations from one country to another. If migrants are perceived as Romani, then there is a great chance of being characterized in various ways, for instance, as 'bogus asylum seekers' (Guy, 2003; Molnar Diop, 2013), 'ethnotourist', 'asylum adventurers' (Vašečka & Vašečka, 2003), 'poverty migrants', 'intrusive beggars' (Benedik, 2010), and 'excessively mobile', 'nomadic' (van Baar, 2011) and 'welfare parasites' (Kóczé & Trehan, 2009). The evocative language creates epistemological and rhetorical borders between 'normal' and 'abnormal' migrants, thereby distinguishing Romani migrants from white migrants in the EU. This discursive practice is used to create a coded racialized language between insider and outsider, to control the social and political boundaries between 'Us' and 'Them' (Hall, 1997, p. 258). Similar epistemic boundaries are created and sustained by various racialized discourses between domestic Romani groups and white local populations (Kóczé & Trehan, 2009).

The migration of Roma in the EU is also distinguished in politico-technical terms. They are known as 'irregular' migrants[1] and also identified as 'security threats' to public order (van Baar, 2015). Huub van Baar expressed concern about the conceptualization of the migration of Roma in terms of 'irregular', rather than 'regular', mobility. One of van Baar's (2012) questions is how 'irregularization' relates to the development of post-socialist neoliberal welfare states in East-Central Europe. Narratives of 'irregularity' are part of discursive and non-discursive practices that contribute to treating Roma differently from other EU citizens. This specific politico-technical approach exacerbates their racialization. I concur with van Baar, who categorizes 'irregularization' as an umbrella term for practices and discourses of orientalization, securitization and nomadization (van Baar, 2015).

The Italian (Hepworth, 2012; Sigona, 2008) and French (McGarry & Drake, 2013; Nacu, 2012) expulsions of Roma in 2008 and 2010 show some striking similarities to the conceptualization of migration as 'irregular', as well as to the nature of racialized political debates that are conditioned by neoliberalism. Davison and Shire (2013, pp. 82–83) refer to the coded meaning of migration that accompanies race and which led to it becoming 'common sense' in neoliberalism. By the same token, when affluent migrants live in a different country we call them expats, but when we are referring to immigration we often connect it with people who are not like 'us'; they are pariahs and not entitled to the same rights. As Davison and Shire succinctly stated, 'whiteness is associated with higher status and wealth, while blackness is associated with poverty and abjection' (Davison & Shire, 2013, p. 83). In this context Roma represent the black Europeans; they are criminal, illegal and not even counted as human (Davison & Shire, 2013, p. 3). Their dehumanization is fortified by the neoliberal state that keeps them outside of the legal boundaries to make them illegal (Goldberg, 2009), cheap and flexible labor for economic exploitation (Bacon, 2013).

European integration, neoliberalism and right-wing populism

The EU enlargement has offered several opportunities and perspectives for Roma. These offers have been hindered by the neoliberal politics of the EU, which are demonstrated by Hermann, who explains how neoliberalism has impacted major policy issues of the EU. Hermann describes, the 'European integration process was used to adopt mainstream neoliberal policies' and to eliminate state social protection that, in the past, gave Europe's 'distinctiveness compared to other countries, notably the United States' (2007, p. 61). The Single Market Strategy, European Competition Policy, Economic and Monetary Integration, and even the European Employment Strategy are intertwined with a neoliberal approach – including elements such as 'free' trade and 'free' capital mobility, monetary restraint and budgetary austerity, the flexibility of labor markets, and the erosion of employment security – contributed to the structural changes in Europe. Davison and Shire (2013) have reflected on how the acceding Eastern European states represented new opportunities for the EU in terms of new markets, cheap labor and good investment opportunities. The EU accession created favorable investment conditions for foreign capital by the privatization of state institutions and the liberalization of the market (Davison & Shire, 2013). However, the neoliberal agenda to liberalize markets, restructure the state and dismantle welfare did not improve the social and economic situation of the disadvantaged population, such as Roma in the new member states. Even though, the social integration and human rights situation of Roma in the Central and Eastern European countries were considered as key issues in the EU pre-accession phase (Sigona & Trehan, 2009). The available pre- and post-accession EU financial resources, as well as various Europe-wide policy initiatives such as the proclamation of the 'Decade of Roma Inclusion 2005–2015',[2] did not created an opportunity for the vast majority of Roma in the new EU countries. They rather remained untouched by the promises of economic liberalization and social inclusion, as well as continuing to face systematic discrimination and state-financed segregation (Sigona & Trehan, 2009).

EU enlargement is also considered a landmark opportunity for Roma to enjoy freedom of movement in Europe. By the same token, migration of Roma – even after enlargement – sparked significant public concern in the EU (Sigona & Vermeersch, 2012). For instance, the expansion of the EU in 2004 (Cyprus, the Czech Republic, Estonia, Hungary, Latvia, Lithuania, Malta, Poland, Slovakia and Slovenia) and 2007 (Bulgaria and Romania) intensified the international and national debate around Romani migrants in Europe, particularly in the post-socialist states. National media and public discourse concerning the restriction and expulsion of Romani people was often carried out with anti-Gypsy rhetoric (van Baar, 2014). In most cases, racist motivation has been used, as simple, vivid and easily memorable language to intensify this alienation, memorably in several cases of expulsion of Roma from various Western countries, including Great Britain, Germany, Austria, Italy, France, Denmark, Sweden and Belgium (Cahn & Guild, 2008).

This concern about Romani migrants is exemplified by the neoliberal agenda: The *securitization of mobility of Roma* in the EU.

The concern, *securitization of mobility of Roma,* has been criticized by both scholars and activists. The representation of Romani migrants as 'nomads' and 'criminals' became gradually embedded in European social and political discourses, thus connected intrinsically to the notion of 'irregular Romani migrants'. One the strongest scholarly critiques was made by van Baar, who notes 'the irregularization of Romani identities and mobilities intensifies the applicability of strategies of criminalization and responsibilization to the situation of the Roma' (van Baar, 2011, p. 205). Later in this article I will focus on two specific case studies in Italy and France, in which the indefinite 'state of exception' (Agamben, 2005) as a case of a neoliberal governmental rationality project became associated with 'irregular Romani migrants'. In the name of security and protection, the government used discourses racializing Romani migration to support a new anti-Gypsy politics in Europe, both overtly and tacitly (McGarry & Drake, 2013; van Baar, 2012).

The development of anti-Gypsy politics operates hand in hand with the development of populism that takes different forms and different political outcomes in Europe. Berezin (2009) suggests that the emergence of populist discourse in Europe has mainly been explained by accelerated Eastern European integration into the EU, which is 'coupled with shifting demographics'. According to Berezin, quantitative changes in demography, such as the increasing numbers of 'non-white' migrants, occurring alongside European integration, has led to an increase in populist discourse. In contrast to Berezin, who stresses the role of immigration in fueling populism, Michael Stewart argues that it 'is a part of a broader shift in European politics' (Stewart, 2012a, p. xx). Stewart explains the unintended impact of European integration from a different perspective, attributing it instead to the rise of cultural politics, which 'focus less on economic issues than cultural differences between peoples' (Stewart, 2012a). Contrary to Stewart, Berezin connects populism with neoliberal social and economic changes, which are conceived more as free market economic policies that dismantle welfare states, privatize public services and intensify income disparities (Brown, 2006).

Fox and Vermeersch (2010) wrote an informative analysis about 'backdoor nationalism' that has emerged in Hungary and Poland over the past two decades as an unintended consequence of EU integration. They identify backdoor nationalism as a phenomenon whereby nationalist and populist political parties and radical nationalist political movements have actually been indirectly encouraged in Central and Eastern Europe by the EU's politics of enlargement. Richard Saull explicitly draws attention to the re-emergence of far-right populist parties and movements in recent years, which should be understood within the context of contemporary socio-economic structures and processes, that have been generated by neoliberal forms of governance (Saull, 2015). Owen Worth succinctly points out the latest specific policies, such as dismantling welfare and the abolition of state subsidies for refugees, which constitute the central elements of the neoliberal ontology (Worth, 2015).

After all, recent migrations of Roma within the EU have been subjected to securitization, racialization, stigmatization and even welfare-chauvinism (Sigona, 2008; van Baar, 2011, 2014). Yet, the interplay between neoliberal social and economic forces, on the one hand, and extreme-right political forces, on the other, has either been relatively disregarded or only discussed implicitly. This article argues for a more thorough examination of contemporary neoliberal governance which has produced and reproduced rhetoric and social mechanisms compatible with the exclusionary politics of the far right. Their politics have been simultaneously targeted and mobilized against Roma. Hence, neoliberal socio-economic structures provide a political means of creating and excluding racialized groups as aliens, non-citizens, permanent criminals, with the tacit support of right-wing populist parties. While harsh anti-Roma discriminatory rhetoric is obvious, the mechanisms of social, economic and political exclusion remain disarticulated, depoliticized and detached.

Italian and French case studies as a test for European integration

In the following two case studies, this article focuses mainly on anti-Romani immigration politics in France and Italy for two reasons. *Firstly*, in the period between 1994 and the present, France and Italy were the central sites of right-wing populism in Europe, although in different ways. In both countries, right-wing political parties' racist rhetoric on Romani populations has been mainstreamed by national politics. *Secondly*, with their recent neoliberal securitization of Romani migration, both countries present the Romani people as 'others' and 'abject citizens' of Europe (Hepworth, 2012; McGarry & Drake, 2013). There are already several scholarly articles that analyze some aspects of Italian and French migration policies directed at Romani migrants, particularly from Romania and Bulgaria, but none of them make the theoretical link with racial neoliberalism (e.g. Clough Marinaro, 2009; Clough Marinaro & Sigona, 2011; Fassin, 2010; Hepworth, 2012; Hermanin, 2011; Sigona, 2011; McGarry & Drake, 2013; Nacu, 2012). This article reflects on the normalization of racialization of Roma and exclusion of racialized Romani migrants, who are associated with illegitimacy and a threat to European citizenship.

Italian right-wing populism

In 1994 in Italy a political party, which has a roots in the Italian fascist past, the *Movimento Sociale Italiano* (MSI) under the leadership of Gianfranco Fini, became part of an Italian governing coalition. This was the first Silvio Berlusconi government (from May to December 1994). Berlusconi allied with MSI and the regional separatist movement, the Northern League (*Lega Nord*), under the leadership of Umberto Bossi. In 1995, MSI became the National Alliance (*Alleanze Nazionale*) and moved towards the center of Italian politics to become the official party of the Italian right. The year 1994 was therefore an important landmark in Italy and throughout Europe, because a political party with a direct connection to a historical fascist party became a legitimate player in European politics (Berezin, 2009). In Italy, this was the period when Yugoslavian Roma were fleeing to Italy from war and post-war persecution. Based on Nando Sigona's account in the '90s, Roma refugees – mainly from Bosnia, Serbia, Macedonia and Kosovo – were treated with 'pre-existing cultural and policy frames rooted in the image of "nomadic Gypsy" [which] normally applied to Italian indigenous Roma and Sinti' (Sigona, 2011). In the 1990s, in his article on the Romani migration in Italy, Giovanni Picker identified the language of the political parties as harsh and dehumanizing against Romani migrants. He claims that this pernicious language became gradually normalized by various political parties, including even left-wing politicians in Italy (Picker, 2012).

French right-wing populism

At the same time in France, the French right movement gradually and systematically inserted itself into French politics. The breakthrough of the French right was much later than in Italy. In April 2002, Jean-Marie Le Pen advanced to the second round of the French presidential elections. During this period, the French right had significantly increased its constituency. The rise of right-wing discourse, including anti-immigration, became further intensified by the campaign of his daughter and successor, Marine Le Pen. Furthermore, her success was confirmed in the European Parliament elections in May 2015. France (similarly to Italy) carried out several expulsions of Romani migrants from Bulgaria and Romania in 2007 and 2008, following the EU accession of these countries (Cahn & Guild, 2008). An Organization for Security and Co-operation in Europe (OSCE) report illustrated through various cases that EU states, including France and Italy, have expelled Roma which is considered a violation of EU legal provisions (Cahn & Guild, 2008, pp. 51–53). The racism against Romani migrants has been appropriated by the extreme right, becoming the epicenter of mainstream governmental politics. According to Alexandra Nacu's account, the summer of 2010 was the culmination of the scapegoating of Romani migrants from new EU members states, such as Bulgaria and Romania. Under the Sarkozy Presidency, Roma immigration became associated with 'insecurity' regarding non-white Romani migrants (Nacu, 2012).

Italian 'emergency legislation'

In 2007, the EU expanded to include Romania and Bulgaria, allowing their citizens freedom of movement to enter and live in any EU member state, including Italy. According to an

OSCE/Office for Democratic Institutions and Human Rights (ODIHR) publication (Sigona, 2008), since this expansion, the media promoted the notion that migrants from Romania and Bulgaria were set to 'invade' Italy. The word 'invasion' was thereby linked to Romani people and accompanied by a racial subtext.

The hostility against migrants has been stimulated by the murder of an Italian woman, Giovanni Reggaini. The homicide was, allegedly, committed by a Romanian Romani male citizen. Shannon Woodcock explores the intersection of gender and ethnicity in the public discourse that was generated by the murder of Giovanni Reganni. She argues that this case generated a specific public discourse on 'dangerous black men' who are sexually threatening to white Italian women. The 'dangerous black man' in this case is Roma (Woodcock, 2010).

This kind of rhetoric is very similar to what has been used in a range of European and colonial nationalist projects in order to justify control over racialized men and white women as objects of the patriarchal structure that maintain the hegemony of white masculinity (Woodcock, 2010).

Sigona (2008) states that as the situation became worse, and as a reaction to anti-Romani public sentiment, Prodi's center-left Italian government issued an 'emergency law' (n. 181/2007) aimed at facilitating the expulsion and repatriation of EU citizens whenever they were perceived to represent a threat to public and national security (Hepworth, 2012).

After the 2008 election campaign which led to the victory of the center-right coalition led by Silvia Berlusconi, the 'emergency law' was extended as part of the 2008 Security Package, triggering criticism by human rights organizations (Merlino, 2009; Sigona, 2011). During a meeting in Naples on 21 May 2008, the Italian Council of Ministers declared a 'state of emergency' in relation to the settlements of nomadic communities in the territory of the regions of Campania, Latium and Lombardy. Later on 25 July 2008, the Italian government passed another decree that extended the state of emergency to the country (Merlino, 2009, pp. 10–11). The following definition explains the consequences of the state of emergency: 'State of Emergency and Power of Ordinance' (Stato di emergenza e potere di ordinanza), states

> [i]n case of natural calamities, catastrophes or other events that, according to their intensity and reach, need to be faced by extraordinary powers and means, the Council of Ministers rules on the state of emergency, establishing its temporal and territorial extension. (cited by Merlino, 2009, p. 10)

The state of emergency suspends and limits the general principles of the rule of law.

This legislative package bundled together legal measures for regulating the free movement of EU citizens with legislation addressing organized crime, '"illegal" migration and urban degradation' (see Hepworth, 2012; Sigona, 2011). The government also appointed three special commissioners to lead the implementation of the Security Package in order to bring an end to the 'emergency situation', which had been fueled and sustained by the media and the rhetoric of populist politicians. The decree authorized the government to order the identification and census of people, including minors, who were living in 'nomad camps'. Besides checking their documents, the identification process also included taking fingerprints, even though this was harshly condemned by international human rights organizations, as well as the European Parliament.

Despite the international outcry and condemnation, the Italian government continued to label and to racialize Romani and Sinti as 'nomadic groups' and 'illegal and criminal immigrants' who were seen as threats to national security and therefore needed to be controlled and repressed. A member of the European Parliament, Sarah Ludford from the Alliance of Liberals and Democrats for Europe (ALDE), raised concerns about the populist and racist political rhetoric that was attached to the implementation of the 'Nomad Emergency Decree'. She made a statement about the discriminatory and illegal method of collecting fingerprints that targeted Roma, posing the question, 'Have we forgotten the history of Nazi and fascist racial persecution?' (Sarah Ludford MEP).[3] Her comparison is similar to the argument of Wendy Brown, who compares to the 'tacticalization' of law to Foucault's formulation of governmentality, which suspends and instrumentalizes the institution of liberal democracy (Brown, 2006, p. 695). Brown elaborates further, explaining that neoliberalism,

> as law is tacticalized or instrumentalized, it is radically desacralized, producing the conditions for its routine suspension or abrogation, and paving ground for what Agamben (2005) drawing on Carl Schmitt's, has formulated as sovereignty in the form of a permanent 'state of exception'. (Brown, 2006, p. 695)

Two days after the extension of the state of emergency to the entire territory of Italy on 27 July 2008, the Interior Minister, Roberto Maroni gave an answer to the European Parliament in a way that twisted the rhetoric about the implementation of the 'Nomad Emergency Decree', justifying it as a humanitarian action and explaining that the government's goal was to give an identity to those living in the nomad camps without ID cards. His strategy was a turning point to de-racialize the discourse, and for this purpose they did not mention 'Roma'; rather, they referred only to 'nomad groups' and 'nomad camps'. Nonetheless, in his speech, Maroni used various historically embedded stereotypical images and racial tropes associated with the Romani people, reinforcing their image as deviant, criminals and nomads (Kóczé, 2014; Kóczé & Trehan, 2009). Robert Maroni's speech in the European Parliament was a shrewd justification of his government's policy, encouraging various other European political parties and governments by providing an example of how they could use racially coded language and discriminatory practice against the Roma in the name of 'social inclusion' or 'humanitarian intervention', without explicit reference to Romani migrants. While invoking the idea that the Italian policy was actually assisting the Roma to secure identity documentation, Maroni reinforced and legitimized widespread, deep-rooted anti-Romani sentiments to mobilize fear and hostility towards Romani migrants from new EU member states.

Edith Bauer from Slovakia and Lívia Járóka, the Romani MEP from Hungary, effectively endorsed the same de-racializing tactic that was employed by Maroni to justify their measures against Roma. They declared: 'What is currently happening in Italy is not an ethnic matter, and we must act against injustice, from whomever it comes'. There is a very cynical element in the statement of Bauer and Jaroka which hints that 'the parties are creating hysteria and use the Romani issue for their own short-term, self-serving interests, and it is easy for them to do so since the Romani civil society organisations are too weak to protest against or to oppose it'. Basically, Bauer and Járóka's account indicates that the remaining left, liberal and Green parties in the European Parliament create a public outcry in order to gain political capital at the expense of the voiceless and victimized Romani.[4]

Romani deportation in France

On 21 July 2010 the French President Nicolas Sarkozy announced a *Déclaration sur la sécurité*. As Alexandra Nacu reported, Sarkozy made a presidential speech which highlighted two events: an episode of rioting in a district of Grenoble following the death of a young man of North African descent, shot during a police search after an armed robbery, and an attack in July 16 on a police station in a small town in Central France by members of families reported to be *Gens du voyage (French Travelers)* (Nacu, 2012, p. 1324). Nacu argues that the unprecedented stigmatization of Romani in the summer of 2010 by the French authorities was intended to misdirect the public from their own struggle with corruption and economic crisis (Nacu, 2012, p. 1323).

This was not the first time that Sarkozy used inflammatory rhetoric against 'immigrants'. This declaration and the intense media campaign against immigrants contributed to the quick deportation of Romani people from France. In this rhetoric, *les gens du voyage* (Romani people who are French citizens) and Romani immigrants from Central and Eastern Europe have become identified as one homogeneous group, which is considered a security threat to France. In his communiqué on 29 July, Sarkozy denounced the 'lawlessness' (lack of legal documentation) that characterized the situation of the Roma coming from Eastern Europe to France as unacceptable (cited by McGarry & Drake, 2013). He also announced a government action plan with regard to 'illegal migrants', namely to demolish illegal Romani sites, which he described as 'being a source of illegal trafficking and the exploitation of children for the purposes of begging, prostitution, or crime' (cited by McGarry & Drake, 2013, p. 82). Moreover, it implied that 'irregularly' residing EU citizens, who were 'abusing' EU citizenship and freedom of movement, should be forced to return to their countries of origin (cited by McGarry & Drake, 2013).

The securitized Romani migration crisis generated tremendous national and international media attention and political debate in France as well as in the rest of Europe. The United Nations, the EU, the Vatican, various international human rights groups, scholars, intellectuals and politicians were opposed to Sarkozy's discriminatory policies. They argued that the policy specifically targeted Roma based on their ethnicity. Therefore, the expulsion of Roma from France was a violation of EU laws prohibiting discrimination and guaranteeing freedom of movement.

In September 2010, news media disclosed the official memo, which revealed that the French government was implementing several administrative guidelines (*circularies*) for authorities to abolish illegal sites. As it turned out, in September the government had already ordered local authorities to target the evacuation of Romani migrants before the violence started in mid-July between police and *les gens du voyage*. The memo was issued in June with a more precise instruction in which authorities were asked for targeted evacuation of illegal settlements and immediate return of Romani migrants from Central and Eastern Europe who were irregularly residing in France. It also identified a number of settlements, which should be eliminated within a 3 month period (at least 100 a month and a target of 300 within 3 months). There was an explicit request in the memo that those settlements that were occupied by Romani should be a priority (Circulare IOC/K/1017881/J du 5 Aout 2010, Paris, Objet: Evacuation des campements illicits, cited in McGarry & Drake, 2013).

When the memo was released to the public, the French authorities were confronted with Europe-wide public condemnation by various international organizations including the European Commission. Viviane Reding, European Commissioner for Justice, accused the Sarkozy government of mass expulsions of Romani people, and of dishonesty in its dealings with Brussels. Furthermore, Commissioner Reding linked the deportation of Romani people to Romania and Bulgaria to Vichy France's treatment of Jews in World War II, concluding that Brussels had no option but to lodge infringement proceedings at the European Court of Justice (Traynor, 2010). As a reaction to the infringement procedure, the French government issued another memo on 13 September to amend the original one. The new memo stated that the police and relevant local officials had evacuated all illegal settlements, regardless of who occupied them. This was meant to show that France had never intended to single out Roma or Travelers (McGarry & Drake, 2013, p. 85). The French government used the same colorblind/de-racialized language as the Italian government used in 2008 by not mentioning the word Roma. Instead, they tacitly referred to them as the 'illegal'.

Viviane Reding's statement on France is reminiscent of the remarks made by Sarah Ludford (MEP) in Italy in 2008. Both Reding and Ludford compared France and Italy's treatment of Romani migrants with the fascist treatment of Jews. The *EU Observer*, an independent online newspaper covered Sarkozy's reaction, stating that

> the French politician said on 15 September that Mrs. Reding's 'unseemly' remarks in effect compare France to the Nazi regime. A plane ticket to one's country of origin in the European Union is not a death train, and is not the gas chamber. (Pop, 2010)

Moreover, it unabashedly articulated France's place in a perceived moral hierarchy of EU states by stating: 'This is not how you speak to a major power like France, which is the mother of human rights.' On 29 September 2010 the European Commission announced a press release stating that they would not pursue the infringement procedure against France. The Commission Press Release (IP/10/1207 European Commission Press Release, 29 September 2010) concluded that: 'The administrative instruction ("circulaire") of 5 August 2010 that was not in conformity with this orientation was annulled and replaced by a different instruction on 13 September 2010.' The new memo persuaded the Commission to withdraw the legal proceedings against France.

Deprivation from political membership

These two case studies suggest that in order to understand the hostile policies of EU member states against the migration of Roma, we must focus on larger economic, social and political restructuring as well as how financial crisis aids rampant nationalism (Fassin, 2010; Sigona, 2014). Fassin explains the 'phobias' and securitization of immigration as a general phenomenon against 'otherized'/racialized groups that are deemed to have biopolitical characteristics, capable of being constructed by political parties as a social threat to 'the nation' and to 'Europe'. People are categorized based on racial or quasi-racial classifications into those who must live and those who may be left to die (Foucault, 2008). Fassin borrows a concept from Claude Lévi-Strauss to explain that these racist and xenophobic discourses are directed against a 'floating signified'. So, the phobia against 'others' such as Romani, Jews or Muslims is a 'rhetorical circulation', which changes focus according to the particular needs of each political moment. In this sense, the 'rhetorical circulation' of Otherness is a scapegoating process, which may tactically change its target, but consistently works according to the same exclusionary logic. However, while Fassin discusses these 'phobias' as a reaction to various kinds of differences (mainly racialized differences), his critique does not tackle the more fundamental question about the ways in which French-ness itself (and Italian-ness, likewise) has been conceptualized and constructed as presumed opposites to Romani-ness, Muslim-ness and Blackness. In order to advances this debate, this article pronounces that contemporary neoliberal economic, social and political constraints produce, and reproduce, a new configuration of colonial racism as the politics of anti-Gypsyism[5] that are embedded in discursive and material realities.

The distinct migrant position of Roma within contemporary Europe is derived from a deep-rooted history of racism. The European racist imagination about Roma in art history (Junghaus, 2015), literature (Trumpener, 1992) and in social and political narratives (Kóczé, 2014; Kóczé & Trehan, 2009) contributes to anti-Roma discourses. The mobility of Roma has been distinguished by irregularization and punitive practices. The notion of irregularization, in a different context, has been discussed by several scholars (De Genova, 2002; McNevin, 2011; Squire, 2011). Based on their conceptualizations, the production of the 'irregularity' of Romani migrants functions as a mode of governmentality. In the cases of France and Italy, governments have used the 'state of emergency' to discursively transform 'criminal' and 'nomadic' Romanians and Bulgarians – as well as Italians and French – into 'abject' European citizens (Hepworth, 2012; Sigona, 2014). Thus, the 'irregularization' of Romani mobility also raises the question of political belonging. According to McNevin (2007, p. 671), in the context of neoliberal globalization, irregular migrants are positioned at the frontiers of politics. Their political position is given by a recognition of their precarious life through their 'state of emergency' (Agamben, 1998; McNevin, 2007). Hence, in McNevin's interpretation, the political claims of irregular migrants have a potential to challenge the social and political practices and attitudes of the neoliberal state which construct them as apolitical and illegitimate. By contrast, European Romani 'irregular' migrants have been able to attract some media attention but have not been able to mobilize enough political support and solidarity to radically contest dominant exclusionary discourses.

Scholarship that 'focuses upon the incarceration of irregular migrants' has been considerably impacted by Giorgio Agamben's theoretical work on the 'state of exception' (Agamben, 1998; McNevin, 2007). Sigona's ethnography in Italian 'nomadic camps' offers a critique of Agamben's conceptualization of the camp as a space of exception or incarceration. Sigona instead argues that 'camp space [is] paradigmatic of stratification and diversification of political entitlements, and obligations are reshaped, bent, adjusted, neglected and activated by and through everyday interactions' (Sigona, 2014, p. 12). Sigona introduces the concept of 'campzenship' which 'captures the situated forms of political membership produced by the camp'. He criticizes that scholarship which overemphasizes the segregating and exclusionary forces of the camps and 'portray[s] them exclusively as spaces of control over a group of people deemed to represent a threat to society' (Sigona, 2014, p. 12). In contrast, he argues, 'campzenship' creates a situated political membership. While this insight is crucial, we should not undervalue the asymmetrical power relations with the external world (governmental authorities, entitled citizens) that mark these camps' boundaries, and delegitimize their political belonging and citizenship. Furthermore, the temporal and spatial construction of the camp serves to create and sustain the politico-technical control and uncertain sociopolitical predicament of Roma. This article argues that permanent 'campzenship', and permanent criminalization sustain the state of insecurity and state of exception that legitimize and normalize precariousness and deprivation of Roma from political membership.

Politics of anti-Gypsyism

Neoliberalism has frequently been conceptualized as a race-neutral discourse, yet several studies show that the functioning of the contemporary global economy is deeply embedded in (while also reconfiguring) histories of colonization and racism (Lentin & Titley, 2011; Roberts & Mahtani, 2010). The operations of the market are always supported by unequal gendered and racialized power relations. As Shiva (2014) explains, contemporary neoliberal capitalism maintains unequal gender and racial relations based on the 'law of exploitation', which is a normative set of 'Western' values that determines our hierarchical relationships. The maintenance of the entitlement to practice exploitation and the denial of racial hierarchy are supported by the neoliberal ideology of meritocracy (Knowles & Lowery, 2012). Meritocracy is the belief system in neoliberalism which does not recognize the historical and social forces that determine people's social conditions and life circumstances, and therefore does not acknowledge the structural discrimination and racism that create enduring obstacles to the improvement of life. One of the basic tenets of this ideology is that those who are at the top or in a very advantageous positions are there, simply based on merit. Consequently, those who are in disadvantaged positions and are under-represented in various parts of the society simply lack merit in some way (Soss, Fording, & Schram, 2011). The lack of success is thus interpreted as an individual failure to work hard, or attributed to personal defects such as laziness, criminality, etc.

In the French and Italian cases, public discourse has also invoked neoliberal tropes to justify mistreatment against Romani migrants. Racialized rhetoric and spatialized material borders maintain the difference between 'us' and 'them'. Based on that, Romani people are fashioned as 'criminals', 'illegals', 'invaders' and 'nomads' who are taking 'our' resources and threaten 'our' security. Across these discourses, the presumed priority and privilege of the (white) Italian-ness and French-ness are maintained and reinforced by the construction of a binary between the ideal neoliberal citizen and those abject 'non-citizens' who inhabit the illegalized 'nomad camp'. The image of Romani migrants reiterated as deviant, antithetical to the very ethos of the free market.

Neoliberal governance, as Zygmunt Bauman suggests, has created a disposable (racialized) surplus labor force, 'populations of migrants, refugees and other outcasts' (Bauman, 2004). In summary, neoliberalism, in interaction with post-socialist domestic industrial and social policies' schemes in particular, has further forced some Roma from Central and Eastern European countries to migrate in order to escape from the violent manifestations of anti-Gypsyism (van Baar, 2011, 2014). Recent Italian and French anti-Roma policies have therefore become test cases, which may have polarized the EU's political elite, but not enough to challenge the neoliberal structural foundations of anti-Gypsyism. As this article has illustrated, Italian and French authorities acted against inter-EU Romani mobility and used coercive force, such as eviction and deportation, and discursive strategies of criminalization to alienate them from the 'color-blind' French and 'white' Italian citizenry. Therefore, promises of 'European' equality, equal opportunity and anti-discrimination protections remain empty. The histories of accumulated social inequalities and the persistent exclusion of Roma from citizenship, as well as a lack of social and political solidarity with their struggles, provide ample reasons for continued and renewed critical scholarly attention to the structure of anti-Gypsyism in Europe.

Notes

1. Undocumented migrants, often referred to as 'irregular', 'illegal', 'unauthorized' or 'clandestine migrants'.
2. The Decade of Romani Inclusion 2005–2015 is an unprecedented political commitment by European governments to eliminate discrimination against Romani and close the unacceptable gaps between Romani and the rest of society. The Decade focuses on the priority areas of education, employment, health and housing, and commits governments to take into account the other core issues of poverty, discrimination and gender mainstreaming. http://www.Romanidecade.org/about-the-decade-decade-in-brief.
3. See: http://www.europarl.europa.eu/sides/getDoc.do?pubRef=-//EP//TEXT±CRE±20080707±ITEM-018±DOC±XML±V0//EN.
4. See: http://www.europarl.europa.eu/sides/getDoc.do?pubRef=-//EP//TEXT+CRE+20080707+ITEM-018+DOC+XML+V0//EN.
5. Anti-Gypsyism used in the text as it is defined by a wide coalition of Roma and non-Roma activists and scholars; 'Antigypsyism is the specific racism towards Roma, Sinti, Travellers and others who are stigmatized as "gypsies" in the public imagination.' http://antigypsyism.eu/?page_id=17.

Disclosure statement

No potential conflict of interest was reported by the author.

References

Agamben, G. (1998). *Homo sacer: Sovereign power and bare life*. Stanford: Stanford University Press.
Agamben, G. (2005). *State of exception*. Chicago: University of Chicago Press.
Bacon, D. (2013). *The right to stay home: How US policy drives Mexican migration*. Boston: Beacon Press.
Bauman, Z. (2004). *Wasted lives: Modernity and its outcasts*. Cambridge: Polity.
Benedik, S. (2010). Harming cultural feelings. In M. Stewart & M. Rövid (Eds.), *Multidisciplinary approaches to Romany studies* (pp. 71–90). Budapest: CEU Press.
Berezin, M. (2009). *Illiberal politics in neoliberal times: Culture: Security and populism in the New Europe*. New York, NY: Cambridge University Press.
Brown, W. (2006, December). American nightmare: Neoliberalism, neoconservatism, and de-democratization. *Political Theory, 34*(6), 690–714.
Cahn, C., & Guild, E. (2008). *Report on the recent migration of Roma in Europe*. The Hague: Organization for Security and Cooperation in Europe.
Clough Marinaro, I. (2009). Between surveillance and exile: Biopolitics and the Romani in Italy. *Bulletin of Italian Politics, 1*(2), 265–287.
Clough Marinaro, I., & Sigona, N. (2011). Introduction anti-Gypsyism and the politics of exclusion: Romani and Sinti in contemporary Italy. *Journal of Modern Italian Studies, 16*(5), 583–589. doi:10.1080/1354571X.2011.622467

Davison, S., & Shire, G. (2013). Race, migration and neoliberalism. In S. Hall, D. Massey, & M. Rustin (Eds.), *After neoliberalism? The Kilburn manifesto* (pp. 176–191). Series: Soundings collections, Lawrence & Wishart: Independent Radical.

De Genova, N. (2002). Migrant 'illegality' and deportability in everyday life. *Annual Review of Anthropology, 31*, 419–447.

Fassin, É. (2010, October 7). Why the Romani? *Theory, Culture & Society*. Retrieved from https://www.theoryculturesociety.org/eric-fassin-why-the-roma/

Foucault, M. (2008). *The birth of biopolitics: Lectures at the collége de France, 1978–1979*. (ed. Michel Senellart, trans. Graham Burchell). Basingstoke: Palgrave Macmillan.

Fox, J., & Vermeersch, P. (2010). Backdoor nationalism. *European Journal of Sociology, 51*(2), 325–357.

Goldberg, D. T. (2009). *The threat of race: Reflections on racial neoliberalism*. Malden: Wiley-Blackwell.

Guy, W. (2003). 'No soft touch': Romani migration to the U.K. at the turn of the twenty-first century. *Nationalities Papers, 31*(1), 63–79.

Hall, S. (1997). The spectacle of the 'other'. In S. Hall (Ed.), *Representation: Cultural representations and signifying practices* (pp. 223–290). London: Sage.

Hepworth, K. (2012). Abject citizens: Italian 'nomad emergencies' and the deportation of Romanian Romani. *Citizenship Studies, 16*(3–4), 431–449.

Hermanin, C. (2011). 'Counts' in the Italian 'nomad camps': An incautious ethnic census of Roma. *Ethnic and Racial Studies, 34*(10), 1731–1750.

Hermann, C. (2007). Neoliberalism in the European Union. *Studies in Political Economy, 79*(Spring), 61–90.

Imre, A. (2005). Whiteness in post-socialist Eastern Europe: The time of the Gypsies, the end of race. In A. J. Lopez (Eds.), *Postcolonial whiteness: A critical reader on race and empire* (pp. 79–102). Ithaca: State University of New York Press.

Junghaus, T. (2015, April). *Romani contemporary Art the epistemic disobedience*. Paper presented at global governance, Democracy and Social Justice Symposium, organized by Wake Forest University and Duke University, Winston-Salem, NC.

Knowles, E. D., & Lowery, B. S. (2012). Meritocracy, self-concerns, and whites' denial of racial inequity. *Self and Identity, 11*(2), 202–222.

Kóczé, A. (2014). A rasszista tekintet és beszédmód által konstruált Romani férfi és női testek a médiában. *Apertúra*, (nyár-ősz).

Kóczé, A., & Trehan, N. (2009). Postcolonial racism and social justice: The struggle for the soul of the Romani civil rights movement in the 'New Europe'. In G. Huggan (Ed.), *Racism, post-colonialism, Europe* (pp. 50–77). Liverpool: Liverpool University Press.

Lentin, A., & Titley, G. (2011). *The crises of multiculturalism: Racism in a neoliberal Age*. New York, NY: Zed Books.

McGarry, A., & Drake, H. (2013). The politicization of Romani as an ethnic other: Security discourse in France and the politics of belonging. In U. Korkut, G. Bucken-Knapp, A. McGarry, J. Hinnfors, & H. Drake (Eds.), *The discourses and politics of migration in Europe* (pp. 73–91). New York, NY: Palgrave-MacMillan.

McNevin, A. (2007). Irregular migrants, neoliberal geographies and spatial frontiers of 'the political'. *Review of International Studies, 33*(4), 655–674.

McNevin, A. (2011). *Contesting citizenship. Irregular migrants and new frontiers of the political*. New York, NY: Columbia University Press.

Merlino, M. (2009). The Italian (In)security Package, *Research Papers Series*, No. 14. CEPS-Challenge Programme.

Molnar Diop, P. (2013). The 'bogus' refugee: Romani asylum claimants and discourses of fraud in Canada's bill C-31. *Refuge, 30*(1), 67–80.

Nacu, A. (2012). From silent marginality to spotlight scapegoating? A brief case study of France's policy towards the Romani. *Journal of Ethnic and Migration Studies, 38*(8 September), 1323–1328.

Picker, G. (2012). Left-wing progress? Neo-nationalism and the case of Romani migrants in Italy. In J. Stewart (Ed.), *The gypsy 'menace': Populism and the New anti-gypsy politics* (pp. 81–94). London: Hurst & Co./Columbia University Press.

Pop, V. (2010, September 15). Paris tells Brussels: 'You do not speak to us like this'. *EU Observer*.

Roberts, D. J., & Mahtani, M. (2010). Neoliberalizing race, racing neoliberalism: Placing 'race' in neoliberal discourses. *Antipode, 42*(2), 248–257. doi:10.1111/j.1467-8330.2009.00747.x

Saull, R. (2015). The origins and persistence of the far-right: Capital, class and the pathologies of liberal politics. In R. Saull, A. Anievas, N. Davidson, & A. Fabry (Eds.), *The longue duree of the far-right: An international historical sociology* (pp. 21–43). Abingdon: Routledge.

Shiva, V. (2014, May 26). We are the soil. *CommonDreams.org*. Retrieved from http://www.commondreams.org/views/2014/05/26/we-are-soil

Sigona, N. (Ed.). (2008, January 21). *The latest public enemy: The case of the Romanian Romani in Italy: The case studies of Milan, Bologna, Rome and Naples*. The research and writing for the report was funded by the OSCE/ODIHR and CPRSI. Published by OsservAzione.

Sigona, N. (2011). The governance of Romani people in Italy: Discourse, policy and practice. *Journal of Modern Italian Studies, 16*(5), 590–606.

Sigona, N. (2014). Eu citizenship, Romani mobility and anti-Gypsyism: Time for reframing the debate? In B. Anderson & M. Keith (Eds.), *Migration: The COMPAS anthology*. Oxford: COMPAS. Retrieved from http://compasanthology.co.uk/eu-citizenship-roma-mobility-anti-gypsyism-time-reframing-debate/

Sigona, N. & Trehan, N. (Eds.). (2009). *Romani politics in Europe: Poverty, ethnic marginalisation and the neoliberal order*. London: Palgrave Macmillan.

Sigona, N., & Vermeersch, P. (2012). Editors' introduction. The Romani in the New EU: Policies, frames and everyday experiences. *Journal of Ethnic and Migration Studies, 38*(8), 1189–1193.

Soss, J., Fording, R. C., & Schram, S. (Eds.). (2011). *Disciplining the poor: Neoliberal paternalism and the persistent power of race*. Chicago: University of Chicago Press.

Squire, V. (Ed.). (2011). *The politics of contesting mobility: Borderzones and irregularity*. London: Routledge.

Stewart, M. (2012a). Foreword: New forms of anti-gypsy politics: A challenge for Europe. In M. Stewart (Ed.), *The Gypsy 'menace': Populism and the new anti-gypsy politics* (pp. xiii–xxxviii). London: Hurst & Co./Columbia University Press.

Stewart, M. (2012b). Populism, Romani and the European politics of cultural difference. In M. Stewart (Ed.), *The Gypsy 'menace': Populism and the new anti-Gypsy politics* (pp. 3–23). London: Hurst & Co./Columbia University Press.

Traynor, I. (2010, September 14). Romani deportations by France a disgrace, says EU. *The Guardian*.

Trumpener, K. (1992). The time of the gypsies: A 'people without history' in the narratives of the west. *Critical Inquiry, 18*(4), 843–884.

van Baar, H. (2011). Europe's Romaniphobia: Problematization, securitization, nomadization. *Environment and Planning D: Society and Space, 29*(2), 203–212.

van Baar, H. (2012). Socio-economic mobility and neo-liberal governmentality in post-socialist Europe: Activation and the dehumanisation of the Roma. *Journal of Ethnic and Migration Studies, 38*(8), 1289–1304.

van Baar, H. (2014). The emergence of a reasonable anti-Gypsyism in Europe. In T. Agarin (Eds.), *When stereotype meets prejudice: Antiziganism in European societies* (pp. 27–44). Stuttgart: Ibidem.

van Baar, H. (2015). The perpetual mobile machine of forced mobility: Europe's Romani and the institutionalization of rootlessness. In Y. Jansen, R. Celikates, & J. de Bloois (Eds.), *The irregularization of migration in contemporary Europe: Deportation, detention, drowning* (pp. 71–86). London: Rowman & Littlefield.

Vašečka, I., & Vašečka, M. (2003). Recent Romani migration from Slovakia to EU member states: Romani reaction to discrimination or Romani ethno-tourism? *Nationalities Papers, 31*(1), 27–45.

Woodcock, S. (2010). Gender as catalyst for violence against Roma in contemporary Italy. *Patterns of Prejudice, 44*(5), 469–488.

Worth, O. (2015). The far-right and neoliberalism: Willing partner or hegemonic opponent? In R. Saull, A. Anievas, N. Davidson, & A. Fabry (Eds.), *The longue durée of the Far-right: An international historical sociology* (pp. 153–172). London: Routledge.

3 Challenging Europe's external borders and internal boundaries

Bosnian *Xoraxané Xomá* on the move in Roman peripheries and the contemporary European Union

Marco Solimene

ABSTRACT
This paper explores, from an ethnographic standpoint, the mobility of a Bosnian Romani community in relation to the xenophobic and anti-Romani discourses that are pervading contemporary Italian and European society in the time of the so-called migrant crisis. The analysis focuses on some so-called *Xomá* families who live dispersed among illegal shanties in the Rome and whose movements and social network protract into other Italian and European cities. The question of mobility is addressed both in terms of local movements within the Roman peripheries and of wider transnational trajectories. Romani mobility appears as a tactical response to processes imposed from above that challenges the forms of governmentality related to the policing of borders and the production of boundaries of the EU and its member-states.

Roma and migrants in the context of Europe's borders and boundaries

This paper explores the mobility of several Bosnian Romani families whose presence, family linkages and activities extend from Rome into other Italian and European cities. By putting these families' social organization and movements into relation with the xenophobic and anti-Romani discourses that are pervading contemporary Italian and European society, I will unravel the tangle of Romani mobility at the local, national and transnational levels with the issue of governmentality. This begs for a preliminary discussion on the role that external borders and internal boundaries, which the persons described herein continually cross, play in the issue of governmentality in the context of both the EU and its nation-states.[1]

Without falling into the trap of 'methodological nationalism' (Wimmer & Glick Schiller, 2002), it can be claimed that nation-states still play an important role in the contemporary Europe (Isin & Saward, 2013a). Nation-states, however, face the reconfiguration and re-conceptualization of their functions, characteristics, structure and limits (Aretxaga, 2003) in light of processes (globalization, transnationalism, migrations, diasporas, etc.) that challenge the national rhetoric of isomorphism between territory, population and culture (Malkki, 1992) and question ideas of national sovereignty and citizenry (Glick Schiller,

2007; Wimmer & Glick Schiller, 2002). People moving across borders represent 'a problem of state policy, national cohesion, racial consciousness and academic study' (Silverstein, 2005, p. 364), and, Fassin (2011) argues, it is precisely because immigrants 'embody the articulation of borders and boundaries' (p. 215) that 'the governmentality of immigration has become a crucial issue of contemporary societies' (p. 213).

Borders and boundaries have geographical, political, social, cultural and identity connotations (Alvarez, 1995; Lamont & Molnár, 2002), but while 'borders' is used in reference to the delimitation of political entities and their legal subjects and thus the exclusion of outsiders, 'boundaries' have to do with the establishment, within these borders, of symbolic differences that lead to distinguishing between members and 'illicit' residents. The analytical distinction between borders and boundaries should not obscure the mutual nature between the policing of external borders and the production of internal boundaries in contemporary Europe (Fassin, 2011). The 'border spectacle' (De Genova, 2002), showing Europe's outposts threatened by tidal waves of 'undesirables', moves inwards and produces internal boundaries that are constructed and maintained by juridico-political categories, such as 'immigrant', 'clandestine' and 'illegal alien', detaining a biopolitical character and subjecting migrants to a regime of illegality, deportability and detainability (e.g. De Genova & Peutz, 2010).

The link between borders and boundaries was highlighted by Stewart (2011), who noticed how the closure to immigrants, enacted by European nation-states between the nineteenth and twentieth centuries, coincided with the involution of policies concerning the Romani population living within national territories. This argument also supports the close connection between migrants and the so-called Gypsies/Roma. The reader should consider that 'Roma' and 'Gypsies' are problematic categories that result from the dialectic between self-ascriptions and ascriptions-by-others, and that the construction of the Romani people as a distinct group and the deployment of different terms to name it are currently object of debate among scholars, intellectuals, activists and politicians. For analytical purposes, in this article I will use the adjective 'Romani' in reference to the actual persons labelled as 'Gypsies' or 'Roma' and identifying themselves as *Roma, Sinti, Gypsies, Manouches, Gitanos* ... I will instead use the terms 'Gypsies' and 'Roma' to reflect the perspective of those who consider themselves as non-Gypsies (or non-Roma) and attach this label to a non-well defined group of people. In Europe, indeed, national rhetoric, juridical-political discourse, the media and collective imagery use the terms 'Roma' and/or 'Gypsies' in reference to a supposed ethnic belonging and socio-cultural specificity, and associate them with Otherness and non-belonging. The terms 'Roma' and 'Gypsies' are thus increasingly becoming politically correct synonyms of race; furthermore, they also hold a biopolitical power that exposes the Romani population to a regime of illegality, deportability and detain-ability similar to that to which migrants are subject (Piasere, 2012; Stewart & Rovid, 2011; Stewart & Williams, 2011; also Clough Marinaro, 2009; Solimene, 2013; Kóczé, 2017).

Several publications (e.g. Piasere, 2004; Stewart & Williams, 2011) have pointed out the crucial role that the Roma play in the construction of European national identity. This argument may be extended to the European level, where uncertainties regarding debates on European identity are accompanied by the certainty that the Roma are excluded from it (Isin & Saward, 2013a). The resemblance between European and national discourses can also be detected in their reference to immigrants and Roma. In regard to immigration, the EU maintains a framework that is strictly based on openness and respect of human and asylum rights and, in fact, many national governments have been issued warnings regarding their treatment of refugees, reluctance to assume their share of asylum responsibilities and breach of the principle of non-refoulement. However, even before the outbreak of the alleged 'migrant-crisis' the EU has also allowed member states to circumvent this framework and apply restrictive exceptions and has also promoted the principle of quotas (with its racializing and criminalizing effects on migrants) and the use of detention and deportation as a legitimate governmental means to deal with immigration (De Genova & Peutz, 2010; Fassin, 2011; Fekete, 2005; Walters, 2009).

Regarding the Roma issue, European society is steeped in anti-Romani racism (Kuychukov, 2012) and 'anti-Gypsyism' has only recently been recognized as a specific form of racism that subjects the people categorized as Gypsies/Roma as a whole group to an othering process of de-humanization and criminalization (Nicolae, 2007). The European Commission has repeatedly expressed concerns about the situation of the Romani population in Europe and admonished national governments for their indifference, and often explicit discrimination, towards the Roma (Ionescu & Stainescu, 2014). This concern has led to the outlining of programmes supporting Roma-related initiatives and the emergence of 'human rights and minority discourses and regimes' that consolidated 'alongside an embryonic Romani political movement' (Sigona & Trehan, 2009, p. 7). Nonetheless, in the EU's discourse, even in its explicitly multi-culturalist and pro-Roma standpoints, anti-Romani sentiments surreptitiously emerge and also seem to be in league with the neoliberal agenda affirmed throughout Europe (Piasere, 2012; Sigona & Trehan, 2009; Templer, 2006).

The point I am making is that just as they are rejected from national citizenry, Europe's Romani people are 'in the EU but not of EU citizenship' (Caglar & Mehling, 2013). The anti-Romani discourse pervading contemporary European society portrays the Roma as nomadic, hybrid and uprooted people who, like immigrants and refugees, threaten the 'sedentary metaphysics' of nation-states (Malkki, 1992). The Roma are thus construed as a social, economic, political and cosmological threat (Piasere, 2012): despite their centuries-long presence in Europe as a 'dispersed majority',[2] they are treated as what Douglas (2002) called 'matter-out-of-place'. Or better: embodying the figure of the trickster, who is 'representative of non-order (rather than just dis-order)' (Piasere, 2012, pp. 171–172), the Roma appear in non-Romani discourses as matter-without-place.

In light of these considerations, we might paraphrase Fassin (2011) and argue that the governmentality of the Roma represents a crucial issue in contemporary Europe, especially in the case of persons, like those presented in this paper, who are non-EU citizens and thus clearly embody the articulation of Europe's external borders and internal boundaries. One more consideration is necessary. 'Europe' is a prototypical category with central members and marginal ones (Piasere, 2012). This epistemological issue is vehicle and expression of power relations within Europe. The Schengen agreements made Europe's internal borders easier to trespass in physical terms, but borders did not vanish at the politico-juridical level and their symbolical relevance increased, thus giving rise to a hierarchy between EU members that favours the neoliberal agenda (Walters, 2009). Besides, different 'Europes' reside within Europe itself and do not coincide. Even when considering the EU alone, which dominates this 'variably overlapping assemblage of institutions, treaties, arrangements, organs, and movements' (Isin & Saward, 2013b, p. 6), borders and boundaries are blurred by the distinction between EU-members and EU-candidates (Walters, 2009), the prospect of withdrawal by EU-members, the presence of Transit Processing Centres in extra-European areas (Fekete, 2005) and the inward expansion of external borders (Andrijasevic, 2010; Templer, 2006).

In this paper, I will present materials collected during a 14-month ethnographic fieldwork study carried out between 2007 and 2008. A great deal of information also emerged during relations with several Romani families that began in 1999 and which I still cultivate. The persons described herein are situated at the far limits of the European and Italian society's xenophobic system. Hailing from Bosnia (non-EU country in the heart of Europe and lacerated by an ethnic conflict that shocked the European conscience), they were temporarily war refugees[3] (thus 'uprooted' and 'displaced'), 'immigrants' (often within national borders illegally) and also 'Gypsies' and 'Nomads'. I will firstly explore the repercussions of their categorization as 'Gypsies', 'Roma', 'Nomads', 'immigrants' and 'illegals' and then address the question of mobility in terms of both local movements within the Roman peripheries and wider transnational trajectories, since these Romani families extend their movements and social network into various Italian and European cities. Since Romani mobility can only be fully understood in reference to non-Romani policies (cf. Beluschi, 2013; Piasere, 2004), I will conceptualize mobility as the result of dynamics inherent to both the world of the *Gağé* (non-Romani persons) and the Romani world, and of the dialectic relation between them. Lastly, I will demonstrate that Romani mobility challenges the forms of governmentality related to the policing of external borders and the production of internal boundaries at local, national and European levels.

About the *Xomá*

This paper explores the movements of a Romani community hailing from Bosnia and that has predominantly been living in Rome for decades. These people, who count about 200 individuals, more than half of which are minors, are organized into large families linked together by a thick web of blood and affinity relationships and cohabitation experiences in the same Bosnian village and the same Roman nomad camps. These people call themselves '*Xomá*' (masc. sing.: *Xom*; fem. sing.: *Xomní*), a term that will hereinafter distinguish my interlocutors from all other Romani persons. As many other Bosnian Romani communities, the *Xomá* define themselves as '*Xoraxané*': this term refers to their Islamic religion,[4] which nevertheless is bland and highly syncretic, even by Bosnian standards (cf. Al-Ali, 2002; Bringa, 1995). The *Xomá* also use the term '*Bosnijako*' (Bosnian), but predominantly in front of *Gağé* and in order to distinguish themselves from other Romani groups (especially Romani migrants from Romania and non-Muslim Slavic Romani communities).

Many *Xoraxané* living in Rome define the *Xomá* as *Čergarja*. This term is generally used in reference to Romani persons who live in tents ('*čerga*' means 'tent' in many Balkan languages) and constantly change abode. As an attributed identity, '*Čergarja*' is interpreted as somewhat pejorative. '*Čergarja*', many assert, 'lack hygiene, culture and parenting abilities; they are the real nomads' (where this term evokes the prejudices and stereotypes Italians attach to the word '*nomade*'). As a self-ascription, however, '*Čergarja*' has no demeaning connotations whatsoever and many *Xomá* proudly assert their identity as *Čergarja*, which, in their view, expresses the freedom and self-determination that most non-

Čergarja would renounce with reticence to movement and the acceptance of seclusion and controls that characterize legal nomad camps (cf. Saletti Salza, 2003; Solimene, 2013).[5]

The *Xomá*'s relationship with Italian society is characterized by a blend of inclusion and exclusion occurring at intersecting levels and produced by the dialectic between enforced processes imposed from above and autonomous choices. First of all, they are categorized as 'Gypsies/Roma/Nomads' (*Zingari/Rom/Nomadi*, terms that have somehow become interchangeable), and therefore they are approached by the Italian authorities through a combination of indifference and discrimination. The Roma are not recognized as a national minority and thus do not legally exist as a group. Nonetheless, they are the object of regional laws issued between 1980s and 1990s, and more recently emergency measures that prompt their racialization and criminalization. Political debate, media and collective imagery construe the Gypsies/Roma/Nomads as foreigners (even though Romani communities have been living in Italy for centuries) and as a culturally and socially underdeveloped group that threatens the Italian society. These anti-Romani discourses radicalized in response to the 'invasion syndrome' triggered by the recent arrival of Romanian Romani migrants. As a result, Italian authorities focused on treating Italy's Romani population as 'social waste', to be contained in nomad camps and/or banned from the national territory (Clough Marinaro, 2009; Clough-Marinaro & Sigona, 2011; Colacicchi, 2008; Piasere, 2012; Simoni, 2005).

The *Xomá* are also labelled as 'immigrants' (and often 'illegals'). Despite having lived in Italy for decades, they are denied Italian citizenship. Once their war-refugee status was lost, many *Xomá* struggled to get a visa (often temporary) and some still lack any official document of identification. This situation exposes the *Xomá* to the marginalization, racialization and criminalization processes inherent to contemporary Italy's immigration policies (cf. Angel-Ajani, 2000; Saitta, 2011). This legally borderline condition, aggravated by the lack of legal permits, adds to the difficulties that Romani persons generally encounter in the Italian labour market (Colacicchi, 2008). As a result, many of the *Xomá*'s economic activities (begging, scrap metal collection and sale of counterfeit merchandise) stand on the threshold between legality and illegality. As such, they perfectly fit within the ambiguities of the Italian social, economic, political and cultural landscape (Solimene, 2016), wherein legality and illegality, formality and informality, rejection and acceptance merge and intertwine (Istituto Nazionale di Statistica, 2005). As for dwelling conditions, most *Xomá* live dispersed among the innumerable nomad camps disseminated throughout Rome's territory.[6] Most settlements are illegal: precarious encampments sprouting up in green areas and interstitial urban spaces, in which the inhabitants have to contend with the weather conditions, the lack of electricity, toilets and water, as well as the constant threat of forced eviction by the police.

Summarizing, the *Xomá* are exposed to the anti-Romani and xenophobic discourses that pervade contemporary Italian society. Perceived as inadmissible and illegitimate aliens, they face ghettoization in nomad camps, evictions, juridical marginality (when not invisibility), exclusion from the formal labour market, harassment by the authorities and grass-root racism. Nevertheless, as I will demonstrate in the following pages, they are relatively integrated in specific peripheries where, especially as single individuals, they are well-accepted (or at least tolerated) by the local population and authorities, who have learned to cohabitate, not without difficulties and occasional contrasts, with the (allegedly) despicable Gypsies/Roma/Nomads.

Rome, between mobility and rootedness

The *Xomá* first arrived in Italy between the second half of the 1960s (during Italy's economic boom) and the mid-1990s, when the war in former Yugoslavia – from which many Bosnians, including a large number of Romani persons, fled (de Koning, 2008) – officially came to an end. Like other Yugoslavian Romani communities, in the past the *Xomá* carried out transnational practices, favoured by easy access to a three-months-stay visa (Lockwood, 1986; Piasere, 2004, pp. 84–86). Today, most *Xomá* only reach out to Bosnia – I paraphrase Glick Schiller (2007) – 'through memory, nostalgia and imagination'. The legal restrictions concerning circulation between Italy and Bosnia (intensified by the *Xomá*'s lack of documents) are joined by: the impossibility to return to the village of origin, nowadays situated in Serbian territory (*Republika Srpska*); the social, economic and cultural hardships that Bosnian returnees face (Al-Ali, 2002; de Koning, 2008); and the deprivation of rights that Romani persons in Bosnia and Herzegovina are subject to (ERRC, 2004; also, Sardelić, 2017). Another significant point is that the *Xomá* do not return to Bosnia because most of their family members now live in Western Europe. This consideration calls for reflection on the *Xomá*'s social organization.

The typical patrilineal-based Bosnian household (Bringa, 1995) has lost its relevance in structuring social ties among Bosnian refugees, whose families were scattered and dispersed in and out of Yugoslavia (Al-Ali, 2002). By contrast, the extended families of the *Xomá* – and more generally of Bosnian Romani refugees (cf. for Italy Saletti Salza, 2003; Saletti Salza & Piasere, 2004) – have maintained a high level of cohesion. Like other *Xoraxané* groups living in Italy (cf. Piasere, 1991; Saletti Salza, 2003), the *Xomá* follow the general rule of patri-viri-locality: roughly speaking, once they marry, the men remain with their parents while the women move to their husbands' dwelling place. The residential extended family is thus ideally made up of a married couple, their unmarried children, and the married sons with their respective wives and children. It functions as an autonomous socio-economic-political entity, whose members share an ideology of reciprocal help and solidarity, which is amply confirmed by their everyday practices.

That of the *Xomá* is a headless, fluid and flexible organization. Families live dispersed and move autonomously, gathering and splitting with extreme facility. Aggregations appear, disappear and continually re-shape and relocate, but clustering is not random. The couple of elderly parents represents the centre around which the various nuclear families of the couple's married sons cluster; but the principle of segmentation also reverberates within the residential extended family, whose nuclear families often split and rejoin among themselves and with other Romani families. In fact, the *Xomá* social network extends beyond familial linkages. Common economic interests, past cohabitation and fortuitous events contribute to establishing social vicinity, thereby affecting the decision of where, and with whom, to live. Thus, *Xomá* families may at times be hosted by distant relatives living in authorized settlements or in a flat; share their encampment with *Goraždakuri* and *Cernogorcuri* (respectively, Romani persons from Goražde, Bosnia, and from Montenegro), who are '*Xoraxané* like us' and practice the same mobility; encamp in a *Rumuni* (as they call Romani persons from Romania) settlement, but possibly at its borders because the '*Rumuni* are different and dirty'.[7]

This combination of segmentation and (re)consolidation places each *Xomá* family within a wide Romani network that extends into various Roman neighbourhoods, wherein each *Xomá* family has reference points in familiar dwelling places (familiar because known, and/or because inhabited by relatives or acquaintances) and in *Gağé* facilities, such as shops, bars and internet points, that are regularly attended when living in the district. Dispersion and mobility do not mean isolation. The world of the *Xomá*, with its ramifications in other Romani groups, may be surprisingly small and the circulation of information through hearsay and gossip is continual. Besides, social ties are continually confirmed and re-constructed through phone-calls and, more importantly, reciprocal visits. The *Xomá* regularly 'sit' (*te bešél*) together drinking coffee, smoking cigarettes, eating and exchanging information (cf. Saletti Salza, 2003). Moreover, celebrations like birthdays and marriages often bring relatives and acquaintances together, and it is generally easy to find *Xomá* and Romani acquaintances in some particular squares, at flea markets, train stations, metal dealers and charitable organizations.

Dispersion and mobility may even preserve relations. The social organization of the *Xomá* responds to their specific horizon of interpersonal relations, wherein the *Xomá* consider themselves as equals, do not accept hierarchies or representation from persons outside the family, do not hide antipathies and harshly react to external interferences in the management of everyday life. Thus, the *Xomá* move to avoid living with families they dislike or are in conflict with, may change settlement to curb animosity after a quarrel with a relative or an in-law, or leave a neighbourhood to avoid a fight escalating into a blood feud. It can therefore be said that relations and social peace are maintained through mobility and dispersion.

The *Xomá* organization can be also seen as a response to the external world, that of the *Gağé*. Mobility and dispersion are a way to escape the authorities' continual attempts to control and repress the Gypsies/Roma/Nomads. The *Xomá* move to avoid an eviction or an incoming police control, and/or to win the benevolence of officers who might appreciate acquiescence to an 'official transcript' (Scott, 1990).[8] By moving, they also dilute their presence among areas patrolled by different police stations[9] and administered by different boroughs.[10] Mobility and dispersion thus diminish *Xomá* visibility within a territory and give the local authorities and population the impression of a light and ephemeral presence. Not only do the *Xomá* keep a low profile by moving continuously between small encampments that appear and disappear as soon as they risk provoking too much disturbance, the *Xomá* also move on a daily basis to carry out economic activities that might produce tension with the local population. Aware that Italians are not fond of beggars on their doorstep or of vans that, in search of scrap metals, further congest the urban traffic, *Xomá* women go begging in the centre and *Xomá* men search for scrap metals across the city's periphery and conurbations. Furthermore, the disjunction between working and dwelling territories means that a constant presence within a working territory can be maintained despite changes of residence.

The *Xomá* therefore combine tactics of spatial mobility and dispersion with local rootedness. Many, indeed, grew up and attended (although intermittently) state schools in Rome's south-western periphery. There, they interweaved personal networks of relations and everyday interaction with the local population (comprised of both Italian citizens and immigrants) despite their movements in and out of the capital area, the collective rejection of Gypsies/Roma/Nomads and the segregating power of the nomad camps. In a counterintuitive way, mobility means that the *Xomà* can remain in a district without creating excessive disturbance to the local population, escape the authorities' control of the urban territory, achieve individual socio-economic integration and remain socially close despite forced displacements, evictions and quarrels and tensions within the *Xomá* community or with the local population.

Transnational landscapes

In the eyes of the authorities, the *Xomá* are among those undisciplined Gypsies/Roma/Nomads, whose lack of documents, legal employment and residence makes them an 'excess of humanity' (Rahola, 2003), in a city like Rome that explicitly set a maximum allowance of Gypsies/Roma/Nomads (Clough Marinaro, 2009). Nevertheless, as argued above, the *Xomá* have maintained their presence in the Eternal city by moving: mobility creates an idea of 'impermanence' which persuades the non-Romani society to accept the very presence of Romani groups and 'it is precisely this definitive character of transitoriness that makes the presence of the [*Xomá*] continuous' (Solimene, 2014, p. 139). I will now turn to wider landscapes and explain how the *Xomá* combine urban mobility with travels across Italy and Europe. Beluschi (2013) demonstrates that the social organization of the Transylvanian *Roma Korturare* migrating to Western Europe varied according to the external political context and thus that the *Korturare* became highly mobile and dispersed in countries (such as France and Italy) that enacted policies aimed at territorial 'cleansing' of the Romani population. Following this lead, I will demonstrate that the presence of the *Xomá* at transnational level reflects, *mutatis mutandis*, the principles underlying their local presence. Once again I will start from the *Xomá* social organization.

As previously discussed, the *Xomá* talk of 'family' (*familja*) in relation to the patri-virilocal family. In a wider meaning, however, *familja* refers to every person who shares blood ties with a *Xom* or *Xomní* on both the paternal and maternal side. Thus, every *Xomá* person has their own *familja*, which, at their death, ceases to exist in that specific composition (cf. Piasere, 1991, about Kosovo's *Xoraxané*). In this extended version, *familja* is a 'transnational family' (Bryceson & Vuorela, 2002) that comprises tens of members dispersed among different districts in Rome, other Italian cities (especially Naples, Geneva, Turin and Milan), Western European countries (France, Spain, Germany and Holland) and, to a minimal degree, former Yugoslavia. Most of the *familja*'s older members know each other personally. At a distance, contacts are maintained through phone-calls, hearsay and, more recently, the Internet. However, the lack of personal and continual contacts between most members weakens the *familja*'s centripetal force. Thus, I use Glick Schiller's (2007) distinction, these extended families represent a 'transnational way of belonging' that only partially result in a 'transnational way of being'. Members of a *familja* are bound by ties that, being defined in terms of 'blood' (*rat*) (predominantly on the patrilineal side), ideally exist independently of any actual experiences of vicinity but nevertheless must be cultivated in order to also be of practical relevance.

This is why relatives pay visits to each other even when living in distant lands. When these visits foresee a long journey, they are often lengthy and thus become intense experiences of vicinity. Events such as marriages, name-giving ceremonies or funerals are good opportunities to meet up again, but travels have a variety of often simultaneous purposes. Visiting a relative may be combined with exploiting economic opportunities that translocal and transnational movements may offer, or fleeing from conflict with other Romani families or from troubles with the local authorities. Lastly, travels also provide the chance to explore the opportunities offered by a territory in terms of housing, employment and access to documents and welfare.

Travels require a starting capital and are risky enterprises: harshness and uncertainties merge with the possibility of unfortunate events (such as accidents) and unlucky encounters (such as police controls, which might result in extortion, abuse of power, or even seizure of a vehicle, detention and/or expulsion). The *Xomá* reduce the risks of uncertainties by moving (when possible) between places either inhabited by *familja* or known through direct and/or indirect experience. Moreover, the *Xomá* lie low by moving in small and agile groups that rarely count more than three nuclear families, and that in specifically exploratory trips, are composed of one nuclear family or a few close relatives. Travel by road is preferred to trains and planes: roads are less controlled and a vehicle grants autonomy of movement. Both cars and caravans are used. A caravan is more detectable as a Gypsy vehicle (the *Xomá*'s caravans are often old and battered, while the cars they use for travelling are usually shiny BMWs or Mercedes). A caravan is also slower and more expensive, but it provides autonomy in terms of dwelling and food preparation. Lastly, the *Xomá* place their hopes on the possibility of avoiding controls and encounters with unfriendly officers, or at least, they hope that being caught with some irregularity – lack of visa, vehicle insurance, passengers exceeding the legal number – they might be able to rely on their interactional skills and get out of trouble by moving the officers' heart (or filling their wallets) (Solimene, 2013). During these encounters, movement might even prove advantageous since the authorities might just be content with handing some Roma over to the neighbouring municipality, region or country – an easy solution often adopted with immigrants and refugees as well. Thus, internal borders act as 'filters' (Walters, 2009) that can be relatively trespassed at both national and EU levels, even by undocumented people (whose major problem is still how to gain entry by crossing national, and particularly the EU's, external borders).[11]

Sometimes, sporadic travels mark the beginning of more assiduous transnational practices, as the following case exemplifies. In 2002, Fikret and Golub[12] (two brothers in their thirties with the prospect of soon being evicted with their families from their settlement) went on an exploratory trip to Marseille (France). Apparently, a regularization provision on the matter of immigration was making visa and public housing more accessible there than in Rome. These were the rumours – actually well-founded (cf. MPI, 2007) – circulating in the *Xomá*'s network, wherein some families had started crossing France to reach Spain. Between 2003 and 2005, Fikret moved regularly between Rome and Marseille, firstly alone or with Golub, and later on also with part of his nuclear family. After obtaining his legal residence in Marseille, Fikret became a reference point for the *Xomá* (belonging to his network) who wanted to try their luck in France. However, Fikret and his nuclear family also maintained a constant presence in Rome, where long periods (even months) were spent with Fikret's brothers and cousins (father's brothers' sons) encamping in the Nomentana district and/or his wife's siblings residing in a legal settlement in the Magliana district. From 2007, when Rome's Romani population was targeted for several years with extremely harsh policies (Clough Marinaro, 2009, 2015), Fikret's stays in Rome became shorter and less frequent and, after a series of events, Golub also moved to Marseille with his family. To my knowledge, the two brothers are now living in Lille and there is no guarantee that they will remain there definitively.

In 18 years I have lost track of many *Xomá* who had left Rome but I have also re-encountered *Xomá* who were back in Rome visiting relatives and/or staying for some time. Halil's family offers a good example of these long-term, almost cyclical, trans-local oscillations. In addition to some family members' occasional travels abroad, Halil's family moved as a whole unit (more than 20 persons) approximately every 10 years. In 1991, they moved to Milan's nomad camps for several months, where one of Halil's sister lived (and where two of Halil's sons were born).[13] Between 2000 and 2002, the family lived in Germany, Berlin and Cologne, where they accessed (temporarily) visa, housing, employment and schooling programmes and where one of Halil's sons married Danka, a *Šiftar* (Albanian) Romani woman born in Beograd. In 2014, exhausted by years of precarious living on riverbanks and with no prospect of improvement, Halil moved with his wife and two sons (one married and with children) to Lille (where his wife's relatives and his cousins Golub and Fikret were living); then they crossed into Holland (where one of Halil's married daughters was living) and eventually arrived in Cologne, where Danka met her father again. Apparently, Cologne's social services offered them social housing and economic support, but after a few months they separated the family members, who are now scattered among different locations. This might trigger a return to Rome, where part of the family (Halil's eldest son, now with his extended residential family, and two younger brothers with their nuclear families) is living, keeping the territory warm and familiar.

Mobility, rhizomes and governmentality

Considering that the *Xomá* are linked together by both kinship and affinity ties, we understand that each *Xomá* person potentially disposes of a widespread network stretching out all over Europe and providing social, economic, cultural and symbolic capitals. In this way they can leave a place knowing that someone will remain there (thus making return possible) and that someone else will mediate with the new territory. The *Xomá* can therefore rely on a network of familiar places, whose level of familiarity and accessibility, however, is highly variable since the *Xomá*'s network continually changes in composition and geographical distribution, as it is the result of flexible and fluid ties whose relevance in drawing the contours of commonality is continuously renegotiated.

These findings confirm Beluschi's (2013) accounts of the *Korturare* migrating to Western Europe: like the *Korturare*, the *Xomá* move for varied reasons and purposes, their families spread out in unclear patterns and may remain scattered, and their choice of whether to stay or leave is always revocable. However, while Beluschi talks of a migratory process from Romania to Western Europe, the *Xomá*'s case is complicated by the fact that there is no easily definable homeland to leave or return to. Without entering into the complex debate about the concept of home opened by migration, diaspora and return migration studies (cf. Cassarino, 2004), I would say that the *Xomá* left their 'homeland', that is, Bosnia, long ago and they do not fantasize about a return, nor yearn for it. Moreover, Rome has partially exceeded Bosnia in conveying the idea of homeland in terms of both identity and everyday practices since many *Xomá*, especially the younger generations, now consider themselves as Romans and Rome is still the place around which the existences and movements of most *Xomá* gravitate. This 'bi-focality' (Vertovec, 2004), however, is moderated by the idea that, as I once heard from a *Xom*, 'we are used to living among the *Gağé* [...] and there is no place that is really ours: we are international'. There is 'no place' because the *Xomá* are hardly acknowledged a place by the non-Romani authorities – and this may lessen the need for a clear definition of homeland (cf. Malkki, 1992). But 'there is no place' also because the movement characterizing the *Xomá* at both practical and symbolical levels (they are *Čergarja*) makes everywhere a potentially feasible place to live in. The pivotal role of Rome comes from my analytical choice and fieldwork experience and I believe that it also reflects the perspective of many *Xomá*. Nonetheless, within the larger picture of the Romani network in which the *Xomá* are embedded, Rome's importance is weakened by the presence of other centres whose relevance depends on the experiences and memories of the place and on the closeness of the persons still dwelling therein. Based on a decentred, fluid and transitory understanding of, and relation to places, the *Xomá*'s presence shows the characteristics of a 'rhizome' (Deleuze & Guattari, 1987): connections between heterogeneous elements, lines of segmentation that make ruptures insignificant, absence of a rigid structure, de-territorialization and multiple entryways.

These premises bring to focus on the *Xomá*'s movements in relation to the question of governmentality. Borders are created to control the movement of people but their effects reach also those who physically trespass them. Likewise, the effectiveness of the deportations and detention goes beyond the number of people actually deported or detained. In other words, it is the regime of illegality, deportability and detain-ability that functions as a biopolitical means to make migrants vulnerable and exploitable (De Genova, 2002; De Genova & Peutz, 2010; Walters, 2009). These considerations could lead to disquieting conclusions. Firstly, if movement is a 'weapon of the weak' (Scott, 1985), the *Xomá*'s mobility signals the heightening of anti-Romani sentiments and xenophobia at both national and EU levels. Secondly and consequently, the *Xomá* might move but would not escape the biopolitical regime targeting those trespassing the EU's borders and boundaries.

However, if the mobility of the *Xomá* is a response to the biopolitical regime, this response echoes De Certeau's (1984) concept of 'tactic'. It does not start from a clearly circumscribed space, it is the result of specific conjunctions, and it wallows in the contradictions and ambiguities of the governmentality of immigration and Roma, making, De Certeau would say, 'another use' of it. Thus, the degree of movement and transgression permitted at borders is useful to the neoliberal governmentality (De Genova, 2002; Walters, 2009), but also accommodates the *Xomaní* agenda. The *Xomá* move across the EU's internal borders knowing that the border spectacle mainly concerns the EU's external borders and therefore, a few Roma crossing the frontier between state-members are rarely symbolically relevant. The *Xomá* also use their 'on-the-move', 'undesirable' and 'social waste' categorizations as leverage to cross borders since authorities have tendency to hand 'social waste' over to the neighbouring borough, municipality, or country. Moreover, the *Xomá* know that being Third-National-Citizens may prove convenient since the non-refoulement principle works better when those seeking asylum or a temporary suspension of expulsion come from Bosnia rather than Romania or Bulgaria (cf. Caglar & Mehling, 2013); and they are aware that state protection and social aids are temporary so, when their advantage comes to a close, they just move somewhere else. Finally, the *Xomá* know that the illegal occupation of houses and/or public land does not trigger an immediate intervention by the police, that deportations and evictions are a display of power rather than a systematic response to the Romani illegal settlements (cf. Clough Marinaro, 2009) and consequently, that the authorities' iron fist of repression can be easily circumvented by moving.

As non-EU citizens, sometimes with no citizenship whatsoever, 'up-rooted', 'rootless', 'immigrants', 'aliens', 'Gypsies', 'Roma' and 'Nomads', the *Xomá* appear and disappear across different boroughs, cities and countries knowing that their mobility, ideally hindered but actually promoted and sometimes forced by non-Romani authorities, gives their presence a character of transitoriness that is the key to their permanence and rootedeness in specific territories. That of the *Xomá* is a tactically mobile and dispersed presence that clashes with and taunts its allegedly illicit character, and thus represents a substantial challenge to the forms of governmentality related to the policing of external borders and the production of internal boundaries of the EU and its member-states.

Conclusions

This paper analysed the mobility of Bosnian *Xoraxané Xomá* whose family linkages and movements extend from Rome into other Italian and European cities. These persons, labelled as 'immigrants', 'Roma', 'Gypsies' and 'Nomads', resolve to mobility and dispersion in order to become locally rooted, tactically wallowing in the contradictions of the non-Romani dominant system. This case study provides further proof that transnationalism results from a complex dialectic between processes imposed from above and those developed from below (cf. Smith & Guarnizo, 1998; Vlase & Voicu, 2013). It highlights that *Xomá* circulation within Europe, even if 'illegal' and ideologically inadmissible, is a fact. Lastly, it further substantiates viewpoints (e.g. Piasere, 2012) that see Europe's Romani population as part of European society and as a people that is able to think of itself in transnational terms but outside the political and cultural box of the nation-state. With their presence and persistence, the *Xomá* challenge the EU's external borders and internal boundaries, almost embodying the ideals that lie behind the concept of Europe. Ironically, their mobility signals the heightening of a regime of illegality, deportability and detain-ability that targets migrants and Gypsies/Roma and yet, as the key to persistence on a territory and challenge to this biopolitical regime, the mobility of the *Xomá* becomes, to use Isin and Saward's (2013a) expression, an incontrovertible act of European citizenship.

Notes

1. Shore (2011) argues that 'European governance is better understood as a new type of neo-liberal "governmentality"' (p. 289); hence my choice of focusing on 'governmentality' rather than 'governance'. As Sending and Neumann (2006) explain, 'a focus on governmentality seeks to analyze the relation "between individuals and the political order from the perspective of the different processes whereby the former are objectified as certain kinds of subject through the ways they are targeted by political power" (Burchell, 1991, p. 119)' (p. 657).
2. As Piasere (2012) argues, the total count of Europe's Romani population comes to about 11 million, more than the population of many European countries.
3. In Italy, as in other Western European countries, war refugees from former-Yugoslavia received only temporary protection (Sardelić, 2017; for Italy, see Brunello, 1996).
4. *Xoraxanó* is a general label used to distinguish Muslim Romani groups from Christian ones (Piasere, 2004).
5. This expression refers to a broad spectrum of state-engineered and externally run settlements that are usually located at the margins of the city territory or outside it. For the recent debate around Italian legal nomad camps and their segregating power, cf. Clough Marinaro (2009, 2015), Piasere (2012) and Sigona (2014).

6. Few *Xomá* live in flats (rented or occupied) or shelters provided by the social services; these, however, are exceptional and highly temporary solutions.
7. On the complex and ambivalent relations between Bosnian and Romanian Romani groups, see Solimene (2011).
8. Moving spontaneously from an encampment shows the will to abide by the question of public order without the police' intervention. This means diminishing the authorities' workload and (officially) acknowledging their authority.
9. With this term I include all the corps of Public Security.
10. The administrative division of Rome's territory does not coincide with the territorialization of public security.
11. To my knowledge, the recent restrictions to cross-border movement within the EU have not heavily affected the *Xomá*, who traverse borders that are not under the spot-light of governmental attention. Of course, future consequences are difficult to predict.
12. All the names of persons in this article are pseudonyms.
13. At the time Halil had two wives.

Disclosure statement

No potential conflict of interest was reported by the author.

Funding

Part of the research underpinning this study was financed by the EEA Financial Mechanism 2009-2014 [project contract n.14SEE/30.06.2014].

References

Al-Ali, N. (2002). Gender relations, transnational ties and rituals among Bosnian refugees. *Global Networks*, 2(3), 249–262.
Alvarez, R. R. (1995). The Mexican-US border: The making of an anthropology of borderlands. *Annual Review of Anthropology*, 24, 447–470.
Andrijasevic, R. (2010). Deported: The right to asylum at EU's external border of Italy and Lybia. *International Migration*, 48(1), 148–174.
Angel-Ajani, A. (2000). Italy's racial cauldron: Immigration, criminalization and the cultural politics of race. *Cultural Dynamics*, 12, 331–335.
Aretxaga, B. (2003). Maddening states. *Annual Review of Anthropology*, 32, 393–410.
Beluschi, G. (2013). *Roma Korturare entre Transilvania y Andalucía: Procesos migratorios y reproducción cultural* (Unpublished doctoral dissertation). University of Granada, Granada.
Bringa, T. (1995). *Being Muslim the Bosnian way: Identity and community in a Central Bosnian village*. Princeton, NJ: Princeton University Press.
Brunello, P. (1996). *L'urbanistica del disprezzo: Campi rom e societá italiana*. Roma: Manifesto Libri.
Bryceson, D. F., & Vuorela, U. (Eds.). (2002). *Transnational families: New European frontiers and global networks*. Oxford: Berg.
Caglar, A., & Mehling, S. (2013). Sites and the scales of the law: Third country national and EU Roma citizens. In E. Isin & M. Saward (Eds.), *Enacting European citizenship* (pp. 155–177). Cambridge: Cambridge University Press.
Cassarino, J. P. (2004). Theorising return migration: The conceptual approach to return migration revisited. *International Journal of Multicultural Societies*, 6(2), 253–279.
Clough Marinaro, I. (2009). Between surveillance and exile: Biopolitics of the Roma in Italy. *Bulletin of Italian Politics*, 1(2), 265–287.
Clough Marinaro, I. (2015). The rise of Italy's neo-ghettos. *Journal of Urban History*, 41(3), 368–387. doi:10.1177/009614421456958

Clough-Marinaro, I., & Sigona, N. (Eds.). (2011). Roma and Sinti in contemporary Italy. *Journal of Modern Italian Studies, 16,* 583–666.

Colacicchi, P. (2008). Ethnic profile and discrimination against Roma in Italy: New developments in a deep-rooted tradition. *Roma Rights Journal, 2,* 35–44.

De Certeau, M. (1984). *The practice of everyday life* (S. Rendall, Trans.). Berkeley: University of California Press.

De Genova, N. (2002). Migrant 'illegality' and deportability in everyday life. *Annual Review of Anthropology, 31,* 419–447.

De Genova N., & Peutz, N. (Eds.). (2010). *The deportation regime: Sovreignity, space and the freedom of movement.* Durham, NC: Duke University Press.

de Koning, M. (2008). *Return migration to Bosnia and Herzegovina: Monitoring the embeddedness of returnees.* Retrieved from http://www.ru.nl/publish/pages/533483/report_bosniaherzegovina_final.pdf

Deleuze, G., & Guattari, F. (1987). *A thousand plateaus: Capitalism and schizophrenia.* Minneapolis: University of Minnesota Press.

Douglas, M. (2002). *Purity and danger.* London: Routledge.

European Roma Rights Centre. (2004). *The Non-constituents. Right deprivation of Roma in post-genocide Bosnia and Herzegovina* (Country Report Series No.13). Retrieved from ERRC website: http://www.errc.org/cms/upload/media/00/28/m00000028.pdf

Fassin, D. (2011). Policing borders, producing boundaries: The governmentality of immigration in dark times. *Annual Review of Anthropology, 40,* 213–226.

Fekete, L. (2005). The deportation machine: Europe, asylum and human rights. *Race & Class, 47,* 64–78. doi:10.1177/0306396805055083

Glick Schiller, N. (2007). Transnationality. In D. Nugent & J. Vincent (Eds.), *A companion to the anthropology of politics* (pp. 448–467). Malden, MA: Blackwell.

Ionescu, M., & Stainescu, S. M. (2014). *Public policies for Roma: Assessment report of national programmes financed by European Union for Roma inclusion.* Bucharest: Pro Universitaria.

Isin, E., & Saward, M. (Eds.). (2013a). *Enacting European citizenship.* Cambridge: Cambridge University Press.

Isin, E., & Saward, M. (2013b). Questions of European citizenship. In E. Isin & M. Saward (Eds.), *Enacting European citizenship* (pp. 178–194). Cambridge: Cambridge University Press.

Istituto Nazionale di Statistica. (2005). *La misura dell'economia sommersa secondo le statistiche ufficiali. Anno 2003.* Roma: Conti Nazionali.

Kóczé, A. (2017). Race, migration and neoliberalism: Distorted notions of Romani migration in European public discourses. *Social Identities.* doi:10.1080/13504630.2017.1335827

Kuychukov, H. (2012). *New faces of anti-Gypsyism in modern Europe.* Prague: NGO Slovo.

Lamont, M., & Molnár, V. (2002). The study of boundaries in the social sciences. *Annual Review of Sociology, 28,* 167–195.

Lockwood, W. (1986). East European gypsies in Western Europe: The social and cultural adaptation of the Xoraxané Romá. *Nomadic Peoples, 21–22,* 63–70.

Malkki, L. H. (1992). National geographic: The rooting of peoples and the territorialisation of national identity among scholars and refugees. *Cultural Anthropology, 7*(1), 24–44.

Migration Policy Institute. (2007). *Immigration and the 2007 presidential elections.* Retrieved from http://www.migrationpolicy.org/pubs/France_Elections05307.pdf

Nicolae, V. (2007). Towards a definition of anti-Gypsyism. In V. Nicolae & H. Slavik (Eds.), *Roma Diplomacy* (pp. 21–30). New York: Idebate Press.

Piasere, L. (1991). *Popoli delle discariche: Saggi di antropologia zingara.* Bari: Laterza.

Piasere, L. (2004). *I rom d'Europa: Una storia moderna.* Bari: Laterza.

Piasere, L. (2012). *Scenari dell'antiziganismo: Tra Europa e Italia, tra antropologia e politica.* Firenze: Seid.

Rahola, F. (2003). *Zone definitivamente temporanee: I luoghi dell'umanitá in eccesso.* Verona: Ombre Corte.

Saitta, P. (2011). Between Kafka and carnevale: An introduction to the immigrant condition in Italy. *Journal of Modern Italian Studies, 16,* 317–320.

Saletti Salza, C. (2003). *Bambini del campo Nomadi. Romá Bosniaci a Torino*. Roma: CISU.
Saletti Salza, C., & Piasere, L. (Eds). (2004). *Italia romaní* (vol. 4). Roma: CISU.
Sardelić, J. (2017). In and out from the European margins: Reshuffling mobilities and legal statuses of Romani minorities between the Post-Yugoslav space and the European Union. *Social Identities*. doi:10.1080/13504630.2017.1335829
Scott, J. (1985). *Weapons of the weak: Everyday forms of peasant resistance*. New Haven, CT: Yale University Press.
Scott, J. (1990). *Domination and the arts of resistance: Hidden transcripts*. New Haven, CT: Yale University Press.
Sending, O. J., & Neumann, I. B. (2006). Governance to governmentality: Analyzing NGOs, states, and power. *International Studies Quarterly, 50*, 651–672.
Shore, C. (2011). 'European governance' or gvernmentality? The European commission and the future of democratic government. *European Law Journal, 17*(3), 287–303. doi:10.1111/j.1468-0386.2011.00551.x
Sigona, N. (2014). Campzenship. Reimagining the camp as social and political space. *Citizenship Studies, 19*, 1–15. doi:10.1080/13621025.2014.937643
Sigona, N., & Trehan, N. (Eds.). (2009). *Romani politics in contemporary Europe: Poverty, ethnic mobilization, and the neoliberal order*. New York, NY: Palgrave.
Silverstein, P. A. (2005). Immigrant racialization and the new savage slot: Race, migration and immigration in the new Europe. *Annual Review of Anthropology, 34*, 363–384.
Simoni, A. (Ed.). (2005). *Stato di diritto e identitá Rom*. Torino: L'Harmattan Italia.
Smith, M. P., & Guarnizo, L. E. (Eds.). (1998). *Transnationalism from below*. New Brunswick, NJ: Transaction.
Solimene, M. (2011). 'These Romanians have ruined Italy': Xoraxané Romá, Romanian Roma and Rome. *Journal of Modern Italian Studies, 16*, 637–651.
Solimene, M. (2013). Undressing the Gağe clad in state garb. Xoraxané Romá face to face with the Italian authorities. *Romani Studies, 5*(23), 161–186.
Solimene, M. (2014). The rootedness of a community of Xoraxané Romá in Rome. In I. Clough Marinaro & B. Thomassen (Eds.), *Global Rome: Changing faces of the eternal city* (pp. 129–142). Bloomington: Indiana University Press.
Solimene, M. (2016). I go for iron: Xoraxané Romá collecting scrap metal in Rome. In M. Brazzabeni, M.I. Cunha, & M. Fotta (Eds.), *Gypsy economy: Romani livelihoods and notions of worth in the 21st century* (pp. 107–126). New York, NY: Berghahn.
Stewart, M. (2011). The other genocide. In M. Stewart & M. Rovid (Eds.), *Multi-disciplinary approaches to Romani studies* (pp. 172–195). Budapest: Central European University.
Stewart, M., & Rovid, M. (Eds.). (2011). *Multi-disciplinary approaches to Romani studies*. Budapest: Central European University.
Stewart, M., & Williams, P. (Eds.). (2011). *Des tsiganes en Europe*. Paris: Éditions de la Maison des Siences de l'Homme.
Templer, B. (2006). Neoliberal strategies to defuse a power keg in Europe: The decade of the Roma inclusion and its rationale. *New Politics, 10*(4). Retrieved from http://wpunj.edu/~newpol/issue40/tenpler40.htm
Vertovec, S. (2004). Migrants transnationalism and modes of transformation. *International Migration Review, 38*, 970–1001.
Vlase, I., & Voicu, M. (2013). Romanian Roma migration: The interplay between structures and agency. *Ethnic and Racial Studies, 37*, 2418–2437.
Walters, W. (2009). Europe's borders. In C. Rumford (Ed.), *Sage handbook of European studies* (pp. 485–505). London: Sage.
Wimmer, A., & Glick Schiller, N. (2002). Methodological nationalism and beyond: Nation-state building, migration and the social sciences. *Global Networks, 2*, 301–334.

4   In and out from the European margins

Reshuffling mobilities and legal statuses of Romani minorities between the Post-Yugoslav space and the European Union

Julija Sardelić

ABSTRACT

This paper traces the mobilities of Romani minorities between the 'old' EU Member States and the non-EU Post-Yugoslav space. It unravels how the mobilities of Romani individuals, who are Non-EU Post-Yugoslav citizens, were different from the mobilities of Roma coming from other post-socialist spaces, now EU Member States. Instead of focusing on motivations for mobility of Romani individuals as some previous work has done, this paper investigates the treatment of these mobilities by different states and the legal statuses these states ascribe to those labelled as Romani migrants. By using the combination historical and socio-legal analysis, this paper diachronically examines the *precarious migrant statuses* of Post-Yugoslav Romani minorities in the old EU, such as Yugoslav labour migrants, Post-Yugoslav forced migrants and subsequently the 'bogus' asylum seekers. The paper points to the interconnectedness of these statuses, but also to their interminable liminality: they are constantly on the verge of being rendered 'illegal' and are hence subject to deportability. I claim that while their legal statuses are being reshuffled, their liminality and interconnectedness also contribute to circular mobilities between the Post-Yugoslav space and the EU. I investigate how these mobilities are not only socially produced, but are also legally and politically conditioned by the hierarchical relationship between the Post-Yugoslav space and the EU. As a side effect of this relationship, Roma are positioned as a racialized minority, treated only as temporary migrants in their 'host country' and without prospects of inclusion in their 'country of origin' as minority citizens.

Introduction

The right of all EU citizens to move and reside in another EU member state than their own (following the Directive 2004/38/EC), was a highly contested even before the debate on Brexit; has started. Many politicians as well as the media often highlighted the position of EU Romani migrants (Parker, 2012; Ram, 2011; Sardelić, 2016) as the basis for challenging this unconditional right: the claim put forefront of these discourses was that when Romani 'nomadic culture' is coupled with the freedom of movement and the 'push-

and-pull' factors from their countries of origin, they will migrate *en masse* towards Western Europe (Matras, 2000). Although such mass migration never occurred, since most Roma remain immobile within their own countries (Cahn & Guild, 2008), the portrayal of Romani migrants as welfare tourists (BBC, 2014) and as criminal gangs remains pertinent. EU Romani mobilities are framed in terms of securitization (see van Baar, 2017), while Roma themselves through the usage of free movement become a new EU *racialized minority* (Imre, 2005, p. 85; Vincze, 2014). In this paper, I extend this argument by claiming that racialization of Romani minority does not apply only to those, who are EU citizens, but also Romani migrants without EU citizenship.

By far the largest number of Roma, who are third-country nationals in the EU, come from the territory of the former Socialist Yugoslavia (Latham, 1999; Matras, 2000; Perić & Demirovski, 2000), particularly from the states on the EU margins: Serbia, Kosovo, Macedonia, and Bosnia and Herzegovina (BIH). I argued in my past work (Sardelić, 2015) that due to multiple war conflicts resulting in the dissolution of the Yugoslav state, their citizenship statuses in the newly established states often became irregular (legally invisible and internally displaced persons, refugees, etc.). Some of other previous scholarly work (Matras, 2000) already disputed the theory of Romani nomadic culture as a driver of migration as well as described other motivations Romani migrants have to migrate.

In this paper, I take a different perspective. I examine what *precarious migrant statuses* (Goldring, Berinstein, & Bernhard, 2009) different states ascribe to those Roma, who are now holding a non-EU Post-Yugoslav passport and have in different periods migrated to the 'old' EU Members States, mainly to Germany. I argue that the legal statuses ascribed to these migrants are far less forthright in the terms of rights, but also exponentially more diverse and precarious than the status of EU citizens. Some of the stories about post-Yugoslav Romani minorities[1] migrating to the EU have also appeared in the national EU media. For example, one of such stories in the French media was about Leonarda Dibrani, a Roma refugee, who was in the middle of her school excursion deported to Kosovo. German media reported on the case of Romani actor Nazif Mujić, who received the Berlinale 'best actor award' for his role in the Tanović' movie 'The Episode in a Life of an Iron Picker'. Despite his fame in BIH, he stated he could barely survive in Bosnia so he later on returned to Berlin as an asylum seeker, where his application was rejected.

These two media stories are the most vivid portrayals of the position of Post-Yugoslav Roma being mobile in and out of the EU Member States. In this paper, I focus on the myriad of mobilities and divergent migrant statuses, which Post-Yugoslav Roma have acquired in the EU after the disintegration of the former Yugoslavia and accompanying war conflicts, such as toleration (Duldung) status, (expired) refugee statuses and subsequently rejected asylum seekers. Some previous scholarly work focused separately on each of these statuses (Kummrow, 2015; Matras, 2000; Sigona, 2003), while others also compared it to the position of migrant Romani EU citizens (Caglar & Mehling, 2013; Solimene, 2011).

However, what is missing is an explicit analysis of the relationship among different migrant statuses of Post-Yugoslav Roma in the EU and how legal policies governing the international relations between the states in question affected the creation of these migrant statuses. For example, the fact that Romani individuals, who were Yugoslav citizens could migrate as temporary workers to Western Europe, while those residing in other socialist countries were more or less immobile, received limited scholarly attention. By using historical contextualization and socio-legal analysis (Scheppele, 2004), I focus on how these migrant statuses are diachronically interconnected and were being reshuffled due to hierarchical relationships between the (Post-)Yugoslav state(s) and certain EU Member States.

I claim that their legal statuses are liminal (Menjívar, 2006) since, in contrast to EU citizen status, their statuses are temporary and are thus always on the verge of 'illegality production' (De Genova, 2002). Most of the migrant statuses in question have been subjected to *liminal legality* (Menjívar, 2006) as a response to the end of Post-Yugoslav war conflicts. In the course of Schengen visa liberalization processes for the Western Balkan countries, the former Yugoslav countries also signed readmission agreements with the European Commission (Kacarska, 2012), which paved a way for the most of Post-Yugoslav Romani migrants to be deportable back to their 'countries of origin'. I argue that the liminal legality of all the statuses embedded in the hierarchical relations between the 'countries of origin' and 'host countries' is accompanied by various racialization processes: the states in question treat Roma as a racialized unwanted minority. They use racialization as a disciplinary legitimation (in Foucauldian manner) for the governing the movement of Romani minorities.

On the basis of this analysis, I claim the mobilities of Post-Yugoslav minorities are not only socially produced (Sassen, 1998), but also *legally* and *politically conditioned* by the aforementioned relationship between the EU and its neighbouring states, which are at different stages of EU accession. I argue that due to such constellations, these mobilities are bound to be circular: most Post-Yugoslav Romani migrants are manoeuvring between their precarious and liminal legal statuses between *chutes* and *ladders* (Goldring & Landolt, 2013) as the host country treats them as 'temporary visitors', and as minority citizens they also have no prospects of full access to rights in their countries of origin. With the analysis of this relationship, I aim to show how the boundaries of the EU work both within, but also beyond its own territory by affecting the *deportability* (De Genova, 2002) and also conditioning mobilities of the most marginalized minorities in the Post-Yugoslav space as well as Europe as a whole.

Contextualizing research on Romani migrations in the EU: overview of theoretical foundation and methodological approaches

Over the last five years, the academic discourse on Roma has significantly shifted from the mere understanding of Roma as a minority in a single national context towards more transnational approaches (Portes, Guarnizo, & Landolt, 1999; Vertovec, 1999). These new approaches moved away from treating Roma merely one-dimensionally as an ethnic or a socio-economic group to a more intersectional (Kocze, 2011) and *transborder* approach (Rövid, 2012), mainly focusing on the transnational migration of different Romani minorities and also their heterogeneous migration practices (Caglar & Mehling, 2013; Grill, 2012; Pantea, 2012, 2013; Sigona, 2015; Vlase & Voicu, 2014; Vullnetari, 2012). As latest studies showed it cannot be simply assumed that the mobility of Romani minorities rests on 'ethnic categorization' or socio-economic disadvantage. All these studies have demonstrated how ethnicity itself is a product of certain hegemonic relations and is not merely the thing in the world, but the perception of the world, to paraphrase

Brubaker (2004). A great number of qualitative research pointed to other distinctive and often intersecting factors that affect migration decision and mobility among Romani individuals, such as gender (Pantea, 2012), other subgroup identity features (Vlase & Voicu, 2014) and social ties between migrating individuals (Pantea, 2013).

Many anthropological and sociological studies focused on the intra-EU migration of Romani individuals holding EU citizenship. Such research in many instances showed how legal equality among EU citizens does not necessarily also mean de facto equality when it comes to freedom of movement (and including non-deportability) within the EU (or at least the Schengen area), which should derive from this citizenship status (Parker & Toke, 2013). Yet less scholarly attention was paid to different precarious (non-)citizen statuses of those Romani individuals who have been crossing borders and migrating between the EU and its neighbouring states, thus falling into the category of third-country nationals. Some researchers conducted a comparative analysis on the basis of case studies in order to describe the difference between Roma holding EU citizenship and those with the asylum seeker status (Caglar & Mehling, 2013). Others, such as for example Julie Vullnetari, analysed the migration of Roma from Albania to Greece and argued that the dichotomy coupled with voluntary/forced migration should be surpassed (Vullnetari, 2012). Furthermore, through his analysis of the position of stateless Romani individuals, who migrated to Italy during the Kosovo conflict, Nando Sigona demonstrated that the boundary between citizenship and statelessness is far more elusive and cannot be simply contemplated from the perspective of binary opposition (Sigona, 2015). In my previous work, I analysed the plethora of non-citizenship statuses, such as legally invisible persons, 'internally displaced', refugees, etc. in which many Romani individuals found themselves as de facto stateless in the Post-Yugoslav space. These individuals are usually left immobile within the Post-Yugoslav space and their opportunities to regularly cross the Post-Yugoslav borders are virtually non-existent (Sardelić, 2015).

This article shifts the focus to that treatment of those non-EU Romani individuals who were able to regularize their citizenship status to the extent they could migrate between the (Post-)Yugoslav space and the EU territory. I especially focus on the mobilities of former Yugoslav citizens towards one particular EU Member State, Germany. Different studies showed that the largest proportion of migrants from the former Yugoslav space move between their country of citizenship and Germany (Castañeda, 2010; Novinšćak, 2009). These studies, however, did not particularly focus on the different types and reasons for the mobilities of Romani minorities, which I aim to do in this paper. Furthermore, while applying the theoretical framework of *liminal legality* (Menjívar, 2006), my paper aims to historically contextualize precarious legal statuses of Post-Yugoslav Romani migrants in the EU. While most of the previous studies did not have a focus on mobilities of Roma during the socialist period, I argue that it is essential to include it in the (Post-)Yugoslav case in order to understand how these statuses are interconnected and were subsequently reshuffled due to their liminality.

This article follows previous theoretical contributions whereby the migration of Romani minorities cannot be simply explained by socio-economic deprivation and ethnic stigmatization, but needs to include the dimension of racialization. In this paper I discuss the migration patterns that are not merely employed by Romani minority citizens, but also by other (Post-)Yugoslav citizens. However, I claim that the precarious liminality of these statuses affected Roma, because they have become the European racialized minority. In this connection I employ the theories on cultural racism (Balibar & Wallerstein, 1991; Gilroy, 1987; Sardelić, 2014a) according to which although the biological foundations of race have been disputed, certain *visible minorities* are still hierarchized by racist discourse practices as culturally different: Roma become visible through their mobilities, which are attributed to them as their essentialized characteristic, rather than the product of different political and legal arrangements among different European countries and their treatment as such.

In term of methodology, I used two main methods in this paper. Firstly, I employed a *socio-historical contextualizing approach* to highlight mobilities Romani (post-)Yugoslav citizens throughout different periods. I couple this approach with the *socio-legal analysis* of their migrant statuses to show how different states rendered them as liminal and precarious on the basis of racialization. Both of these approaches are supported by two fieldworks[2] I carried out in 2010 and 2012, respectively, in all the post-Yugoslav states. In the first fieldwork, I conducted semi-structured interviews with 20 individuals from different post-Yugoslav Romani communities, who highlighted their experiences with mobilities and migration. In the second fieldwork,[3] I conducted 54 elite interviews with representatives of post-Yugoslav national authorities as well as human rights and Romani NGOs and international organizations that were dealing with the position of Roma and their mobilities.

Historicizing mobilities of Post-Yugoslav Romani minorities: managing labour migration in the socialist Yugoslavia

There was a common misconception in public debates that Romani minorities were a 'nomadic' social group before being sedentarized by different socialist states with assimilationist approaches (Barany, 2002; Crowe, 2007; Matras, 2000). With their portrayal as nomads, Roma were a racialized and hence visible minority perceived as being far from a model socialist citizen. Therefore, different policies of most socialist states strived to include them in the working class with other majority citizens (McGarry, 2010; Stewart 2012): in the case of Roma that meant that they had to be 'disciplined' by controlling their movement. However, such 'inclusion' by assimilation through the control of their mobility did not simply mean their sedentarization, as it is usually assumed. By examining assimilationist policies towards Roma that different socialist states pursued, we can also find many mobility instances of Romani minorities in the form of relocation enforced by the states. For example, many individuals in the Socialist Czechoslovakia categorized as Roma residing on the Slovak side were relocated to the Czech part since many industrial centres and factories were concentrated there. Although this was the official stance, the other latent reason for such relocation was to prevent the 'uneven' concentration of Romani populations in only a certain area (Kochenov, 2007). Due to such 'relocations', up to 25,000 Romani individuals faced problems in access to citizenship in the Czech Republic after the *velvet divorce* of the Czech Republic and Slovakia, (Kochenov, 2007; Sardelić, 2015). Similar relocations also took place in the Socialist Hungary, where many previously rural Romani communities were in fact dismantled as their inhabitants had to migrate to urban and industrial centres in order to pursue their employment, usually as low-skilled factory workers (Szalai, 2003; Ladányi & Szelényi, 2006). What was, however, common to all socialist states aligned with the USSR was the officially closed border for emigration. Roma, as other citizens, could mostly not migrate abroad.

Most socio-historical sources, however, emphasize that policies towards Romani minorities in the former Socialist Yugoslavia were diametrically opposed to other socialist states (Barany, 2002; Crowe, 2007; Latham, 1999). They were inclined to officially treat Roma as an 'ethnic group' rather than a social class. Therefore, Roma were granted various cultural rights. On the basis of the Yugoslav ideology of 'Brotherhood and Unity', they were partially included in the state-constructed ethnic hierarchy of constitutive nations-nationalities-ethnic groups. However, the main difference was that the rights of constitutive nations and nationalities (term used for groups categorized as national minorities) were linked to certain territories, while the rights of 'ethnic groups' were not territorially conceptualized. Roma were categorized as dispersed and were hence not linked to any particular territory: they were perceived as being a mobile population per se. Yet the approach to mobilities of Romani minorities within the former Yugoslavia was diametrically different from other socialist states. Firstly, the policy of integrating Roma through the working class and the practice of forced labour was never fully implemented in the Yugoslav context (Barany, 2002, p. 140). Hence, similar planned (forced) relocations to disperse Romani populations around Yugoslavia did not occur. The largest part of the Romani population remained in Serbia, Macedonia and Kosovo.

Although relocations were never a state-wide policy towards Roma, there were a few significant local relocations. For example, the largest Romani municipality in the world, Šuto Orizari, on the outskirts of the Macedonian capital of Skopje was created in 1963 after a massive earthquake in Skopje. Instead of rebuilding the centuries-old central Romani neighbourhood of Topaana, it was decided that most of Topaana's previous inhabitants could either relocate to integrated neighbourhoods or to the newly built municipality of Šuto Orizari in the suburbs of Skopje (Crowe, 2007, p. 224). By the 1980s, Šuto Orizari had a population of 80,000 and was considered the exemplary case of Yugoslav multiculturalism (Crowe, 2007, p. 225). Although Romani minorities from Skopje's neighbourhood of Topaana could, in theory, claim their historical connectedness to this territory, this was not considered in their case. They were racialized as the imagery of a nomadic Roma prevailed and hence they were in this context regarded as the population that could be relocated.

Although most cases of Roma mobilities were not 'orchestrated' by the state, they were dependent on different state policies in the Socialist Yugoslavia, also taking into account in particular international agreements. Firstly, some Romani individuals found jobs as workers in factories. In order to do so, many of them migrated across the republican borders. For example, on the one hand, there were many instances of migrations in republican border areas such as the Socialist Autonomous Province of Kosovo and the Socialist Republic of Montenegro (Zahova, 2010). On the other hand, there were many migration patterns from economically less developed republics (i.e. Serbia, Macedonia) to more developed ones, mainly to Slovenia and to a lesser extent to Croatia (Komac, 2007). Yet such mobilities were not limited only to Romani individuals. The consequences of these migrations were particularly felt by Romani individuals after the disintegration(s) of Yugoslavia when they had difficulties accessing citizenship at their place of residence (Sardelić, 2015).

The most distinctive feature of the Socialist Yugoslavia was that its borders were not as 'hermetically sealed' as in other socialist states. From the 1960s, Yugoslav citizens were able to cross borders for shorter periods, but also to pursue employment abroad for longer periods of time. Many individuals from Romani communities were employed in alternative informal economic niches, which were at least unofficially tolerated by the Yugoslav authorities (Sardelić, 2013). One such economic niche was, in fact, informal trading in 'capitalist' goods that were (illegally) imported to Yugoslavia, most typically from Italy, one of the interviewees from the Romani communities stated. While such trading was by no means confined to the traders who identified themselves as belonging to Romani minorities, some interviewees from Romani communities claimed that this was the main source of income for many Romani individuals, while it was just a supplementary source for others. Such mobilities, which included border crossings, were in fact only temporary and they were dependent on the return of these informal traders. However, some Romani individuals informally settled in Italy already at the time of the Socialist Yugoslavia. It is, therefore, no coincidence that during the war conflicts following the disintegration of the former Yugoslavia, some Romani individuals fled to Italy (Sigona, 2003; Solimene, 2011).

The most distinctive approach of the Socialist Yugoslavia that also affected the mobilities of Romani individuals was the permissive policy towards its citizens finding temporary employment abroad (Novinšćak, 2009; Zimmerman, 2014) in other states (Austria, Switzerland, etc.) and particularly in the Federal Republic of Germany (FR Germany). This was officially made possible by the signing of a bilateral agreement between the FR Germany and Yugoslavia in 1968. The non-allied Yugoslavia was the only socialist state at the time that allowed its citizens to work outside its borders in the 'West' (Zimmerman, 2014, p. 95). While the FR Germany needed additional workers due to its booming economy, the Socialist Yugoslavia to a certain extent applied this approach to address unemployment of the rural population (Novinšćak, 2009, p. 124). Yet the 1968 bilateral agreement stipulated that they could live in Germany only on a temporary basis and could at the time not acquire German citizenship. However, after they had lived in the FR Germany for five years they were entitled to permanent residence and after three years to family reunification (Ruhs, 2006). This temporary foreign worker programme was attractive for almost one million of Yugoslav citizens, primarily due to wage differences (Molnar, 1997). Although there was an embargo on accepting new workers after 1973 due to the oil crisis (Novinšćak, 2009), many new workers still migrated from Yugoslavia to the FR of Germany on the basis of the right to family reunification or in many instances became undocumented workers due to previous social ties. In 1978 the remittances from Yugoslav workers abroad accounted for 25% of GDP in Yugoslavia (Baković, 2014, p. 675).

According to the Yugoslav census on citizens living abroad from 1981, a significant proportion of temporary foreign workers identified themselves as Roma (1981). However, most studies dealing with Yugoslav workers in Germany did not address the issue of the percentage of non-dominant minority populations who gained employment abroad in this manner. Yet four analyses on the position of Romani minorities in the former Yugoslavia briefly mentioned that they were also mobile due to this policy and many of them took on temporary employment abroad, particularly mentioning Germany (Cherkezova, 2014, p. 5; Latham, 1999, p. 209; Matras, 2000; Zahova, 2010, p. 252). It was emphasized during my interviews with different representatives of Roma NGOs in Serbia, Kosovo and Macedonia that many Romani individuals also became 'guest workers' in the FR Germany. Similarly to the rural population, Romani individuals also solved their employment status by becoming mobile and seeking work abroad. This mobility was thus on the one hand conditioned by the agreement with the FR Germany. On the other hand, it was also conditioned by the ambiguous position of Romani minorities in Yugoslavia: not all were included in the working class through assimilationist policies as was the case in other socialist states so they had to find alternative niches of employment, similarly to other disadvantaged populations. Some of these migrant workers returned to Yugoslavia as their regularized legal status in Germany was linked to their employment contracts. Some came back and also returned to Germany afterwards, even if they continued working as undocumented migrant workers.

The FR of Germany did not officially consider itself an immigrant state in this period, although many work migrants settled there instead of returning to their states of origin (Castañeda, 2010). Nevertheless, the expectation that most temporary foreign workers will return to Yugoslavia was a myth (Novinšćak, 2009, p. 143). Even after the 1973 embargo on the new import of workers, many more decided to stay and create their new life in Germany, which also included starting a new family. One of the interviewees stated Romani migrants in Germany formed more ties among themselves than with their other Yugoslav co-citizens who attached a certain stigma to them. This meant that many Romani individuals started families in Germany with other Roma, who were Yugoslav citizens but originated in other Socialist Republics, hence holding different republican citizenship, which became important after the disintegration (Sardelić, 2015).

While some were able to keep their employment, those whose employment contracts ended often became undocumented work migrants and were manoeuvring between the *chutes* and *ladders* of their precarious migrant statuses (Goldring & Landolt, 2013). Furthermore, their position became more complex with the start of the Yugoslav disintegration at the end of the 1980s and particularly at the beginning of the 1990s. While they did not cross any Yugoslav borders at the time, since they were already outside Yugoslavia, the creation of new borders in Yugoslavia profoundly affected their position. They entered the FR Germany and the other EC Member States as Yugoslav citizens with a temporary right to stay, now the 'country of origin' disintegrated and they were transformed into Post-Yugoslav citizens making it very unclear where they could return to since their state of origin no longer existed, but also because they were a non-dominant minority in each newly established state, while their status in the host country was reshuffled.

Post-Yugoslav Roma crossing borders and Post-Yugoslav borders crossing Roma: liminal 'conflict management' statuses in the EU

During the violent disintegration of Yugoslavia, many Romani individuals had to flee their homes as well. This was particularly the case with Roma, Ashkali and Egyptians (RAE) from Kosovo, who became one of the largest long-term displaced populations within and beyond the Post-Yugoslav borders, amounting to up to 120,000 or 90% of these minority populations (Caglar & Mehling, 2013; Matras, 2000; Perić & Demirovski, 2000; Sardelić, 2015). As Krasniqi (2015) argued, RAE were *invisible* minorities; they were not initiators of the conflict in Kosovo, but were caught between territorial demands of the majority population and the more dominant minority population; without territorial demands of their own. Their displacement was collateral damage of the war conflicts, but also of the redefinition of citizenries in the newly established states. Besides being displaced within the former Yugoslav territory (Sardelić, 2015), many fled to Italy (Sigona, 2003). Some regularized their refugee status, while others who arrived directly just after the Kosovo conflict finished, were not entitled to asylum (Perić & Demirovski, 2000). They became the largest stateless group in Italy without being *de jure* recognized as such (Sigona, 2015).

Germany was again one of the main destinations for Romani minorities who fled during the Yugoslav wars (Perić & Demirovski, 2000). Both elite interviews, as well as interviews with the individuals from the Roma community, showed, that those who fled to Germany did not do so because of their knowledge of the German asylum system and generous welfare benefits for refugees, but because they had previous *transnational* ties (Vertovec, 2004). Following the contemporary migration theory, this was not surprising due to the fact that communities had been previously formed in Germany during the period of bilateral agreements on temporary foreign workers (Van Hear, 2003, pp. 29–30). However, after the reunification of Germanies, the 1993 Asylum Law became much stricter in granting refugee status (Castañeda, 2010). Therefore, in Germany, all of the individuals self-identifying as Roma and fleeing the war conflict in the former Yugoslavia acquired precarious temporary statuses, which were liminal from the beginning. According to UNHCR (2011), as many as 12,000 RAE from Kosovo received 'toleration' status or 'Duldung' in German rather than refugee status, similar to Romani individuals from other Post-Yugoslav states. This status is defined as 'temporary suspension of deportation'.[4] However, in this context refugee status was also temporary and could be revoked. It did not offer the possibility of full and permanent integration into German society. In 2010, Kosovo passed the Law on Readmission and signed a readmission agreement with Germany (ESI, 2015), while other Non-EU Post-Yugoslav countries signed readmission agreements with the EC as a part of visa liberalization processes (Kacarska, 2012). This made Romani individuals with 'Duldung' and other forced migration statuses deportable. Many of them were in fact deported in a very brutal manner: police authorities came to their place of residence in the middle of the night and gave them a very short time to pack their most necessary belongings before they were put on charter flights, thereby deporting them to their country of origin, which used to be Yugoslavia that in fact no longer existed (UNICEF, 2011). This was also confirmed by my interviewees in several different Post-Yugoslav states besides Kosovo. As some of them stated, it was not clear to them, but not even to state authorities, where they could be deported to since the common state disintegrated. As mentioned in the previous section, there were some families created between Romani individuals from the same state of Yugoslavia, but from different Yugoslav socialist republics. These Yugoslav socialist republics later became independent. Furthermore, some families were created between individuals with different precarious migrant statuses (i.e. temporary migrant workers and those with 'Duldung' status), while their children were often born in Germany. In the new constellation, their statuses were also often reshuffled. For example, a person with the previous temporary foreign worker status now had very limited opportunities to work under 'Duldung' status (Castañeda, 2010), but also ended up with different citizenship.

One of the interviewees from a Roma community in Croatia stated that he was deported from Germany to (Non-EU Post-Yugoslav state at the time) Croatia with his mother and siblings, while their father was deported to Serbia. After the Yugoslav disintegration, the father acquired Serbian citizenship, while the mother and the children obtained Croatian citizenship. The family was broken up as the parents were now deported to two different countries and were separated for several years. One of the children from this family 'discovered' that he was Roma only after his deportation,[5] when they resettled in one of the Roma communities without running water and electricity. He did not speak any of the languages of his new (and his mother's old) environment, neither local Romani nor Croatia's majority language, but only German. Due to higher unemployment rates and discrimination towards Roma, the parents were unable to get employment in the places they were deported to. When the interviewee turned 18, he tried to return to Germany, but was deported back and was prohibited from entering the Schengen area. In turn, he started leading what was stereotypically considered a 'Romani way of life' (in inadequate housing conditions and without employment prospects) on the basis of the act of deportation to a country with no connecting factors. His mobility (and with it deportation) was conditioned by an external readmission agreement between two countries and he became racialized by the act of deportation. While he tried to find again a *latter* to return, to what to him was subjectively the 'country of origin' (Germany), he was thrown down the *chute* (Goldring & Landolt, 2013), which radically worsened his position and his problem was not addressed by the state. Similarly, as the interviewee from my research, many Romani children born in Germany were deported from the only country they knew as home (UNICEF, 2011).

EU 'Visa-free' mobilities: Post-Yugoslav Roma as 'bogus' asylum seekers

Another layer of precarious migration statuses was added after the visa liberalization process in the Schengen area was completed for certain Post-Yugoslav countries, such as Macedonia and Serbia, after 2008 (Kacarska, 2012). In 2010, the number of asylum seekers in Germany from these two countries increased by up to 200% (Spiegel, 2011) and in 2013, one in six of all applications for asylum was from these two countries, and BIH (Deutsche Welle, 2014). All three countries were added to the list of safe countries by the German Bundesrat after the visa liberalization was concluded (European Council on Refugees and Exiles, 2015). During the so-called 'European refugee crisis' (on 24th October 2015), the new Law for acceleration of the asylum procedures came into effect. According to this Law, Germany also added other Western Balkan countries to their safe countries list: Kosovo, Montenegro and Albania (Aida, 2015). As demonstrated by Liza Kummrow (2015, p. 20), while during 2009 before the visa liberalization process was concluded, 5460 asylum applications came from Serbia and 930 from Macedonia, in 2014 30,810 pplications were from Serbia and 10,330 from Macedonia. In 2014 76% of these applications were made in Germany (Kummrow, 2015, p. 21). Yet what was indicative was the fact that almost 90% of the asylum seekers in question self-identified as Roma (Hauser, 2014). For example, in 2014, there were 8906 asylum applications from Macedonia to Germany, out of which 6931 self-identified as Roma. Similarly, there were 27,148 asylum seekers this year in Germany, out of which 25,582 identified as Roma: only 53 from these 2 groups were granted asylum. Similar statistics was also observed a year before (Kummrow, 2015, p. 21)

In 2013, the asylum seekers from the Western Balkans triggered a heated debate in the European parliament (EP). In turn, MEPs voted to include a 'visa-free regime suspension mechanism' for the countries in question, which would be activated in the event of an even greater influx of asylum seekers. According to the EP, the application of such measure would strengthen minority rights for the Roma at their country of origin and hence eliminate the reasons for applying for asylum in the first place (Sardelić, 2014b). However, this instead caused racial profiling on the border whereby many Romani individuals were not allowed to leave their own country (Kacarska, 2012). The rationale behind it was that in order to keep the free movement for all citizens, the free movement of certain citizens paradoxically had to be impeded, that is the movement of the racialized minority. While the EP visa-free regime suspension mechanism was supposed to send a message to the countries in question about the need to protect minority rights so that these 'bogus' asylum seekers would not be coming to the EU, this in reality resulted in more violations of human rights of these minorities, such as not allowing them to leave their own country by the means of racial profiling on the border (Kacarska, 2012; Sardelić, 2014b). In the way these mobilities were managed, the racialization of Romani minorities was the most evident result of the hierarchical relations between the non-EU Post-Yugoslav countries and EU Member States.

According to interviews, I conducted in different Post-Yugoslav countries, while some Romani individuals were in fact persecuted, others lived in unbearable conditions. Therefore, they stated that their asylum application was actually one of survival strategies. As stated repeatedly in some of the interviews, many of these individuals, for example, applied for asylum to survive winter because they could not afford to pay heating bills. Most of them were aware they would be deported back to different Post-Yugoslav countries.

Furthermore, there was a clear connection between those Romani individuals who possessed refugee or 'Duldung' status and 'bogus' asylum seekers. Helene Hauser (2014) reported, a large proportion of these 'false' asylum seekers previously lived in Germany: many of them were actually born in Germany to the parents who had refugee status, which was later revoked. From their perspective, they were returning to what they perceived as their country of origin, which was Germany and not any of the Post-Yugoslav states. Their mobility back to Germany was conditioned by the previous act of deportation to the post-Yugoslav states, but also by the fact that their legal status was temporary and hence liminal in the place where they were actually born.

Moreover, the above-described mobilities of Romani minorities are linked to many more instances of ambiguous EU policies towards the non-EU Post-Yugoslav states. For example, in the case of Sejdić and Finci versus BIH, the European Court of Human Rights ruled in favour of the applicants. The ECtHR case revolved around the Dayton Agreement that was drafted by international powers and constituted the basis for the post-conflict Bosnian Constitution. According to the Bosnian constitution, only those identified as belonging to Serbian, Croatian or Bosnian communities could run for presidency. That effectively meant that Bosnian citizens who identified themselves as belonging to a Romani or Jewish minority could not run for presidency in their own country, which Dervo Sejdić and Jacob Finci challenged (Sardelić, 2014b). ECtHR ruled that BIH needs to change its constitution so that the members of minority groups could run for presidency. This change has not come into force to date. Introducing these changes became part of the EU conditionality for BIH. In 2014, the European Commission thus decided to freeze (Instrument for Pre-Accession Assistance) funds for BIH since it did not comply with the ECtHR decision (Sardelić, 2014b). A big proportion of these funds were also earmarked for the improvement of the position of minorities. Thus the EC decided to use this measure for this purpose, while at the same time restricting funds for the building of infrastructure that would improve the position of vulnerable minorities. During the visa liberalization process, one of the benchmarks for the Post-Yugoslav countries in question was the improvement of the citizenship status and rights for Romani minorities. It was highlighted during this process that many Romani individuals in Serbia, Macedonia and BIH, respectively, lack personal identification documents, which would be the first guarantor of their rights (Kacarska, 2012; Sardelić, 2013, 2016). Different legal NGOs in the region were struggling to acquire proper personal identification documents for many Romani individuals. However, many of these individuals did not see a passport as a possibility to access citizenship rights, which were as in the aforementioned case non-existent, but as a 'ticket' to mobility towards other countries. This brings us back to the story of Nazif Mujić, a Bosnian citizen, who in the meantime returned to Berlin to apply for asylum and his application was rejected.

Conclusion

In this paper, I conducted a socio-historical investigation of the mobilities of Romani individuals who are third-country nationals mobile between the EU and the non-EU Post-Yugoslav space. In contrast to Romani migrants holding EU citizenship, Post-Yugoslav Romani migrants acquired a wide range of diverse migrant statuses in the EU such as labour migrants, refugees and persons with toleration status. Following Schengen visa liberalization processes many of them became rejected asylum seekers. Although some of these statuses were considered to be in the domain of forced migration, while others were characterized as economic migration, they all had certain common characteristics that distinguished them from migrants with the status of EU citizenship. Their statuses were not only precarious, but also temporary and liminal, thus all these individuals could be deportable. This legal liminality was an essential part in the control of their freedom of movement. While the equality of all EU citizens was challenged in the case of Romani migrants, when it comes to the Roma who are third-country nationals, the restrictions of freedom of movement and unequal precarious migrant statuses were usually legitimized and even reinforced by their racialization.

I showed in this paper that the migration statuses assumed by the Post-Yugoslav Romani individuals in the EU, particularly Germany, cannot be considered as being 'Romani mobilities'. I argued that Romani migrants from the former Yugoslav space were a part of wider migration patterns that were also taken by their other co-citizens. However, in the case of Romani individuals, the reasons for such mobilities were specific, usually due to the status they had in their states of citizenship, where they have been often treated as a non-dominant, but also racialized minority not linked to any territory and mobile per se. In contrast to other (Post-)Yugoslav citizens, their mobilities were racialized as their essentialized cultural trait: they were not treated as the product of their position in the state of origin and the host state, and also not as conditioned by legal arrangements and the relationship between them.

I argued that the migrant statuses of Post-Yugoslav Romani individuals were interconnected and often reshuffled due to circular mobilities between the EU and the Post-Yugoslav space. Circular mobilities were the direct product of migration control, including deportation, which prevented Romani migrants from settling permanently in host states. Yet for many of them, it was unclear which country was de facto their country of origin and which was their host country: what was supposed to be their country of origin was a country they had never been to. In the last instance, we can see that the boundaries between economic and post-conflict mobilities are blurred, yet they convey multi-layered inequalities that the Post-Yugoslav Romani minorities face.

Notes

1. By using the term Romani minorities I want to acknowledge the Post-Yugoslav hybrid and heterogeneous multitude of populations that in the political context of EU usually fall under the common denominator of Roma (Simhandl, 2009). However, in the Post-Yugoslav space, these populations besides Roma or even Gypsy identify themselves by means of different names, such as Ashkali, Egyptians, Xoxorane, Sinti, Bayash, Vlach, etc. Secondly, I use the term minorities not in order to simply align my research with the terminology of many states, but to signal that all these populations share their non-dominant, that is, minority position. This can be deduced both from their position within the Post-Yugoslav space as well as within the EU as a whole. Hence, the term Romani minorities does not only cover individuals who self-identify themselves as belonging to one of the above-mentioned groups, but are also externally categorized as such. As I aim to show in this paper such labelling can thus have many consequences, also when it comes to legal statuses.
2. Part of the fieldwork was supported by European Research Council funding scheme within the CITSEE Project (grant number 230239) based at the University of Edinburgh, and another part by the European Social Fund, which funded my PhD studies.
3. While the fieldwork was conducted earlier, the findings are the result of research during my Max Weber Fellowship at the European University institute.
4. Source: http://www.refworld.org/docid/50b740df2.html.
5. Similar issues on Romani individuals who were deported from Germany were reported by film director Želimir Žilnik in his documentary 'Kenedi goes home'. Žilnik's movie and some other reports mostly focus on returnees to Kosovo. However, I highlighted the case from Croatia and Serbia in order to show that deportation did not only happen in the case of Kosovar citizens, but also in other contexts.

Acknowledgements

I would like to thank the special issue's editors Can Yıldız and Nicholas De Genova as well as Marco Solimene and Huub van Baar for the invaluable comments on this paper.

Disclosure statement

No potential conflict of interest was reported by the author.

ORCID

Julija Sardelić http://orcid.org/0000-0002-2206-4369

References

van Baar, H. (2017). Contained mobility and the racialization of poverty in Europe: The Roma at the development-security nexus. *Social Identities*. doi:10.1080/13504630.2017.1335826

Baković, N. (2014). Tending the "Oasis of Socialism." Transnational political mobilization of Yugoslav economic emigrants in the FR Germany in the late 1960s and 1970s. *Nationalities Papers, 42*(4), 674–690. doi:10.1080/00905992.2014.880831

Balibar, E., & Wallerstein, I. M. (1991). *Race, nation, class*. London: Verso.

Barany, Z. (2002). *The East European gypsies*. Cambridge: Cambridge University Press.

BBC. (2014, November 11). EU 'benefit tourism' ruling is common sense, says Cameron. *BBC*. Retrieved from http://www.bbc.com/news/uk-politics-30002138

Brubaker, R. (2004). *Ethnicity without groups*. Cambridge, MA: Harvard University Press.

Caglar, A., & Mehling, S. (2013). Sites and scales of law: Third country nationals and EU Roma citizens. In E. Isin & M. Saward (Eds.), *Enacting European citizenship* (pp. 155–177). Cambridge: Cambridge University Press.

Cahn, C., & Guild, E. (2008). *Recent migration of Roma in Europe*. Retrieved June 2, 2017, from http://www.osce.org/hcnm/78034?download=true

Castañeda, H. (2010). Deportation deffered: 'Illegality', visibility and recognition in contemporary Germany. In N. De Genova & N. M. Peutz (Eds.), *The deportation regime* (pp. 245–261). Durham, NC: Duke University Press.

Cherkezova, S. (2014). Potential Romani migrants from the Western Balkans. *Roma Rights*, (1), 5–15.

Crowe, D. (2007). *A history of the gypsies of Eastern Europe and Russia*. New York, NY: Palgrave Macmilan.

De Genova, N. P. (2002). Migrant 'illegality' and deportability in everyday life. *Annual Review of Anthropology, 31*, 419–447.

Deutsche Welle. (2014, September 19). "Doubts about western Balkans as 'safe Countries of origin'" *Deutsche Welle*. Retrieved from http://www.dw.com/en/doubts-about-western-balkans-as-safe-countries-of-origin/a-17933918?maca=en-rss-en-top-1022-rdf

ESI. (2015). *Kosovo's activities to receive a roadmap*. Retrieved June 2, 2017, from http://www.esiweb.org/index.php?lang=en&id=451

European Council on Refugees and Exiles. (2015). *Safe countries of origin: A safe concept?* Retrieved June 2, from https://www.ecre.org/wp-content/uploads/2016/06/AIDA-Third-Legal-Briefing_Safe-Country-of-Origin.pdf

Gilroy, Paul. (1987). *'There ain't no black in the union jack'*. Chicago, IL: University of Chicago Press.

Goldring, L., Berinstein, C., & Bernhard, J. K. (2009). Institutionalizing precarious migratory status in Canada. *Citizenship Studies, 13*, 239–265. doi:10.1080/13621020902850643

Goldring, L., & Landolt, P. (2013). *Producing and negotiating non-citizenship*. Toronto, ON: University of Toronto Press.

Grill, J. (2012). 'Going up to England': Exploring mobilities among Roma from Eastern Slovakia. *Journal of Ethnic and Migration Studies, 38*, 1269–1287. doi:10.1080/1369183x.2012.689187

Hauser, H. (2014). Blitzverfahren-German Asylum procedures for Roma from Western Balkan Countries. *Roma Rights*, (1), 71–79.

Imre, A. (2005). Whiteness in post-socialist Eastern Europe: The time of the gypsies, the end of race. In A. J. Lopez (Ed.), *Postcolonial whiteness: A critical reader on race* (pp. 53–78). Albany: SUNY Press.

Kacarska, S. (2012). *Europeanisation through mobility: Visa liberation and citizenship regimes in Western Balkans* (CITSEE Working Paper 2012/21). Edinburgh: University of Edinburgh.

Kochenov, D. (2007). EU influence on the citizenship policies of the candidate countries: The case of Roma exclusion in the Czech Republic. *Journal of Contemporary European Research, 3*(2), 124–140.

Kocze, A. (2011). *Gender, ethnicity and class: Romani women's political activism and social struggles* (Unpublished PhD thesis). Budapest: CEU.

Komac, M. (2007). *Priseljenci*. Ljubljana: INV.

Krasniqi, G. (2015). Equal citizens, uneven communities: Differentiated and hierarchical citizenship in Kosovo. *Ethnopolitics, 14*(2), 197–217. doi:10.1080/17449057.2014.991152

Kummrow, L. (2015). *To what extent has the EU visa liberalization process contributed to further discrimination of Roma community in Serbia and Macedonia?* (Unpublished MA Thesis). University College London, London.
Ladányi, J., & Szelényi, I. (2006). *Patterns of exclusion: Constructing gypsy ethnicity and the making of an underclass in transitional societies in Europe* (1st ed.). Boulder: East European Monographs.
Latham, J. (1999). Roma of the former Yugoslavia. *Nationalities Papers, 27*(2), 205–226. doi:10.1080/009059999109037
Matras, Y. (2000). Romani migrations in the post-communist era: Their historical and political significance. *Cambridge Review of International Affairs, 13*(2), 32–50. doi:10.1080/09557570008400297
McGarry, A. (2010). *Who speaks for Roma?* New York, NY: Continuum.
Menjívar, C. (2006). Liminal legality: Salvadoran and Guatemalan immigrants' lives in the United States. *American Journal of Sociology, 111*(4), 999–1037. doi:10.1086/499509
Molnar, I. G. (1997). The sociology of migration from the former Yugoslavia. *Journal of Ethnic and Migration Studies, 23*(1), 109–122. doi:10.1080/1369183x.1997.9976578
Novinšćak, K. (2009). The recruiting and sending of Yugoslav 'Gastarbeiters': Between socialist demands and economic needs. In U. Brunnbauer (Ed.), *Transnational societies, transterritorial politics* (pp. 121–144). München: Oldenbourg.
Pantea, M. (2012). From 'making a living' to 'getting ahead': Roma women's experiences of migration. *Journal of Ethnic and Migration Studies, 38*, 1251–1268. doi:10.1080/1369183x.2012.689185
Pantea, M. (2013). Social ties at work: Roma migrants and the community dynamics. *Ethnic and Racial Studies, 36*, 1726–1744. doi:10.1080/01419870.2012.664282
Parker, O. (2012). Roma and the politics of EU citizenship in France: Everyday security and resistance. *Journal of Common Market Studies, 50*(3), 475–491. doi:10.1111/j.1468-5965.2011.02238.x
Parker, O., & Toke, D. (2013). The politics of a multi-level citizenship: French Republicanism, Roma mobility and the EU. *Global Society, 27*(3), 360–378. doi:10.1080/13600826.2013.790785
Perić, T., & Demirovski, M. (2000). Unwanted: The exodus of Kosovo Roma (1998–2000). *Cambridge Review of International Affairs, 13*(2), 83–96. doi:10.1080/09557570008400300
Portes, A., Guarnizo, L., & Landolt, P. (1999). *Transnational communities* (1st ed.). London: Routledge.
Ram, M. (2011). Roma advocacy and EU conditionality: Not one without the other? *Comparative European Politics, 9*(2), 217–241. doi:10.1057/cep.2009.17
Rövid, M. (2012). *Cosmopolitanism and exclusion : On the limits of transnational democracy in the light of the case of Roma* (Unpublished PhD Thesis). Central European University, Budapest.
Ruhs, M. (2006). The potential of temporary migration programmes in future international migration policy. *International Labour Review, 145*(1–2), 7–36. doi:10.1111/j.1564-913x.2006.tb00008.x
Sardelic, J. (2013). *Romani minorities on the margins of post-Yugoslav citizenship regimes* . CITSEE Working Paper No. 2013/31. Retrieved from https://ssrn.com/abstract=2388859
Sardelić, J. (2014a). Antiziganism as cultural racism: Before and after the disintegration of Yugoslavia. In T. Agarin (Ed.), *When stereotry meets prejudice: Antiziganism in European societies* (pp. 201–222). Stuttgart: Ibidem Verlag.
Sardelić, J. (2014b). Romani minorities and the variety of migration patterns in the Post-Yugoslav space. *Roma Rights, 1*, 15–22.
Sardelić, J. (2015). Romani minorities and uneven citizenship access in the Post-Yugoslav space. *Ethnopolitics, 14*(2), 159–179. doi:10.1080/17449057.2014.991154
Sardelić, J. (2016). The position and agency of the 'irregularized': Romani migrants as European semi-citizens. *Politics*. doi:026339571666853
Sassen, S. (1998). *Globalization and its discontents*. New York, NY: New Press.
Scheppele, K. (2004). Constitutional ethnography: An introduction. *Law and Society Review, 38*(3), 389–406. doi:10.1111/j.0023-9216.2004.00051.x
Sigona, N. (2003). How can a 'nomad' be a 'refugee'? Kosovo Roma and labelling policy In Italy. *Sociology, 37*(1), 69–79. doi:10.1177/0038038503037001445
Sigona, N. (2015). Campzenship: Reimagining the camp as a social and political space. *Citizenship Studies, 19*, 1–15. doi:10.1080/13621025.2014.937643
Simhandl, K. (2009). Beyond boundaries? Comparing the construction of the political categories 'gypsies' and 'Roma' before and after the EU enlargement. In N. Sigona & N. Trehan (Eds.),

Romani politics in contemporary Europe: Poverty, ethnic mobilization, and the neoliberal order (pp. 72–93). Basingstoke: Palgrave Macmillan.

Solimene, M. (2011). 'These Romanians have ruined Italy'. Xoraxané Romá, Romanian Roma and Rome. *Journal of Modern Italian Studies, 16,* 637–651. doi:10.1080/1354571x.2011.622471

Spiegel. (2011). *Wave of Roma rejected as asylum seekers.* Retrieved June 2, 2017, from http://www.spiegel.de/international/germany/from-serbia-to-germany-and-back-wave-of-roma-rejected-as-asylum-seekers-a-764630.html

Stewart, M. (2012). *The gypsy 'menace'.* New York, NY: Columbia University Press.

Szalai, J. (2003). Conflicting struggles for recognition: Clashing interest of gender and ethnicity in contemporary Hungary. In B. Hobson (Ed.), *Recognition struggles and social movements: Contested Identities, agency and power* (pp. 188–215). Cambridge: Cambridge University Press.

UNICEF. (2011). *No place to call home: Repatriation from Germany to Kosovo as seen and experienced by Roma, Ashkali, and Egyptian children.* Prishtina: UNICEF.

Van Hear, N. (2003). *New diasporas* (1st ed.). London: Routledge.

Vertovec, S. (1999). Conceiving and researching transnationalism. *Ethnic and Racial Studies, 22,* 447–462. doi:10.1080/014198799329558

Vertovec, S. (2004). Cheap calls: The social glue of migrant transnationalism. *Global Networks, 4*(2), 219–224. doi:10.1111/j.1471–0374.2004.00088.x

Vincze, E. (2014). The racialization of Roma in the 'new' Europe and the political potential of Romani women. *European Journal of Women's Studies, 21,* 435–442. doi:10.1177/1350506814548963

Vlase, I., & Voicu, M. (2014). Romanian Roma migration: The interplay between structures and agency. *Ethnic and Racial Studies, 37,* 2418–2437. doi:10.1080/01419870.2013.809133

Vullnetari, J. (2012). "Beyond 'choice or force': Roma mobility in Albania and the mixed migration paradigm". *Journal of Ethnic and Migration Studies, 38,* 1305–1321. doi:10.1080/1369183x.2012.689191

Zahova, S. (2010). *Refugee migrations of Roma, Ashkali, and Egyptians to Montenegro and their impact on the communities' social and cultural development.* In: N. Sigona (Ed.), *Proceedings of International Conference Romani Mobilities in Europe: Multidisciplinara Perspective* (pp. 251–256).

Zimmerman, W. (2014). *Open borders, nonalignment, and the political evolution of Yugoslavia* (1st ed.). Princeton: Princeton University Press.

5 On the threshold
Becoming Romanian Roma, everyday racism and residency rights in transition

Rachel Humphris

ABSTRACT
This article examines the reaction of welfare state actors and 'Romanian Roma' migrants to the political environment on migration in the UK. Based on the ethnographic fieldwork between January 2013 and March 2014, the article focuses on how processes of everyday racism infused understandings of the legal framework for European migrants' residency rights. The article first explores how state actors developed ideas about 'Romanian Roma families' as opposed to 'Romanian-not-Roma families' in a context marked by pervasive uncertainty about legal entitlements, welfare restructuring and decreasing resources. Second, I draw on new migrants' accounts to identify their perceptions and understandings of discrimination placed within their previous experiences of racism and state violence. The article argues that processes of racialisation are subtly enfolded into everyday life shaping the narratives through which both welfare state actors and new migrants understand their situated experiences and future plans. The article reveals the small and mundane practices that reproduce racialised hierarchies which maintain the notion of 'Roma' as a group with particular proclivities and the affects for their socio-legal status as European migrants in the UK.

Introduction

Dikh! Murre fatsa si Romania, murre lila si Belge! (Look! My face is Romanian,[1] my papers are Belgian!)

This short statement from Serban to his cousins illustrates the main concern of this article. Serban, who moved to the UK from Brussels in December 2013, called HMRC[2] (Her Majesty's Revenue and Customs) to book himself an interview for a UK social security number (known as a National Insurance number or NINo).[3] He was surprised to hear that he had a choice of dates, times and locations for the interview, including an interview in two days. He was surprised because he had just called to make a similar appointment for his Romanian wife, Anca, and she received an appointment scheduled for three weeks' time, falling after the change in transitional restrictions for Romanians in January 2014.

Transitional restrictions were imposed on Romania and Bulgaria (henceforth A2) when they acceded to the European Union in January 2007 and remained in place for seven years until January 2014. These migration controls were more restrictive than those imposed previous European Union accession migrants (Ciupijus, 2011; Cook, Dwyer, & Waite, 2011; Currie, 2016; Somerville, 2007) and constrained A2 migrants' labour market mobility leaving them more vulnerable to precarious work (Fox, Moroşanu, & Szilassy, 2015). Although A2 migrants were entitled to exercise their right of free movement to enter the UK, they had to achieve a 'qualifying status' within three months to remain legally in the country.[4] In addition to this legal change, the interpretation of these restrictions in practice shifted throughout the course of my fieldwork, including the definitions of 'genuine self-employed work' and 'right to reside' which were crucial to gaining a 'qualifying status' to remain legally within the UK.

Returning to Serban's comment, the distinction between his 'Romanian face' and his 'Belgian papers' caused his cousins to laugh because the HMRC seemingly did not know that Serban was 'Romanian' because of his Belgian passport. His cousins were sure the distinction made between Serban and Anca was further proof of the rumours circulating through families at this time that Romanians were 'not liked' in the UK. Furthermore, because the appointment fell after the transitional restrictions had ended, they believed their situation would be worse after January 2014. Many conversations between family members focused on trying to gain a NINo interview before the end of 2013 as it was increasingly believed that the ending of transitional restrictions would usher in increased refusals and removals.

This article explores why these new migrants (living in the UK for less than five years)[5] believed 'England didn't like Romanians' and would 'close the door' following the withdrawal of transitional restrictions, particularly when they were told by welfare state actors that it would be easier to gain a NINo *after* January 2014. Crucially, the article explores new migrants' own understandings and perceptions of racialisation, where they come from and how they are identified in everyday practices. Research with East European migrants has revealed reports of discrimination (Favell & Nebe, 2009; Kraler & Kofman, 2009; Spencer, Ruhs, Anderson, & Rogaly, 2007). But as highlighted by Fox et al. (2015), it has proven difficult to observe and measure the different combinations of 'biological and cultural indicia' that reproduce systems of racial domination (2015, p. 733). This article uses a different approach. It explores how processes of racialisation can be revealed through encounters, and stories of encounters, between new migrants and welfare state actors. It argues that the uncertainty created during this time could itself be seen as representing a process of racialisation leading to dilemmas for new migrants and state actors alike.

First, I explain my methodology before describing the conceptual framework which builds on anthropological perspectives of the state and the position of state actors as relationally embedded in local contexts. Second, I review the perspectives of new migrants who make sense of legal regulations through rumours and previous experiences of racism and state violence. Third, the article explores how state actors developed ideas about 'Romanian Roma families' as opposed to 'Romanian-not-Roma families'. State actors' mechanisms of labelling (re)produce certain expectations and perceptions of those identified as 'Roma families' which infused narratives that are passed between them. These narratives are then mobilised to justify particular courses of action and normalise practices of withdrawing support for families identified as 'Roma'. Fourth, I draw on new migrants' accounts to identify their perceptions and understandings of discrimination placed within their previous experiences of racism and state violence. I use these accounts to explain how and why new migrants imagined their status would be affected by the ending of transitional restrictions and identify how perceptions of discrimination affect the assessment of truth claims, their incorporation into belief systems and decision-making for the future. Finally, I demonstrate how this uncertainty shifts identities and narratives of belonging. The accounts demonstrate how processes of racialisation are subtly enfolded into everyday life shaping the narratives through which state actors and new migrants understand their situated experiences. The article concludes to argue that the creation of a context of pervasive uncertainty is representative of processes of racialisation, or at the least, provide the techniques to obscure these processes.

Methodology

This article draws on long-term ethnographic work with living with three new migrant families in the UK between January 2013 and March 2014.[6] The new migrants most often referred to themselves as 'Romanian', however, were keen to point out to me that the language they spoke (between each other and in the home) would not be understood in the shops in Romania. Most of the new migrants addressed in this article spoke *romanes* in the home, a predominantly oral language spoken by those who are identified as Roma (Matras, 2013).

Over the course of 14 months spending my everyday life with 20 extended new migrant families I observed numerous interactions of various lengths between new migrants and welfare state actors (health visitors, education family liaison workers; welfare advisors; Children's Centre workers; social workers; housing officers; health and safety officers and volunteers from a local Baptist Church). I also attended multi-agency meetings and accompanied welfare state actors on home visits. Living in the homes of new migrant families and following their networks and connections over many months revealed the complex relations of acts, expectations and perceptions on which different practices became prevalent and routine. Stories about the consequences of changing residency rights were rife at this uncertain time. The implementation of transitional restrictions noticeably changed and became the topic of stories and conversations among and between new migrants and welfare state actors alike throughout 2013. The clearest indication of this shift was the increasing refusals of NINo and assessments that these migrant families did not have a 'right to reside' in the UK. The inconsistent application of transitional regulations and lack of clear guidance led to increasing uncertainty for welfare state actors at the front line of service provision provoking dilemmas when they advised new migrants about their residency status.

At the front line of uncertain residency rights

The use of the term 'front-line workers' specifically alludes to those who assume the 'face of the state', referring to the notion that state forms can be 'located' in everyday practices (Mountz, 2003; Trouillot, 2001). The state operates not as a locatable object but as a located series of networks through which governance takes place. As Wendy Brown remarks, the state is a 'significantly unbounded terrain of powers and techniques, an ensemble of discourses, rules and practices, cohabiting in limited, tension-ridden, often contradictory relation with one another' (1992, p. 24). In this formulation, state actors and their 'clients' are examined as a series of relations. Locating the state in interactions allows the incorporation of the situated perspectives of actors to be brought to the fore. State actors, who are themselves relationally embedded (Thelen, Vetters, & von Benda-Beckmann, 2014, p. 7), have to reconcile the idealised versions of bureaucratic practice held in policy with the everyday and often incoherent enactment of those policies when faced with individuals (Mountz, 2003, p. 627). This process becomes more highly contested when these policies are in flux and seem to be rapidly shifting. Front-line workers' decision-making has most widely been discussed as bureaucrats' 'discretion' (Lipsky, 2010). Focusing on the perspective of street-level bureaucrats allows an analysis of the negotiations that take place within these interactions and how they become sites where different narratives emerge, are contested, and are either re-inscribed or transformed. The meanings made in these everyday encounters are crucial as they are the sites of the delivery of public services, the implementation of state policy and where decisions around access to state resources take place. Dubois, drawing on Bourdieu's idea of 'state acts', notes that they are 'inseparably symbolic and material, relying on abstract categories and on concrete objects – consisting of both discourses and bureaucratic routines – that shape the perceptions of the people as well as their material situations' (2014, p. 38).

In addition, the decisions of front-line workers were becoming increasingly crucial to the life chances of new migrants due to two changes to front-line bureaucratic work. First, front-line workers were decreasingly employed directly by the Local Authority creating complex partnership and co-commissioning arrangements (Forbess & James, 2014). The fragmentation of public services, the imposition of financial targets in welfare services, the rise of 'new public management' (Andersen, 2005; Barry, Berg, Chandler, & Ellison, 2007; Clarke, 2005), the co-option of for-profit logics in the state bureaucracy, public–private partnerships increasingly guided by commissioning and co-governing, and transformations within civil society have elevated the significance of forms of governance based on targets, measures and reduced resources (Born & Jensen, 2005; Clarke & Newman, 1997). Second, migration controls were being increasingly diffused to the front line, a process which Yuval Davis has termed 'everyday bordering' (2013, 2017). The interactions between front-line workers and their 'clients' therefore provide a privileged position from which to examine how representations provide meaning to front-line workers, how they act on those representation and with what consequences (Tervonen & Enache, 2017).

Everyday racism and rumour publics

Attention to how encounters between front-line workers and new migrants shape future decision-making helps to identify forms of 'everyday racism' (Essed, 1991) and connects the structural forces of racism within everyday 'routine' and sometimes 'mundane' situations (Billig et al., 1988). The ideological dimensions of racism can then be linked to daily attitudes and reproduction of racism can be interpreted in terms of experiences in everyday life. Focusing on the complexity of lived experiences is vital for understanding the processual and shifting nature of racialisation and is pivotal to avoid reductionist accounts of social relations (Balibar, 1998; Hall & Du Gay, 1996). Examining experiences and subsequent actions of new migrants and front-line workers provides insights into how the narratives of belonging that condition racist structures are situated (Brah, Hickman, & Mac an Ghaill, 1999) and how previous experiences of racism can shape the interpretive lenses through which truth claims about legal systems are assessed and incorporated into systems of belief. As Essed elaborates: 'the experience of everyday racism is a cumulative process. New experiences are interpreted and evaluated against the background of earlier personal experiences, vicarious experiences and general knowledge of racism in society' (1991, p. 8). It is crucial to account for new migrants' own understandings and perceptions of racism and the contexts within which they emerge. This article provides an account of where assessments of discrimination came from, how these assessments were used to comprehend (racist) events and the consequences for future decision-making.

In the particular case of these new migrants, the consequences of legal restrictions and residency rights circulate in a social field that has an excess of stories and rumours about how to make a life in the UK, such that the repetition, or what Butler (1997) terms reiterability, constitutes the way new migrant families understood their situated experiences. These stories of interactions with front-line workers act as improvised news in the absence or rejection of more formal and verifiable news. The stories therefore offer an interpretative frame for those participating in their circulation. This resonates with what Harney has called 'rumour publics' (2006, p. 276), where people make use of the knowledge they possess to solve problems, make sense of changing or uncertain conditions and construct explanatory narratives in the face of fluid and ambiguous situations (Shibutani, 1966; Stewart & Strathern, 2004).

Word of mouth communication of 'unsubstantiated' information extends into wider social fields. The information is 'substantiated' to the extent that it is received by word of mouth from an interpersonal relationship and is subjectively evaluated against standards of experience, knowledge and the trust in or prestige of those from whom one receives the news. The assessments of stories of encounters with front-line workers and new migrants are therefore contingent on prior knowledge and the relationship between those exchanging information. They contain a judgment of the person claiming, the claim itself and the context in which the claim is spoken. As de Certeau expresses:

> 'believing' designates a relation to the other that precedes me and is constantly occurring. Citation appears to be the ultimate weapon for making people believe. Because it plays on what the other is assumed to believe, it is the means by which the 'real' is instituted. To cite the other on their behalf is hence to make credible the simulacra produced in a particular place ... to cite is thus to give reality to the simulacrum produced by a power, by making people believe that others believe in it, but without providing any believable object. (1984, pp. 188–189)

De Certeau's analysis of how truth claims are incorporated into systems of belief takes on particular salience in the context of these new migrant families and the uncertain situation created by transitional restrictions. First, because almost all of the adult new migrants were illiterate and therefore had severely curtailed access to sources of information. Information was exchanged almost entirely through oral transmission and memory. The credibility of the speaker and the plausibility of their speech are assessed on particular forms and norms of performance linked to social position. Second, new migrants' previous and current situations and their own understanding of the palpability of racism inflect their evaluation of interactions and accounts of encounters. Almost all of the new migrants addressed in this article had previously directly or indirectly experienced eviction, deportation, imprisonment or had a child taken into the care of social services. These experiences seemed to change the contours of plausibility when assessing narratives about the future and had particular consequences for interactions with state actors and how changing residency rights were interpreted and understood.

Becoming 'Romanian Roma'

Front-line workers distinguished Roma from their Romanian co-nationals in subtle but consequential ways. Roma women were primarily identified by the way they dressed; wearing a long handmade skirt (*fuwsta*) and headscarves arranged tightly round their head (*diklo*). However, this also led to confusion when families who did not dress in this way were also identified as Roma either through speaking *romanes* or through association with the Roma Pentecostal Church (*khangheri*). This confusion provides an indication of the how 'the Roma' were treated as a generic group despite wide variations across all axes of differentiation. The new migrants in this article come from three different areas in Romania (a large city, a town and a rural area) and have widely diverging experiences, migration trajectories and legal statuses. Front-line workers recognise this diversity; however, they endeavoured to retain an idea of distinct 'Romanian Roma' and 'Romanian-not Roma' groups. As argued in the introduction to this Special Issue, this can be seen as an effect of a larger process of EU institutionalisation and racialisation of those identified as 'Roma'. When I visited homes with front-line workers, they often commented that they knew a Roma house before they entered because all the windows were open and, if there was a garden in front of the house, it did not conform to notions of orderly and tidy space, with rubbish, chairs or children's pushchairs outside.

A distinction between 'Romanian-Roma' and 'Romanian-not-Roma' was introduced and repeated between front-line workers when they met at bimonthly 'multi-agency' meetings. The aim of these meetings was to bring together those who provided education, health and welfare support to new migrants for information sharing and to ensure that front-line workers were not duplicating work. The ambiguous legal situation of these new migrants, who were citizens of an EU member state but were not able to access state resources, was a new phenomenon for many front-line workers, and their organisations. Legal information was available; however, these guidelines did not reflect the rapidly shifting interpretations of the transition restrictions. Rather than receiving guidance from team leaders, front-line workers were considered to be the 'experts' on the situation of these new migrants and the different regulations and legal statuses that affected their clients. When debate regarding transitional restrictions increased in the media leading to a moral panic regarding the number of A2 migrants that might settle in the UK (Allen, 2014), front-line workers were consulted and asked to provide reports on the possible impact on their services, particularly schools and early years' education.

Front-line workers discussions at these meetings provide a lens to grasp their understanding of the changing legal framework in January 2014 and how this bled into their daily activities, infusing the expectations and perceptions of those identified as 'Roma'. In one such meeting in November 2013, Paula, an education diversity officer expressed the view that those who were working long hours in low-wage jobs and not applying for a NINo were 'doing the right thing' by waiting until transitional restrictions were lifted. She provided the example of a 'Romanian-not-Roma' married couple who were working for 14 h a day for £80 in a factory and a cleaning company. It was agreed that 'Romanian Roma' should also be waiting for January 2014 when transitional restrictions would be lifted. It was eluded during these meetings that 'Romanian Roma' were misusing front-line workers' time and resources by trying to obtain a NINo in 2013, particularly when they were unlikely to be granted a NINo due to increasingly strict interpretations of the transitional restrictions.

Romanian Roma families were also distinguished from their national counterparts using old tropes of nomadism and a desire for living in caravans rather than houses. Rosemary, a family liaison volunteer for a primary school, was working with a new migrant family who she identified as Romanian Roma because she had received their referral from the pastor of the Roma Church. She commented that there were no toys in the house because 'it is like living in a wagon isn't it? If your whole family is living in one room then you don't keep things do you?' She also presumed that the family would not stay in the local area. She noted that 'I wouldn't be surprised if they suddenly disappear' and did not pursue contact with them when they did not respond to her initial attempts support them. Attention to these small mundane practices identifies how different socio-political and legal statuses can be (re)produced. Different practices for 'Roma families' developed and became routine as experiences were shared between front-line workers. For example, front-line workers would often visit Roma family homes unannounced because it was believed that Roma did not keep appointments (Humphris, 2017).

However, front-line workers also expressed personal experiences of discrimination and frustration with the terms on which they were able to fulfil their roles. The contradictions in front-line workers' narratives highlight their own ambiguous positions regarding whether, and if so, how, to support these new migrant families. It also shows how their understandings of the future after transitional restrictions shaped, and provided justifications for, their present actions. These narratives emerged at multi-agency meetings. Lisa was a family support worker who was subcontracted by the local government to assist 'Gypsy, Roma and Travellers' with welfare claims and to ensure that they were accessing their entitlements. She commented,

> they are going to put another obstacle in their way. They are not going to make it easy. They will say something like you have to have an offer of a job before you can have a National Insurance Number or something like that. They [HMRC] are not giving them [a NINo] unless they [Roma] can show that they are self-supporting. This didn't used to be the case. But they don't just want to see a bit of income they want to see that you can really support yourself otherwise you don't get anything.

Paula concurred surmising that 'they [Roma] might not ever be able to get good jobs. At the moment lots are doing car wash for cash-in-hand but the Albanians don't want to give them a contract – they will just find somebody else'.

However, these perspectives were not shared with new migrant clients. The end of transitional restrictions in January 2014 was presented as a time of hope for a better future. Lisa also expressed this different view of the future to me in an interview I conducted in her office. She was well aware of the problems that her clients faced acknowledging the discrimination attributed to being identified as 'Roma', informed by media portrayals:

It is the same as when black people came – we weren't allowed in the same pubs as the white. They have got bad stigma for themselves. All communities have got stigma but they are new to the UK. You can see why people see them in this. I only saw in the paper the other day, a Romanian selling his daughter as a slave – as a working girl for him. Then you are seeing them in the streets begging. As someone who has never been alongside them – they are not getting to know them … Before (January 2014) it was self-employed, selling the Big Issue, but that was with their culture. It was cleaning cars but that was with their culture. Now they can go out into the factories. These other cultures will see these Romanian people, as the people they are, not as the stigma. You will see a lady working in Wilkos. That is how these barriers start coming down – it's just getting the bosses to give them a break, you know? They are up against a brick wall. As long as people have these views about Roma people they are going to find it really difficult to get jobs – really difficult. I sent her [Maria, a new migrant mother] down to the Job Centre to get a list of employment agencies and we sat there and we rang them all for her and they asked what nationality: 'Oh they are Roma'. It's got to take a few bosses to start employing them.

Lisa's account demonstrated her awareness of the individual situations that those identified as Roma faced when trying to find employment and drew on her own experience as a visible minority. She acknowledged that 'Roma' are unlikely to get jobs due to the stereotypes that had proliferated in media reports and the structural conditions that dictated their working opportunities. She assigned her own work a degree of futility in the face of these categorisations. Lisa attributed the intensity of discrimination Roma faced to their 'newness' in the area which she believed would fade in time. However, she also drew on an idea of an easier but undetermined future to justify her own decisions to defer support to new migrants until after transitional restrictions had been lifted.

The idea of a future that would be less marked by discrimination with fewer regulations was mobilised when front-line workers interacted with new migrant clients. Front-line workers also told some Roma clients that NINo would not be issued before January 2014. This statement provided front-line workers with the justification to defer helping new migrants with their NINo claims until after January 2014. However, these assertions served to undermine their credibility when stories spread that others had gained a NINo. These actions also fuelled rumours that England 'didn't like us'. Therefore, in some cases even when front-line workers were sympathetic and trying to be helpful to those they identified as Romanian Roma (because they were also speculating about what changes with the transitional restrictions will actually mean) they ended up appearing to mislead new migrants and created conditions that exacerbated uncertainty.

Failed encounters and uncertain futures

The decision regarding whether to help a new migrant family or not was highly contingent on the person who had referred the family and how they presented themselves at initial meetings with front-line providers, which usually took place in their homes (Humphris, 2017). From six front-line workers (one health visitor, two Children's Centre workers, one education diversity officer, one welfare advisor and one housing officer), one never mentioned transitional restrictions, one previously dealt with welfare benefits but had stopped because the regulation were 'too complicated', an education officer, welfare officer, one Children's Centre worker told some families they would help and in other cases would withdraw support and one Children's Centre worker helped one family because of shared religious beliefs.

Front-line workers were not trained in the intricacies of the legal situation for A2 migrants and complicated legal regulations increased their wide areas of discretion (exacerbated by the withdrawal of legal aid[7]). Front-line workers understandings were infused with uncertainty about legal regulations and how they should be interpreted, their own job security and decreasing resources and wider fears regarding the trajectory of legislation about migration and welfare. Drawing on these understandings, practices developed which reinforced new migrants' perceptions that they were gaining a bad reputation, were not wanted in England and should gain a NINo before transitional restrictions were lifted in January 2014.

The consequences of the context of uncertainty can be illustrated through Georgetta, a new migrant mother, and her experience of a 'failed encounter' with Lisa. When Lisa arrived at Georgetta's house in September 2013, Lisa found Georgetta had no NINo and no other documents or receipts. Georgetta was working as a household cleaner but was often paid in furniture or food rather than money. Georgetta was also not aware that she needed to keep receipts or have business liability insurance. Moreover, Lisa found that her housing contract was not 'valid' because she was renting from a private landlord who would not provide her with receipts or a legal rental agreement. Lisa sat on the couch in the front room and sifted through the documents, bills and other papers including solicitor letters regarding a car accident that involved Georgetta's husband. Lisa could not find an order to the papers. Georgetta could read and write in Romanian and she often told me she attended school for 10 years. She also told me that she only spoke Romanian in her family and learned *romanes* when she married her husband, Rosvan. However, she could not read or write in English. Rosvan could not read or write in Romanian or English. Rosvan watched the action from the other side of the room but was silent. Lisa told Georgetta that she could not help her until Georgetta had a NINo. Lisa also explained to Georgetta that she should wait until January (in three months) when the rules would change. Lisa assured her it would be easy to get a NINo in January 2014.

When Lisa left the house the family was confused and frustrated. Rosvan exclaimed that his son's wife had given birth in England, his granddaughter was 'English' (*englezoika*), and therefore 'they must help us'. This was based on the actions of another family member who had received child benefit for their daughter who was born at the same time. However, Rosvan did not know that this family member had gained refugee status and therefore was eligible for social support. He believed Lisa's withdrawal and refusal of help was an indication that 'England is closing the door'. This encounter plunged the family into a sense of confusion, unsure about what course of action to take next or where to seek advice. Lisa made the decision not to help Georgetta gain a NINo due to resource constraints, shifting bureaucratic structures and lack of training about complex legal entitlements. Lisa justified her actions to me by combining ideas from the multi-agency meetings and her own experiences. She felt she would be wasting her time and creating hope for nothing if she helped Georgetta with a futile NINo application. In addition, she would have to invest a lot of time and resources without a successful result. She was under increasing pressure achieve results by her organisation due to funding demands from the local government. Therefore, Lisa used the idea that it would be easier to gain a NINo after transitional restrictions had been lifted in order to justify her withdrawal of support.

In contrast, Georgetta believed that she had 'gone straight' by getting an invoice book, cleaning jobs, business cards and a mobile phone and therefore felt as though she had been mistreated. This feeling was exacerbated when she found out two of her extended family members had gained NINo before January 2014. Georgetta felt she had received misinformation decreasing the credibility of front-line workers and the plausibility of the words that they spoke. This vignette demonstrates the different situated positions of front-line workers and new migrants. For front-line workers, withdrawing support was a response to the wider context of employer discrimination of Roma, shifting NINo requirements and front-line workers' own employment situation which was based on results and targets. For new migrants, they understood their experiences and assess their plans for the future through the stories and rumours told by other family members and their own past experiences.

Previous encounters in different migration contexts were also drawn on and folded into understandings of the legal status change in January 2014. When attending a church service at the end of October 2013 Margereta, a new migrant mother, immediately asked me whether I thought she would be 'put out' of her house when England 'closes the door'. I asked her whether she was paying rent and she confirmed that she was staying with a family who were paying rent to a private landlord. I asked her why she thought she would be moved from her house. She answered that she had heard it on the Romanian televised news and from other mothers who did not have a NINo. Margereta moved to England in June 2013. She proudly showed me a photograph of herself with her son when they lived in Montpellier but she told me she was sent back to her village in Romania in the previous year. She left her son with her parents while she tried to gain work in England. She was extremely anxious and often asked me how she could live in a flat by herself so she could bring her son to join her. Margereta increasingly believed she would not be able to get 'good work' (such as cleaning in contrast to begging which was considered 'hard' (*zurelli*) work), would not be able to bring her son to join her in England and conversely would be sent back to Romania.

Attention to these stories particularly bearing in mind that many could not read and write revealed migrants' subjective understandings of the legal systems in which they were subject and they provide comment on their own economic and legal situation and how previous experiences were mobilised to make sense of current situations. Margereta's anxieties provide a glimpse of how she understands her position within situated migrant hierarchies. It specifically locates her desires within a work trajectory and imagined future for her and her son. However, her previous experience formed part of her assessment of possible futures in the UK, shaping her understanding of regulations and she eventually returned to Romania.

Racialised practices and identity formations

The affects of this generalised condition of uncertainty shifted many new migrants' relationship to the Roma Church (*khangheri*). The effects of processes of racialisation through the perceived lack of any clear information about what was going to happen in January 2014 shaped the narratives through which new migrants understood their experiences and their decision-making strategies.

Many new migrants began attending the *khangheri* shortly after they arrived in the UK. The Roma Church developed from small meetings organised by Violeta, one new migrant mother. She told me she had made a 'promise' to Jesus when he saved her eldest son from meningitis. At first, the religious services took place in Violeta's house and were attended by up to 10 members of her extended family. In 2013, precipitated by the arrival of Grigore and Dan from a different village in Romania and with the support of a local vicar, the Roma Church expanded to a large service. It took place in a rented Methodist Church on Sunday evenings and attracted up to 25 extended families. The context and structure of services was highly contested and fluid. Those who attended regularly described themselves as 'Pentecostal' or 'baptised' (*bokhaimey*). I was often told that the *khangheri* provided 'a straight path' and where 'God washes the heart'. The experiences of two brothers, Dan and Grigore, demonstrate the interrelationship between the Church, residency rights and understandings about uncertain futures that are based on previous and current experiences of everyday racism.

Dan and Grigore applied for NINos at the same time and had very similar backgrounds and work experience. Grigore gained a NINo on his first attempt. He followed the advice of a Romanian solicitor in London. He did not ask the pastor of the *khangheri* to accompany him to his NINo interview, which was considered unusual by other members of the Church. In contrast, Dan was refused four times on the grounds that he could not prove he was engaged in genuine self-employed work. Dan had been following the advice of the pastor, who accompanied him to his NINo interviews. Dan was convinced that the pastor's presence was the reason he did not gain a NINo. He believed that the pastor did not know what to do and could not 'speak well'. This was distressing for Dan not only because he felt he had made the wrong choice, but also because his assessment of credibility in the pastor was based on his Pentecostal faith. His wavering trust in the pastor caused him to question not only his actions in this matter but his wider life choices, including moving to the UK with his family, and religious beliefs.

When Dan received the news that he had failed his NINo interview for the fourth time he despaired, lying on down on the sofa in the downstairs room of his house with tears in his eyes. He questioned his actions, which had been shaped by his religious beliefs. These beliefs had led him to follow the advice of the pastor because this was the 'straight path'. He explained to me that his heart was turning 'black' and that he needed to pray and wash his heart. He was angry which seemed to be heightened by the poor quality of his house. He was getting into debt by sustaining the house which he thought was making his children unwell. He compared his situation to his brother's who was able to afford a better quality house and could 'eat well, drink well and sleep well'. He blamed the pastor and stopped attending the *khangheri*. In addition, his wife, Christina, told me that Grigore was not coming to the house anymore and contact between the brothers seemed to cease because Grigore would not help Dan pay his debts. Dan told me he was planning to move to France where he had previously gained work but was unsure because he had a previous conviction for stealing (which he strongly denied). He considered moving alone, without his family but his wife Christina did not want to be alone to look after their five small children. As previous and current discrimination coalesced at a particular moment he understood his experience through the lens of the failure of his own decision-making and faith in the Pentecostal Church. Dan's experience isolated him from his family and the Church. Previously, he had thought that if he took the 'straight path' that he would gain security for his family in the UK, however, his experience made him reevaluate his future and whether his family should move elsewhere. His choices were curtailed by his previous migration experience and the general context of uncertainty that had been created around the changes in the legal framework. However, he believed the reason for his situation was due to the pastor and by extension his own faith. He was plunged into a deep sense of despair and doubt, not only about his future decisions but also his religious faith. The consequences of previous experiences of racism pervaded everyday life for new migrants, affecting aspects of family relationships, decision-making and extended to religious identities. The uncertain conditions and shifting, complex regulations were propagated, and in some cases, exacerbated by front-line workers and provided the context through which new migrants understood these situated experiences.

Conclusion

Shifting assessments of transitional restrictions including the changing definitions of 'self-employment' and growing numbers of refusals of NINos and the 'right to reside' changed the contours of plausibility about the future after transitional restrictions had been lifted. The strategy of front-line workers acted to increase the salience of transitional restrictions but also decreased their credibility when they offered advice about what would happen in January 2014. These actions lead to a generalised condition of uncertainty that could itself be seen as representing a process of racialisation or at the least, allowed racist practices to be veiled and obscured.

This article has demonstrated how and why new migrants believed that front-line workers 'don't like us' and England would 'close the door' following the end of transitional restrictions in January 2014. These statements also indicate the impact of political and legal uncertainty on migration decision-making and narratives of belonging that occur well before formal legal changes in residency rights. It also contributes to our knowledge of how different new migrants are treated differently in everyday practice as opposed to their portrayal as a homogenous group in media and public discourses. In addition to Fox et al.'s (2014) reports about the hidden racism and racialisation of all Romanians, this article demonstrates how subtle differentiations are made at the front line of services adding further complexity to the lived experiences of racism and the particular pervasiveness and consequences of being identified as 'Roma'. This is vital when those at the front line are bestowed with wider discretionary duties as immigration regulations and welfare requirements become increasingly complex and fused (Yuval-Davis, 2013; Yuval-Davis, Wemyss, & Cassidy, 2017).

Crucially, the article has placed the experiences of new migrants identified as 'Romanian Roma' in relation to front-line workers and their own histories and backgrounds as visible minorities working in organisations that were responding to austerity policies and reductions in personnel and resources. Local processes of labelling and categorisation effect and are woven into front-line workers own understandings and experiences of racism. As such, the article places the experiences of these new migrant families within the historical specificity of contemporary socio-political dynamics and within wider racialised 'minority' social formations (cf. Introduction to this Special Issue).

The ethnographic cases presented here suggest that considering stories as social facts from which people draw meaning has implications for thinking about how histories of discrimination and racism pervade everyday life and decision-making for the future. Through the everyday representations and practices of migrant arrangements and interactions with front-line workers that were produced and circulated in localised sites, new insights can be gained on the implementation and effects of legal regulations. In the cases offered here, stories about residency rights, fears for the future and encounters with front-line workers offered subjective perspectives on the interconnections between situated racialised migrant hierarchies and strategies to gain legal status. Such stories may help explain how certain practices are condemned, condoned, justified or rationalised from particular perspectives and in specific locations. A strict focus on legal regulations and implementation overlooks how new migrants make sense of regulations through previous experiences in various 'elsewheres' including life histories marked by discrimination and unfair treatment. Representations and understandings of those regulations provide meaning to those involved, and explains how they may act on those representations and under what conditions. For migrants whose settlement strategies depend upon subjective evaluations of opportunities and dangers when they have been previously faced with harsh treatment and state violence, these narratives provide a key source of information to assess against their own transnational experiential knowledge.

Notes

1. Serban (and almost all other families) referred to themselves as 'Romanian' and never 'Roma'. They would sometimes tell me that a particular person or church did not like 'Gypsies' or 'Tsigane', the Romanian pejorative word for Gypsies. This is perhaps more surprising as Serban self-identifies as Romanian but was born and lived the majority of his life in Belgium.
2. HMRC is a non-ministerial department of the UK Government responsible for the collection of taxes and the payment of some forms of state support.
3. Two quota based schemes were also introduced for work in the low-skilled labour market. Job Centre assessors performed interviews to assess whether an individual has a qualifying status. If so, the individual was issued with a National Insurance Number (NINo). UK Job Centres were restructured in 2002 to form Jobcentre Plus which amalgamated the Employment Service and the Benefits Agency. In 2011, Jobcentre Plus was dissolved as a separate government entity and now refers to the public facing brand of the Department for Work and Pensions.
4. Romanians and Bulgarians were required to hold a qualifying status in order to live in the UK for more than three months. A qualifying status was defined as being self-employed, economically inactive and self-sufficient, student and self-sufficient, a family member accompanying or joining an EU national who satisfies one of the other statuses, or a pensioner.
5. I use the term 'Romanian Roma' in this article when referring to their relationships with front-line workers as this was how front line service providers identified and categorised these families. The modes of categorisation are discussed in the following section of the article. At all other times I use the term 'new migrant' families as they had all resided in the UK for less than five years. This characteristic was the only common defining feature that I could find between the families referred to here. The new migrants I live with have widely varying migration trajectories, legal statuses, nationalities, languages, religions, family structures, educational backgrounds and are engaged in a range of economic activities. Legal status includes UK citizens, refugee status (UK, Belgium, Canada), A2 migrants, irregular migrants and those who might be considered 'over-stayers' from Brazil and Argentina. In addition, the legal category of some migrants changes around them due to 2007 and 2014 accession arrangements. Entitlements also widely differ between and among families due to different places of birth, background, education, employment and family position and how these characteristics are perceived and brought to bear by others. Therefore, although

they are identified by state actors and religious volunteers as 'Romanian Roma', I found no common characteristic between all the different families apart from their newness in the local area. The most prevalent common characteristic is speaking *romanes* in the home. However, some new migrants I encounter only speak Romanian, and although they seem to understand *Romanës*, do not speak this language. I was also told by new migrants that two women were 'gadje' (non-Roma) and had learnt *romanes* when they got married.
6. This fieldwork formed part of my doctoral research project which aimed to address how new migrants make place in a diverse urban environments. Over the course of 14 months I was in contact with more than 220 new migrants. I interviewed 39 individuals in the local authority and 14 individuals who worked for NGO's, charities and religious organisations. I attended many formal and informal meetings and gatherings. Interviews were tape recorded and transcribed in full. Field notes were taken throughout the course of the fieldwork and were analysed using NVivo 8 and thematic analysis. Ethical approval was gained through the University of Oxford CUREC process for social science researchers.
7. Areas of Social Welfare Law advice were taken out of scope by Legal Aid, Sentencing and Punishment of Offenders Act 2012.

Disclosure statement

No potential conflict of interest was reported by the author.

References

Allen, W. (2014). *Bulgarian and Romanians in the British National Press: 1 December 2012 – 1 December 2013*. Oxford: The Migration Observatory. Retrieved from http://www.migrationobservatory.ox.ac.uk/wp-content/uploads/2016/04/Report-Bulgarians_Romanians_Press_0.pdf

Andersen, J. G. (2005). *The changing face of welfare: Consequences and outcomes from a citizenship perspective*. Bristol: Policy Press.

Balibar, E. (1998). The borders of Europe. *Cultural Politics, 14*(4), 216–232.

Barry, J., Berg, E., Chandler, J., & Ellison, M. (2007). Contested terrains within the neo-liberal project: The re-organisation of services for children in Europe: Gender, citizenship and the forging of New Public Management within professional child care social work practice in Europe. *Equal Opportunities International, 26*(4), 331–351.

Billig, M., Condor, S., Edwards, D., Gane, M., Middleton, D., & Radley, A. (1988). *Ideological dilemmas: A social psychology of everyday thinking*. London: Sage.

Born, A., & Jensen, P. H. (2005). Individualising citizenship. In J. G. Andersen, A.-M. Guillemard, P. H. Jensen, & B. Pfau-Effinger (Eds.), *Changing face of welfare: Consequences and outcomes from a citizenship perspective* (pp. 151–167). Bristol: Policy Press.

Brah, A., Hickman, M. J., & Mac an Ghaill, M. (1999). *Thinking identities: Ethnicity, racism and culture Thinking Identities* (pp. 1–21). London: Springer Press.

Brown, W. (1992). Finding the man in the state. *Feminist Studies, 18*(1), 7–34.

Butler, J. (1997). *Excitable speech: A politics of the performative*. Hove: Psychology Press.

Ciupijus, Z. (2011). Mobile central eastern Europeans in Britain: Successful European Union citizens and disadvantaged labour migrants? *Work, Employment and Society, 25*(3), 540–550.

Clarke, J. (2005). New labour's citizens: Activated, empowered, responsibilized, abandoned? *Critical Social Policy, 25*(4), 447–463.

Clarke, J., & Newman, J. (1997). *The managerial state: Power, politics and ideology in the remaking of social welfare*. London: Sage.

Cook, J., Dwyer, P., & Waite, L. (2011). The experiences of accession 8 migrants in England: Motivations, work and agency. *International Migration, 49*(2), 54–79.

Currie, S. (2016). *Migration, work and citizenship in the enlarged European Union*. Oxford: Routledge Press.

de Certeau, M. (1984). *The practice of everyday life*. Berkeley: University of California Press.

Dubois, V. (2014). The state, legal rigor, and the poor: The daily practice of welfare control. *Social Analysis*, 58(3), 38–55.

Essed, P. (1991). *Understanding everyday racism: An interdisciplinary approach*. Newbury Park, CA: Sage Press.

Favell, A., & Nebe, T. (2009). Internal and external movers: East–West migration and the impact of EU enlargement. In A. Favell & E. Recchi (Eds.), *Pioneers of European identity: Citizenship and mobility in the EU* (pp. 205–223). Cheltenham: Edward Elgar.

Forbess, A., & James, D. (2014). Acts of assistance: Navigating the interstices of the British state with the help of non-profit legal advisers. *Social Analysis*, 58(3), 73–89.

Fox, J. E., Moroşanu, L., & Szilassy, E. (2015). Denying discrimination: Status, 'race', and the whitening of Britain's New Europeans. *Journal of Ethnic and Migration Studies*, 41(5), 729–748.

Hall, S., & Du Gay, P. (1996). *Questions of cultural identity*. London: Sage.

Harney, N. (2006). Rumour, migrants, and the informal economies of Naples, Italy. *International Journal of Sociology and Social Policy*, 26(9/10), 374–384.

Humphris, R. (2017). Borders of home: Roma migrant mothers negotiating boundaries in home encounters. *Journal of Ethnic and Migration Studies*, 43(7), 1190–1204. doi:10.1080/1369183X.2016.1227698

Kraler, A., & Kofman, E. (2009). *Family migration in Europe: Policies vs. reality project report*. Amsterdam: Amsterdam University Press.

Lipsky, M. (2010). *Street-level Bureaucracy, 30th Ann. Ed.: Dilemmas of the individual in public service*. New York, NY: Russell Sage Foundation.

Matras, Y. (2013). Mapping the Romani dialects of Romania. *Romani Studies*, 23(2), 199–243.

Mountz, A. (2003). Human smuggling, the transnational imaginary, and everyday geographies of the nation-state. *Antipode*, 35(3), 622–644.

Shibutani, T. (1966). *Improvised news: A sociological study of rumor*. London: Ardent Media.

Somerville, W. (2007). *Immigration under new labour*. Bristol: Policy Press.

Spencer, S., Ruhs, M., Anderson, B., & Rogaly, B. (2007). *Migrants' lives beyond the workplace. The experiences of Central and East Europeans in the UK*. York: Joseph Rowntree Foundation.

Stewart, P. J., & Strathern, A. (2004). *Witchcraft, sorcery, rumors and gossip*. Cambridge: Cambridge University Press.

Tervonen, M., & Enache, A. (2017). Coping with everyday bordering: Roma migrants and gatekeepers in Helsinki. *Ethnic and Racial Studies*, 40(7), 1114–1131.

Thelen, T., Vetters, L., & von Benda-Beckmann, K. (2014). Introduction to stategraphy: Toward a relational anthropology of the state. *Social Analysis*, 58(3), 1–19.

Trouillot, M. R. (2001). The anthropology of the state in the age of globalization: Close encounters of the deceptive kind. *Current Anthropology*, 42(1), 125–138.

Yuval-Davis, N. (2013). *A situated intersectional everyday approach to the study of bordering* (Euborderscapes Working Paper 2). Retrieved from http://www.euborderscapes.eu/fileadmin/user_upload/Working_Papers/EUBORDERSCAPES_Working_Paper_2_Yuval-Davis.pdf.

Yuval-Davis, N., Wemyss, G., & Cassidy, K. (2017). Introduction to the special issue: Racialized bordering discourses on European Roma. *Ethnic and Racial Studies*, 40(7), 1047–1057. doi:10.1080/01419870.2017.1267382

6   Care-full failure

How auxiliary assistance to poor Roma migrant women in Spain compounds marginalization

Ioana Vrăbiescu and Barak Kalir

ABSTRACT
In Spain, the national and local authorities boast in recent years about their progressive programs for the integration of Roma migrants from Romania. Many state efforts to work with Roma on their integration are specifically directed at women. Economic integration into the waged labor market is considered a major goal as it, supposedly, leads to the empowerment of Roma migrant women while also securing decent standards of living for entire families. This article argues that integration programs adversely result in the further discrimination and exclusion of those they pretend to relief. This adverse result is produced through a two-tier intervention in the lives of Roma families. The caring state works with a general category of 'vulnerability' for targeting populations, in which Roma migrant women are specifically incorporated through designated social programs. The performance of Roma as the subject–object of these programs is carefully evaluated. According to these evaluations, Roma women often fail to meet the normative standards of 'good mothers', 'decent wives', and 'diligent workers'. Subsequently, to deal with 'failing subjects', the disciplining state, a-la Foucault, inflicts an array of penalties on Roma women and their families: cut-offs of social benefits, evictions from poor dwellings, withdrawal of children's custody, and forced removals to Romania. We thus argue that initiatives by the caring state (and civil society) often prescribe or go hand-in-hand with repression from the correcting state. In welfare states, social programs can thus conclusively 'evidence' existing stereotypes about marginalized Roma families and about women in particular.

Introduction

Exploring the views and practices of civil servants and civil-society actors who deal with 'vulnerable migrants', this article exposes how gendered social perceptions and welfare state practices in Spain compound the marginalization of female Roma migrants.[1] The article traces the ways in which the state authorities and NGOs assess and govern the integration of migrant women, who apply for social benefits and other assistance. We argue that a *caring move* by the left hand of the state and civil society often goes hand-in-hand

CONTACT Ioana Vrăbiescu   i.vrabiescu@uva.nl

© 2017 The Author(s). Published by Informa UK Limited, trading as Taylor & Francis Group
This is an Open Access article distributed under the terms of the Creative Commons Attribution-NonCommercial-NoDerivatives License (http://creativecommons.org/licenses/by-nc-nd/4.0/), which permits non-commercial re-use, distribution, and reproduction in any medium, provided the original work is properly cited, and is not altered, transformed, or built upon in any way.

with a *repressive move* by the right hand of the state, resulting in the further marginalization and exclusion of Roma migrants in general, and of Roma women in particular (cf. Clark, 2008). To be sure, we interrogate here a particular pattern of exclusion and marginalization that is applied to Roma migrant women, but we are well aware of the possibility that this same pattern is also applied to other vulnerable and racially marginalized migrant women, for example, undocumented migrants from Africa (Rogozen-Soltar, 2012).

We draw on feminist debates on social work and the patriarchal structuring of welfare state (Alber & Drotbohm, 2015; Halberstam, 2011; Hochschild, 1979) and on the critics of street-level bureaucratic practices towards the racially marginalized poor (Clark, 1999; Wacquant, 2009). The vast literature on social work has shed important light on the 'commodification of emotions' and 'deprofessionalization' emphasizing that the motivations of caregivers cannot only result from personal and ideological convictions about doing good and/or financial incentives (Dominelli, 2002). Among other things, critics have unveiled the wavering notion of 'vulnerability' as a working category (Brown, 2016) and have problematized the feminization of care for vulnerable subjects (Dominelli & Hoogvelt, 1996). Dominelli (2002, p. 10) convincingly argues that in much of social work 'women, as the majority of basic grade workers, [are] controlling other women in their homemaking, child nurturing and elder caring capacities whilst holding out the carrot of retraining for an elusive job'. Viewed from an intersectional perspective, the intricacies of patriarchy lead certain women to inflict violence on other women. In Spain, the vast majority of social workers, NGO workers, trainers, and officials who are in charge of carrying out interventions with 'vulnerable' migrants are females (Alonso-Villar & Del Río, 2008; Carrasco & Recio, 2001). Highlighting the negative effects of EU policies towards Roma, critics have pointed out how implementation of European strategies and recommendations to alleviate the poverty of Roma imposes at the same time multiple vulnerabilities on the target group (Fekete, 2014; Vermeersch, 2012).

Empirical research on social workers as street-level bureaucrats (Lipsky, 1980) revealed their ability to maneuver between 'professional decisions' – predicated on having access to the intimate lives of people – and 'discretionary power', which, building on trust-relationship, leaves the door open for unaccountable decisions (Evans & Harris, 2004; Prendergast, 2007). Even when social workers are trained for non-discriminatory and non-offensive attitudes (Ellis, 2011; Fook, 2016), in their daily interactions with clients, 'culture has been used as a cover to justify racist policies and procedures' (Lavalette & Penketh, 2014, p. 14; see also Kalir & Wissink, 2016). The so-called cultural competences of social workers are pertinent for an analysis of welfare policies and practices towards Roma migrants in Spain.

Our argument builds on the notion of the 'failed' subject of integration policies (Paulle & Kalir, 2014) in leading state authorities to withdraw their protection to migrants and even inflict penalties on those who prove to be undeserving or non-integrating. The penalizing of 'failure' mirrors the state's need of 'good' subjects who fit with neoliberal-infused measurements and business-like models of efficiency and profitability.

The Spanish authorities and civil-society actors work with a particular idea of vulnerability that is largely predicated on the condition of women in society: vulnerability to gender-based violence and precarious living circumstances. This caring state[2] appears to have incorporated feminist critique about the double marginalization of migrant women (Yuval-Davis, 2006). In Spain, social interventions are initially welcomed by

Roma families who struggle to make ends meet. In soliciting assistance, Roma women regularly express their perceived vulnerabilities to social workers: illiteracy, demanding household duties, and the impossibility of finding jobs. This input from Roma women is, however, often assessed differently by the social workers. As we show, there are two situations in which Roma migrant women come into contact with the social services. First, in order to obtain social provisions, women approach the territorial social services according to their place of residence. Second, social services are propelled by the right hand of the state or their own ideological convictions to intervene in the life of the families and to correct what they consider to be deviant behavior.

Social workers habitually reach out to Roma women by attending to their role as *mothers*. Given the hegemonic patriarchal idea of the household, it is women who are considered responsible for bringing up children. Social programs are on offer for both parents who are approached by social workers when dealing with migrant families. However, men are often present only in the first meeting, after which they either decide that this is 'women's business', or prefer to stay away from state surveillance. The ease with which the 'disappearance' of men from social programs is accommodated, or explained away, by both spouses and state/NGO actors is itself a manifestation of widely entrenched gendered perceptions regarding the position and role of women (and men) in the household.

Once the connection between the caring state and Roma families is established, other types of interventions and programs become available specifically for women: language courses, sexual and reproductive education, labor market accession, etc. An integral part of all social interventions is a systematic monitoring and careful evaluation of the progress made by those serviced (Humphris, 2016). It is here, we argue, that the caring state is transformed into a mechanism for surveillance and control over the lives of women and their families. Care workers become part of the lives of Roma families, analyzing, and monitoring continuously their living conditions, normative behavior, achievements in the labor market, and so forth. In the eventuality of a negative assessment by care workers, there is likely to be a subsequent move to penalize the family. Among the punishments that can be inflicted in case of an assessed 'failure' are: discontinuation of social benefits and housing, child abduction to state custody (Vrăbiescu, 2016), intrusive surveillance of family life and so-called voluntary return programs to one's country of origin (Kalir, 2017). In this sense, gendered boundaries and predicaments are transformed in the remaking of the nation-and-state's borders that justify the exclusion and potential removal of 'failed' and 'revolting' subjects (Tyler, 2013).

Methodology

Throughout Spain, social services have been privatized and decentralized since the 1980s, transforming the ancient administrative structures that were under the direct tutelage of the central Spanish government into territorial services managed by regional and local institutions. This post-Franco shift furnished a modality of reforming the state in line with hegemonic neoliberal ideas. In the 1990s, regional authorities obtained the full control over implementation procedures and institutions representing the left hand of the state: education, healthcare, and social protection. This decentralization has allowed institutions to transform departments into independent programs run through public–private collaborations. Thus, entire departments at the regional and local levels have been privatized leading to a conglomerate of programs managed by NGOs and private companies under the coordination of a small number of civil servants. For example, in Barcelona, only five civil servants are employed in the social services of the local authority and they coordinate around 40 projects involving several NGOs and private companies.

The article builds on non-consecutive fieldwork conducted in the years 2013–2016 mostly among those working on the implementation of programs dedicated to Romanian Roma living in the areas *El Gallinero*, *Cañada Real*, and *Delicias* in the Madrid region, and in different locations throughout the Metropolitan Area of Barcelona. We conducted 30 in-depth semi-structured interviews mostly with civil servants, officials in the regional government, and social workers employed either in NGOs or in private companies. In discussions with interlocutors, there was ample room for them to express their vision of the system for which they worked. In addition, we interviewed several Roma women who participated in social programs.

In the following section, we discuss the social dynamics and institutional configurations that frame social interventions, which end up certifying the non-integration or 'failure' of Roma migrants and, thus, legitimize in the eyes of the Spanish authorities punitive measures. We then move on to present several case studies that illustrate two different ways in which the 'exclusion through inclusion' (De Genova, 2013) of impoverished Roma women is produced by the caring state. Although different from one another, the promotion of wage labor for poor women and the criminalization of the Roma migrants, both reflect a double burden that is put on the shoulders of Roma migrant women: not only is their productive work discounted and reproductive work stigmatized, but they regularly run the risk of being subjected to penalties from the sanctioning state (Gandhi, 2017).

From vulnerable migrants to *failed* subjects of integration

Scholars have pointed out the widespread inability of vulnerable people to surmount existing institutional barriers that stand between them and social benefits (FitzGerald, 2016; Heaslip, 2015), stressing the difficulties of the poor in presenting themselves as 'victims' or in demanding assistance from state agencies (Helms, 2013). Following Fineman (2010), we highlight the gap and tension between *vulnerability* as lived reality and as defined for the purposes of state interventions (with the latter also determining what is an adequate assistance). People might feel vulnerable and fight against vulnerability or they might not be in a position to understand the complexity of social and structural constraints that lead to their marginalization. State policies, on the other hand, are guided by a humanitarian logic towards those categorized as vulnerable (Mackenzie, Rogers, & Dodds, 2014). Although it should be considered a continuous process of state learning regarding who is vulnerable and how to adapt assistance accordingly, bureaucratic inertia fixates the definition and thus not allow for new groups to be included. In practice, the caring state fails to address the specific position of migrants and vulnerability remains a point of continuous negotiation between excluded people and those in charge of managing social interventions (Jovanović, 2015).

From a state perspective, preponderantly migrant women, and especially Roma, fit in to the existing category of vulnerable group.[3] In a succession of vulnerable identities: migrant, woman, Roma, and poor, social services construct a methodological working category. Increasingly, migrants play the role of the tolerated Others who receives state aid only when able to prove their bodily marks of violence (Fassin, 2011). The state, through gender mainstreaming, attends to women as a vulnerable group by mostly providing quotas in politics, engaging in positive discrimination and sponsoring shelters for victims of domestic violence (Jaggar, 2002). EU and national policies recurrently consolidate Roma as a vulnerable group through the work of expert classifiers (Surdu, 2015).

Paradoxically, the condition of possibility that allows a state to refrain from providing basic needs to marginalized and excluded people is the vulnerability dimension (Abramovitz, 1996). Vulnerability becomes the condition for the state to exercise benevolent interventions manifested in offering provisions and protection. Concomitantly, by allegedly addressing 'vulnerable groups' generously, the authorities prepare the ground for a potential punitive exclusion. The threshold is 'documented evidence' that ostensibly proves migrants' inability to integrate, transforming the figure of the vulnerable migrant into the failed subject of inclusion.

Within this state framework, social workers in the third sector mold their actions and programs. In Madrid, in a slum neighborhood where a few hundred Roma migrants live, civil servants, NGO workers, and church representatives are all offering services to poor migrants. As Roma migrant women are often targeted as the main subjects for integrative policies and charity programs, various types of interventions are offered to them. An example of how the participation of Roma women in social programs is assessed was given by Javier, a priest leading an activist church in Madrid:

> Another NGO sets-up training classes for young women because there is a problem. A reality that they see as a problem, namely, the age [of mothers]. At their first pregnancy the mothers are 14–16 years old. Well, this is cruelty. I don't know if this is good or bad, but for the health … They then set a project that theoretically is fantastic: to train these young women … then the husbands know how to use contraceptives. However, in practice, these people [NGO workers] set-up the training some 3 km away. So then they organized a bus. Great, but now the problem is that these are women … children in general and babies are dependent on women. We can argue whether this is macho attitude, but changing it is really hard, especially in a community where the cultural features are very strong. In the bus they didn't allow mothers with babies, because there were no facilities, or it was not planned … Then the women [did not attend and] failed the training. The assessment then was to suspend the training because the women were not interested in participating. This circus, according to my experience with excluded people, happens frequently. We do things for people without looking at their reality. Logically, people then 'fail', and the guilty one is the other.

Coupled with a challenging economic background, the legal framework in Spain leads to the exclusion of numerous migrants from basic social provisions such as education, health, and training for the job market (Garcés-Mascareñas, 2013). Without the support of a professional team, consisting of civil servants and social workers, migrant women often cannot obtain basic social services and access formal employment. Gatekeeping access to basic state provisions, NGO workers customarily select and determine those who qualify to take part as 'clients' in the mediated process of integration (Rogozen-Soltar, 2012). In the case of Roma migrants, this is usually done by involving 'cultural mediators' who are supposedly expert in transmitting mainstream norms and values to clients. This constellation produces the dependency of poor migrants on their positive interactions with social workers. Although we did not conduct a comparative research with other marginalized groups in Spain, it stands to reason that the approach of social workers towards Romanian Roma is predicated on an entrenched pattern of engaging racially marginalized groups like *Gitanos* in Spain (Lago Ávila, 2014; Vallhonrat et al., 2015).

There are two levels of categorization when it comes to Romanian migrants in Spain. First, there is the generalizing category of 'Romanians' when referring to Roma and non-Roma Romanians, and even to other migrants from Eastern Europe in Spain. To this homogenizing and stigmatizing category – often used by anti-immigration politicians from the right wing[4] – many non-Roma Romanian migrants strongly react by distancing themselves from Roma, calling them 'ethnics' and reinforcing anti-Roma racism. This approach from non-Roma Romanians contributes to the consolidation of the term *Gitanos del este* (Eastern European Roma) to designate Roma from Romania as a separate inferior category of migrants in the eyes of civil servants and social workers in Spain. Here is how one official at the Catalan Immigration Department shared with us his view of the Romanian Roma:

> It is their culture that makes them live precariously, that makes them live at the margins of everything. (…) Gypsies from Romania are pariahs, they don't have a good relationship with the Romanians and neither do they have a good relationship with the [Spanish] Gypsies.

The value of wage labor and the (in-)visible work of migrant women

Social services oscillate in their interactions with Roma women between providing social benefits while monitoring and evaluating their deservingness. Exploiting the ambiguity left between social policies and gendered roles, social workers use their discretionary power to alternate the ways they address families with children, either as vulnerable clients or as fully responsible adults. When a *family* demonstrates the ability to financially look after the children, social services become more supportive; but when a *mother* has no income, she risks losing her children to state custody (cf. Empez Vidal, 2014).

Local social workers are the first to assess the situation of families and to decide whether to offer material provision and to urge women to: search for work, follow training for waged jobs, learn the local language (Spanish in Madrid, Catalan in Barcelona), and manage health issues (especially concerning reproductive life). These programs rely on local and regional budgets and are run by specialized companies or third-sector organizations, in line with a neoliberal move towards privatization of the social services. Special collaborations between local authorities and private services such as *Xarxa ROMEST* (Barcelona) and *Comisión Población Excluida* (Madrid) bring together experts to share experiences and to advance methodologies of working with Roma migrants as a 'vulnerable group'.

The excluded individuals – citizens or migrants – are those to whom the state ascertains their inability to obtain the minimum living standards. The social services implement policies for social inclusion, demanding that the target population, women and men alike, comply with certain conditions. The most important condition is to have a work place or to be looking for one. Helena, a civil servant in the municipality of Barcelona, explained the case of Marina, a single mother who was recently evicted:

> She considered herself a Romanian. She has all the markers of this type of a Roma from Romania. This mistrust, this … unwilling to relate to the services, but at the same time

she needs help. I worked for ten years with autochthonous Roma in a very depressed neighborhood ... so the first thing that I thought was 'this girl is a Roma'. So, I asked her openly. She said 'yes', but that she is not doing ... well ... anything [wrong]. Fine. It was only to understand what I could observe: this contiguity, this difficulty to plan and to imagine a future, which you can detect when working with Roma. This was a young lady who lived by selling cloths and having social benefits ... our attempt was to build for her a plan for getting work. It was like 'You came to Spain. Don't you have a daughter and don't you want something better for her than what you are doing now? This will happen only if you follow a process.' But she is a person who at first is very nice but then doesn't accept what you tell her.

This is a prominent example of how a mistrustful civil servant who entertains deep-seated stereotypes regarding Roma is blaming the victim for her distrustfulness of the system and its functionaries. Furthermore, measuring the capacity of people to integrate into the formal (waged) labor market reveals entrenched capitalist and patriarchal normativities that often result in the 'failure' of poor migrants. As noted earlier, gender dynamics render women the prime target group for social workers, as men often abandon their participation not least because they must work (mostly informally and for long hours) in order to meet the family's basic needs. Being employed in informal or semi-formal jobs, migrant men can benefit little from social programs that cannot offer them access to provisions. Importantly, having a formal job or a 'criminal record' prevent one from applying for social benefits. '[The social workers] tried to reach the men and bring them to talk. First men were coming too. But then they were not coming anymore' said Jena, an NGO social worker in Barcelona.

State authorities reaffirm and perpetuate the men's role as breadwinners and women's role as caregivers, while the social services push migrant women to obtain waged employment. This gender bias is institutionally perpetuated based on assessing vulnerable migrant women through programs aimed to correct a given situation but without considering the intersectional dimension of exclusion. A Roma migrant woman living in a slum in Madrid rhetorically asked:

> Where should I go to look for work? Look at me, I'm 55, my husband is in prison, and I have nephews to take care of. Who's going to employ me? They [social services] should really look at people and give benefits to those who have no means for living.

Focusing on the integration of poor migrants to the waged labor market, the manager of the social services in Barcelona despondently explains the shortcomings of the current scheme:

> When they work with scrap-metal I have the same problems as with all families for accession to the labor market. [They say] 'I can live from scrap-metal' thus the inclusion in the labor market is not so interesting for them. This is important because if you already can make a living, what can I offer you? A training that is not work in order to find work that I don't have, whereas you already have work.

Officials are thus left to enforce the rules of a lacking scheme whose shortcomings are evident to them as well as to potential clients. Civil servants clearly need to justify the imposition of rules of conduct on clients, as expressed by Jena:

> You are coming to ask for help. It is not me who says you cannot do it. It is your decision as an adult person. But if you come here it is because you cannot make it with the money you earn.

For Darius, a municipality Counselor for social rights in Barcelona, Roma migrants do not relate to the idea of social protection, thus legitimizing special state interventions.

> The social services have no obligation to finance special programs for excluded populations. Ensuring the basic needs is enough. But through these specific social programs (...) we have the intention to bring this population [Roma] in contact with social services, a population that does not feel beneficiary of social services, or that has no intention to be beneficiary of social services, largely because they do not consider it necessary because they already have another modality of subsistence that has nothing in common with social protection.

The social services consistently rationalize their intervention as providers of support and as superintendents of the lives of migrant women. While defending their interventionist approach, officials 'know' that poor migrants prefer not to ask for aid from social services than to suffer the consequences of their prescribed 'failure'.

An important way in which street-level agents explain their dealings with Roma has to do with their own sense of working under difficult condition to achieve the best for their clients. In Spain, institutions that are in charge of family policies often claim to be underfunded and professionally ill-prepared to deal with vulnerable subjects. Social workers regularly express frustration with the situation on the ground and vent bitter feelings of not being able to accomplish their job. Yet, rather than pointing the finger at the Spanish authorities, many street-level agents condemn Roma for not equally doing their best to make the system work. In this dynamic of getting frustrated by work for institutions but ending up blaming the victims, emotions play a major role (Anderson, 2014; Hochschild, 1979). Here, we spotlight how prevailing 'tiredness' among civil servants and in particular medical personnel underlines the anticipation of a 'failure' on the part of migrant Roma women. As one NGO social worker in Barcelona pointed out, there is a widespread mixture of exhaustion and mistrust in dealing with pregnant Roma women: 'I think that many civil servants are tired of spending resources [on Roma], that even when we reserve space for these people, they at best come for one visit and after... well, in general there is no continuity'.

It is crucial to our argument that in formally categorizing Roma women and families as 'vulnerable', civil-society actors and state authorities clearly take stock of the intersection between, gender, ethnicity, and economic/social/cultural marginalization in society at large (Kóczé & Popa, 2009; Oprea, 2004). However, in practice, social workers seem to ignore intersectionality and instead they apply the mainstream normative standards to the evaluation of their clients. Evoking emotional challenges and fatigue, civil servants regularly abandon any special attention for the particular position of Roma women in their assessment.

From provision to control: instrumentalizing social services

In 2004, the Vincle Association[5] was commissioned by the Catalan government to conduct research and to publish a report on the situation of Roma migrants in Catalonia.[6] According to the Vincle Report (2006), Roma migrant children were portrayed as 'delinquents' and as being at risk of getting exploited by their own families (e.g. mothers with children begging in the street). Immediately after, the Catalan government launched a tender for running a special program to attend to Roma children at risk. Vincle won the tender and since 2008 it manages social interventions with Roma migrant children under the supervision of the General Direction of Services for Child Protection (hereafter DGAIA), which has sub-units collaborating with the local social services and with the police unit for minors. Although having no Roma employees or specialized expertise on Roma, Vincle presents itself as an association that professionally manages programs for Roma migrants (both Gallego-Portuguese and, more recently, from Eastern Europe).

Vincle's program for managing Roma migrants is premised on the idea of a 'population trapped between criminality and [state] protection', as put by one social worker. These are mostly poor migrant families that may apply to social services, but, to secure their subsistence, may also resort to criminalized street gathering (Duneier & Carter, 1999). The right hand of the state (the police), together with the left hand of the state (represented here by DGAIA), commissioned Vincle to survey Roma migrant families and to evaluate the life conditions of children in particular. A team consisting of a social worker and an interpreter visit the families in their dwellings, offering special benefits while applying standards of evaluation for child well-being and family values. Emma's view, as social worker in Vincle, on interventions with Roma conveys the institutional concern with monitoring and controlling a suspected and criminalized population:

> We entered this world from the families. We contacted many of them through Gendarmerie [*Mossos d'Esquadra*], through the office that deal with detainees, or in the Justice Court after they got released to their parents. The task was to go to the neighborhoods and enter into these families. Well, the idea was to create trust and to learn about their real life. To observe minors, teenagers in a family and then to decide to which needs we could respond, in order to fulfill our duty towards DGAIA. Eventually you realize that ... well ... what mostly concerns DGAIA is to guarantee a few minimal benefits for the minors.

The penetration into the intimate family sphere and its evaluation by Vincle serves as instructive information for DGAIA in subsequently deciding on the type of intervention. In fact, it was not uncommon for DGAIA to take Roma children into state custody based on Vincle evaluations (Vrăbiescu, 2016). Once the state withdraws the custody of the migrant parents, they are left with an abusive option: to see their children, the family should 'voluntarily' return to Romania. The parents should prove they have better living conditions in the country of origin (e.g. permanent dwelling) and commit to return 'home' (Kalir, 2017). The Spanish authorities then consent that the family can reunite and leave to Romania.

The twisted outcome of the control and assistance program induced by the child protection institution is that some parents, being poor migrants, would accept an abusive relationship of surveillance by social workers. Families that enter the child protection institution potentially receive more benefits from the state, but these benefits come with a stricter control by social workers who ask the parent/s to spell out the income and expenditures, to show commitment to find formal employment, to prove their care for children (supervising homework, bringing children to school, etc.). The motivation for some poor families to accept the stricter monitoring by DGAIA instead of the local social services is the bigger 'carrot' in the form of higher monetary rewards. As one NGO worker put it: 'Maybe they have more generous funds, who knows.'

The state repressive position becomes obvious when social workers prefer to act against minor women and mothers despite their pronounced vulnerability. In many of the interviews conducted with social workers, the views of Roma migrant women included stereotypical verdicts about family structure and 'early marriage' and sexual relations. Discussing the case of what street-level agents called 'imprisoned daughters-in-law', social workers condemned the marriage of young women who live with the husband's family. Social workers emphasized 'early marriages' and 'parental responsibilities' among the difficulties encountered while helping Roma migrants to become successful integrated subjects.

In one case, a social worker at an NGO was called to the hospital to attest the paternity of a new-born child. The Roma family that was expecting a baby was known to the social workers. That was the reason the hospital notified the NGO once the woman arrived to deliver the baby. The personnel were suspicious about the father because he was white, thin, and younger than the mother, and his family name differed from the one on the mother's identity document. When the NGO social worker arrived at the hospital, the couple indeed admitted that another man was the biological father. They went on to explain that they were afraid that if the father 'looked like' Roma the child might be taken into state custody immediately after birth (as had happened to them before).

Another case of a 15-year-old mother who just gave birth at the hospital in Barcelona was analyzed during our interview with the emergency department's manager of DGAIA. That evening the hospital alerted DGAIA, which instantly revoked the custody of the new-born baby who was then taken away by the police. The authorities could have sheltered the mother together with her baby in a center for minor mothers but decided not to. The official told us that DGAIA had been informed by an NGO worker who suspected that the girl was part of a gang because she was seen together with other Roma who were known for robbery. The DGAIA official then added that although the mother had no criminal record, this was an 'obvious case', claiming that 'the girl has been obliged to marry a man in the gang in order to force her afterwards into robbery'. Eventually, a few weeks later the parents rescued the child from state custody and fled to Romania.

The abusive intervention in the life of migrant women, and especially minor mothers, force them to return to Romania in order to maintain the family unit intact. The state is actually inflicting violence on women, revoking the custody of their children, with no reasonable grounds and no protection offered. Thus, the outcome of state interventions that start with upholding the ideal of child protection and helping vulnerable women turns out, in practice, to be the reverse of what institutions claim. In the case of Roma migrants the adverse result leads to further marginalization, exclusion from state protection and provisions, and potential removal from Spain.

Conclusion

By offering state provisions and charitable assistance in the first place, civil servants and third-sector workers intervene in the lives of migrant Roma women under conditions of strict surveillance and control. These interventions are a double sword: on the one hand, they create dependency while attracting marginalized and impoverished migrants with serious incentives offered; on the other hand, they legitimize the surveillance and justify, in the eyes of state authorities, potential penalties. Roma migrant women are conditioned by their failure to keep struggling to integrate within schemes that de facto exclude, stigmatize and punish them.

An operative two-tier system is propelled by a neoliberal notion of individualization, measurement, assumed responsibility, and consequential 'gain or pain'. Roma families, and more specifically women, are individualized and assessed according to a normative yardstick that represents the values and expectations of care workers (often a proxy to 'mainstream' Spanish society). Thus, the category of vulnerability is negotiated, in practice, between the marginalized Roma women and social workers, who de facto do not address but reproduce multiple-discrimination. Street-level agents and social workers offer provisions and protection, and, at the same time, they control and regulate the lives of their subjects according to patriarchal norms and neoliberal standards. Within the assemblage of political decisions, bureaucratic practices, and the discretionary power of social workers, some basic rights are recurrently contested, turning vulnerable migrants into failed-integrated subjects. Poor Roma migrant women are surveyed and assessed, categorized as failed-integrated subjects, and then punished.

The cases we presented showed two modalities of gendered intervention on the part of state and civil-society actors in which women's labor in the household and child rearing is disregarded or under-valued and men's (and women's) informal jobs are condemned. Negotiations between state agents and marginalized migrants are dynamic but never take place in a balanced fashion given the disparity of power positions. The reproductive life and working activities of Roma migrants are continuously rendered suspect and stigmatized. The imbalanced power relation twists the outcome of social intervention; instead of alleviating marginalization, state authorities act with confidence against the most vulnerable people, among them poor migrant Roma women.

Notes

1. We use the term 'Roma migrants' to refer to the Spanish state's working category of 'Gitanos del este' (Eastern European Roma). Both these terms refer principally to Romanian Roma migrants.
2. We hereafter use the 'caring state' to refer both to Spanish authorities and to civil-society actors who engage 'vulnerable groups'. Not simply shorthand, this analytically meant to highlight that most NGOs and private companies providing care services in Spain are heavily, if not entirely, financed by the state. We thus underscore that the caring state has been NGOfied and privatized.
3. See National Strategy for the Integration of Roma in Spain 2012–2020. Retrieved February 4, 2017, from http://ec.europa.eu/justice/discrimination/files/roma_spain_strategy_es.pdf.
4. See the case of Albiol, a politician running for office in Badalona, who was tried for xenophobic anti-Romanian and anti-Roma racial incitement (Cros, 2013).
5. Vincle, first a private company, later functioned as an NGO bidding for projects with the Catalan government and the local authorities in Barcelona. Since 2014 Vincle has completely converted in an NGO managing sub-contracted programs mostly addressing Roma migrants.
6. According to Pajares (2007), the Roma from Romania represent 5–8% of the total Romanian migration in Catalonia, which amounts to around 7–8000 people.

Acknowledgements

The authors would like to thank Can Yıldız and Nicholas de Genova for their helpful guidance and instructive notes during the preparation of this article. A special gratitude is extended to Prof. Colin Clark for his close reading of an earlier draft and the many wonderful suggestions and engaging comments he provided.

Disclosure statement

No potential conflict of interest was reported by the authors.

Funding

This work was supported by the European Research Council [ERC-Starting grant number 336319].

References

Abramovitz, M. (1996). *Regulating the lives of women: Social welfare policy from colonial times to the present*. Boston, MA: South End Press.
Alber, E., & Drotbohm, H. (Eds.). (2015). *Anthropological perspectives on care: Work, kinship, and the life-course*. New York, NY: Springer.
Alonso-Villar, O., & Del Río, C. (2008). *Occupational and industrial segregation of female and male workers in Spain: An alternative approach* (ECINEQ WP 2008-84). Society for the Study of Economic Inequality.
Anderson, B. (2014). *Encountering affect: Capacities, apparatuses, conditions*. Surrey Ashgate.
Brown, K. (2016). *Vulnerability and young people: Care and social control in policy and practice*. Bristol: University of Bristol, Policy Press.
Carrasco, C., & Recio, A. (2001). Time, work and gender in Spain. *Time & Society, 10*(2–3), 277–301.
Clark, C. (1999). Race, ethnicity and social security: The experience of gypsies and travellers in the United Kingdom. *Journal of Social Security Law, 6*(4), 186–202.
Clark, C. (2008). Introduction themed section care or control? Gypsies, travellers and the state. *Social Policy and Society, 7*(1), 65–71.
Cros, B. (2013, November 19). Xavier García Albiol será el primer alcalde juzgado por su discurso xenófobo. *El Diario*. Retrieved from http://www.eldiario.es/catalunya/Xavier-Garcia-Albiol-discurso-xenofobo_0_198080964.html
De Genova, N. (2013). Spectacles of migrant 'illegality': The scene of exclusion, the obscene of inclusion. *Ethnic and Racial Studies, 36*(7), 1180–1198.
Dominelli, L. (2002). *Feminist social work theory and practice*. New York, NY: Palgrave Macmillan.
Dominelli, L., & Hoogvelt, A. (1996). Globalization and the technocratization of social work. *Critical Social Policy, 16*(47), 45–62.
Duneier, M., & Carter, O. (1999). *Sidewalk*. New York, NY: Farrar, Straus and Giroux.
Ellis, K. (2011). 'Street-level bureaucracy' revisited: The changing face of frontline discretion in adult social care in England. *Social Policy & Administration, 45*(3), 221–244.
Empez Vidal, N. (Ed.). (2014). *Dejadnos Crecer. Menores Migrantes Bajo Tutela Institucional* [Let us grow up. Minor migrants in state custody]. Barcelona: Virus Editorial.
Evans, T., & Harris, J. (2004). Street-level bureaucracy, social work and the (exaggerated) death of discretion. *British Journal of Social Work, 34*(6), 871–895.
Fassin, D. (2011). The trace: Violence, truth, and the politics of the body. *Social Research, 78*(2), 281–298.
Fekete, L. (2014). Europe against the Roma. *Race & Class, 55*(3), 60–70.
Fineman, A. M. (2010). The vulnerable subject and the responsive state. *Emory Law Journal, 60*(251), 1–41.
FitzGerald, S. A. (2016). Vulnerable geographies: Human trafficking, immigration and border control in the UK and beyond. *Gender, Place & Culture, 23*(2), 181–197.
Fook, J. (2016). *Social work: A critical approach to practice*. London: Sage.
Gandhi, A. (2017). The sanctioning state: Official permissiveness and prohibition in India. *Focaal, 77*, 8–21.
Garcés-Mascareñas, B. (2013). *Reconsidering the 'policy gap': Policy implementation and outcomes in Spain* (Working Paper Series 18). Barcelona: GRITIM UPF.
Halberstam, J. (2011). *The queer art of failure*. Durham: Duke University Press.
Heaslip, V. (2015). *Experience of vulnerability from a gypsy/travelling perspective: A phenomemological study* (Unpublished doctoral dissertation). Bournemouth: Bournemouth University.

Helms, E. (2013). *Invisible victims: An analysis of human trafficking vulnerability and prevention in Bulgarian Romani communities* (Unpublished doctoral dissertation). Denver: University of Denver.

Hochschild, A. R. (1979). Emotion work, feeling rules, and social structure. *American Journal of Sociology, 85*, 551–575.

Humphris, R. (2016). Borders of home: Roma migrant mothers negotiating boundaries in home encounters. *Journal of Ethnic and Migration Studies, 43*(7), 1190–1204.

Jaggar, A. M. (2002). Vulnerable women and neo-liberal globalization: Debt burdens undermine women's health in the global south. *Theoretical Medicine and Bioethics, 23*(6), 425–440.

Jovanović, J. (2015). *Vulnerability of Roma in policy discourse on combatting trafficking in human beings in Serbia: Perspectives of the national policy actors* (Working Papers Series, 2015/4). Budapest: Center for Policy Studies, CEU.

Kalir, B. (2017). Between 'voluntary' return programs and soft deportation: Sending vulnerable migrants in Spain back 'home'. In Z. Vathi & R. King (Eds.), *Return migration and psychosocial well-being* (pp. 56–71). New York, NY: Routledge.

Kalir, B., & Wissink, L. (2016). The deportation continuum: Convergences between state agents and NGO workers in the Dutch deportation field. *Citizenship Studies, 20*(1), 34–49.

Kóczé, A., & Popa, R. M. (2009). *Missing intersectionality. Race/ethnicity, gender, and class in current research and policies on Romani women in Europe*. Budapest: Central European University.

Lago Ávila, M. J. (2014). El otro Madrid: El chabolismo que no cesa. Actuación autonómica en políticas de realojamiento e integración social 1997–2010. *Estudios Geográficos, 75*(276), 219–260.

Lavalette, M., & Penketh, L. (Eds.). (2014). *Race, racism and social work: Contemporary issues and debates*. Bristol: Policy Press.

Lipsky, M. (1980). *Street-level bureaucracy: Dilemmas of the individual in public services*. New York, NY: Russel Sage Foundation.

Mackenzie, C., Rogers, W., & Dodds, S. (Eds.). (2014). *Vulnerability: New essays in ethics and feminist philosophy*. Oxford: Oxford University Press.

Oprea, A. (2004). Re-envisioning social justice from the ground up: Including the experiences of Romani women. *Essex Human Rights Review, 1*(1), 29–39.

Pajares, M. (2007). *Inmigrantes del Este: Procesos migratorios de los Rumanos* [Eastern migrants: Migration process of Romanians]. Barcelona: Icaria editorial.

Paulle, B., & Kalir, B. (2014). The integration matrix reloaded: From ethnic fixations to established versus outsiders dynamics in the Netherlands. *Journal of Ethnic and Migration Studies, 40*(9), 1354–1374.

Prendergast, C. (2007). The motivation and bias of bureaucrats. *The American Economic Review, 97*(1), 180–196.

Rogozen-Soltar, M. H. (2012). Ambivalent inclusion: Anti-racism and racist gatekeeping in Andalusia's immigrant NGOs. *Journal of the Royal Anthropological Institute, 18*(3), 633–651.

Surdu, M. (2015). *Those who count: Expert practices of Roma classification*. Budapest: CEU Press.

Tyler, I. (2013). *Revolting subjects: Social abjection and resistance in neoliberal Britain*. London: Zed Books.

Vallhonrat, X. C., Casasayas Garbí, Ò, Muñoz Romero, F., Diaz Giner, P., Díaz Molinaro, M., Tatjer Mir, M., & Larrea Killinger, C. (2015). Shantytowns in the city of Barcelona: Can Valero, La Perona and El Carmel. *Revista D'etnologia de Catalunya, 40*, 18–28.

Vermeersch, P. (2012). Reframing the Roma: EU initiatives and the politics of reinterpretation. *Journal of Ethnic and Migration Studies, 38*(8), 1195–1212.

Vincle Report. (2006). *Gitanos procedents de l'Europa de l'Est a Catalunya. Informe encarregat i elaborat per l'associació Vincle por el Departament de Benestar i Família* [Roma coming from Eastern Europe to Catalonia. Report commissioned and written by Vincle Association for the Department of Welfare and Family]. Catalunya: Generalitat de Catalunya, Departament de Benestar i Família.

Vrăbiescu, I. (2016). Roma migrant children in Catalonia: Between the politics of benevolence and the normalization of violence. *Ethnic and Racial Studies*. doi:10.1080/01419870.2016.1229491

Wacquant, L. (2009). *Punishing the poor: The neoliberal government of social insecurity*. Durham, NC: Duke University Press.

Yuval-Davis, N. (2006). Intersectionality and feminist politics. *European Journal of Women's Studies, 13*(3), 193–209.

Index

A2 migrants (UK) 81–95; 'qualifying status' 82
Agamben, G. 38, 42, 45
Albania 68, 74
anti-Gypsyism 28, 29, 46–47, 52
Aradau, C. 3, 10, 11, 26
assimilationist policies, socialist states 69–72
asylum 12, 26; 'bogus' 36, 74–75; claims rejected 21; EU respect for rights 51–52; German law after reunification 73; Germany 30, 66, 74–75, 76; Italy 73; non-refoulement principle 60
Avoiding the Dependency Trap (UNDP Report) 24

backdoor nationalism 39
Balibar, É. 4, 69, 84
Barcelona 99, 101–103, 105
Barker, M. 29
barriers, geopolitical for Roma 25
Bauer, Edith 42
Bauman, Z. 46
Belgium, 1999 Roma deportations 31
Beluschi, G. 53, 57, 59
Berezin, M. 38, 39, 40
Berlusconi, Silvio 40, 41
biopolitical development 19, 23, 24–25, 27
boomerang effect 23
borders: compared to boundaries 51; contained mobility 25–30; epistemological and rhetorical 36–37, 46; free/unfree mobility 9–13; governmentality and 60–61; internal boudaries and 50–53; post-Yugoslavia 72–74; racial profiling on 75; socialist states' closed 69–70; socialist Yugoslavia 71; *Xomá* mobility and 60
Bosnia: challenge to constitution in ECtHR 75–76; *Xomá*, links with 53, 55, 59
Bossi, Umberto 40
boundaries: blurred 18, 23, 27; borders and 50–53; epistemic 36–37
Bourdieu, P. 84
Breaking the Poverty Circle (World Bank Report) 24
Brexit 6, 65
Brown, W. 35, 39, 42, 83

Bulgaria 30, 35, 38, 39; expulsion of Romani migrants from France 40, 44; Italian emergency legislation 41; transitional restrictions in UK 81–82
Butler, J. 85

'campzenship' 45–46
caring state, Spain 97, 98, 99
Catalonia, Vincle Report 103–105
Čergarja 53–54, 60
children: German deportations 73–74; Kosovo Roma in Germany 30; mothers resonsible for 98; Roma migrant in Catalonia 103–104; Sarkozy rhetoric 43; State custody in Spain 101, 103–104, 105; *Xomá* extended family 55, 59
circular mobilities 65–77
citizenship: 'abusing' EU citizenship in France 43; campzenship 45–46; Czech Republic 69; development programs and 24; different statuses 68; 'Duldung' status and 73–74, 76; in EU but not of 52; EU enlargement and 2, 3; EU-ropean 1, 6, 12; freedom of movement and 10, 12–13, 68; German denied 71; irregularities in post-Yugoslav states 66, 68, 70, 73; Italian denied 54; Roma as problem 11; technologies of 27–28; *Xomá* 54, 61
civil servants/society actors, Spain 96, 99–105
colonialism 23
Comisión Población Excluida 101
conflicts, changing nature of 21–22
contained mobility 25–31
Council of Europe (COE) 23
crime/criminality: anti-Gypsyism 46–47; criminalizing effects of quotas 52; emergency measures 45–46; Italian emergency legislation 40–42; policing of Roma 12–13; Roma women in Spain 99, 105; Sarkozy rhetoric 43; securitization 38, 39; securitizing trends 26; stigma of mobility 11; transnatonal crime policy communitarized 25; Vincle program managing/controlling 104; *Xomá* in Italy 54
Croatia 70; deportees from Germany 74

cultural discourse, Roma representation in 36
cultural racism 69
Czechoslovakia 69

'dangerous black men' 41
Davison, S. 37
Dayton Agreement 75
De Certeau, M. 60, 85
Decade of Roma Inclusion 2005–2015 24, 38
dependency trap 24
deportability, permanent state of (Duldung arrangement) 30
deportation: 'Duldung' status 73–76; forced mobility 19, 26; France 43–44
development: biopoliticization of 24–25, 30–31; change in approach to 22; contained mobility 25–30; development-security nexus 18–34; institutional developmentalism 20–21; neoliberalization of 24; reproblematizing 21–25
differential inclusion 27, 29
'dilemmatic spaces' 29
Dominelli, L. 97
Douglas, M. 52
Du Bois, W.E.B. 2, 3
Dubois, V. 84
Duffield, M. 19, 21, 22, 23, 25, 27, 29, 30, 31
'Duldung' staus 30, 66, 73, 75

employment: A2 migrants in UK 81–95; activation work in Slovakia 28; deportees from Germany 74; employment rights stripped 12; European Employment Strategy 37; free movement and 10; labour migration in Yugoslavia 69–72; residency status and NINo in UK 81–94; Spain 100, 102; Xomá in Italy 54
Escobar, A. 18, 21
Essed, P. 84, 85
ethnicity 1–2, 7–8; Bosnia conflict 53; ethnic group in socialist Yugoslavia 70; ethnic minority 5; product of hegemonic relations 67–68; Roma and/or Gypsies belonging 51
ETP Slovakia 28
EU Observer 44
EU-ropean: citizens 11–12; 'problem' 3, 9
European apartheid 4
European Commission: 2004 report on Roma 20; admonished national governments 52; directive 2004/38 9–10; freezing of funds to Bosnia (BIH) 76; reaction to French evacuation memo 44
European Court of Human Rights (ECtHR) 75–76
European Court of Justice 44
'European minority' 5
European national identity 51–52
European Parliament: 2015 elections 40; human rights issue in Italy 41; Maroni speech 42; visa-free regime suspension 75

European Union (EU) 2, 35; development approaches 22; different Europes 52–53; enlargement and neoliberalism 37–39; Framework for National Roma Integration Strategies up to 2020 24; freedom of movement 3, 11–12, 25, 35–36, 38, 40–41, 43, 65–66; human rights framework 52; infringement proceedings against France 44; internal market 25; Maastricht Treaty 20; transitional restrictions 81–82; violation of laws by France 43
everyday racism 84–85, 91
eviction: display of power 60; neoliberal form of governance 36; state-enforced mobility 11, 19; Xomá move to avoid 56

family, Xomá in Rome 55–56
fascism 40, 42, 44
Fassin, É. 39, 44–45
Fekete, L. 3, 4, 7, 11, 52, 53, 97
Fineman, A.M. 99
fingerprints 41–42
Fini, Gianfranco 40
forced immobility 19, 26
Foucault, M. 20, 23, 42, 44
Fox, J. 13, 39, 82, 92
France: 2010 expulsion of Romani 26, 37, 43–44; 2007/8 Romani expulsions 40; bilateral agreement with Romania 30; infringement proceedings by EU 44; post-2007 Roma deportations 31; right-wing populism 36, 39, 40
freedom of movement 3, 11–12, 25, 35–36, 38, 40–41, 43
front-line workers (UK) 81–95; basis of decisions to help Roma 88; contradictions in narratives 87; dealing with A2 migrants in UK 86; decreasing credibility 90; wide areas of discretion 89

gağé 53, 56, 59
gender: 'dangerous black men' 41; politics of anti-Gypsyism 46–47; women Roma in Spain 96–108
General Direction of Services for Child: Protection (DGAIA) 104
Germany: asylum applicatons 30, 66, 73, 74–75, 76; bilateral agreement with Kosovo 30; bilateral agreement with Yugoslavia 71; deportations from 73–76; Duldung arrangement 30, 66, 73, 75; safe coutries list 74
Glick Schiller, N. 50–51, 55, 57
Global North/South 18–19, 23, 27
governmentality 42, 45, 50, 51, 52–53; Xomá movements and 60–61
Grenoble 43
Guglielmo, R. 5, 21

INDEX

Harney, N. 85
Hepworth, K. 5, 10, 11, 12, 35, 36, 37, 39, 41, 45
HMRC 81, 82, 87
Holocaust 2
Honig, B. 29
human rights: ECtHR 75; EU and respect for 52; French deportations 43, 44; Italan state of emergency 41; neoliberalism and 35; Roma in enlarged EU 20
human security 21, 22, 23, 24, 28, 31
Hungary 38, 39, 42, 69

immigration quotas 52
institutional developmentalism 20, 24
integration policies, failed 97
international governing organizations (IGOs) 18, 23, 24, 28
irregularization 26, 36, 37, 38, 45
Italy 35, 39, 71, 73; 2008 Roma expulsions 37; categorization of Gypsies/Roma/Nomads 54; emergency legislation 40–42; right-wing populism 40 *see also Xomá*

Járóka, Lívia 42

Korturare 57, 59
Kosovo 66, 70; bilateral agreement with Germany 30; conflict 68; German safe country list 74; Law on Readmission 73; Roma, Ashkali and Egyptian (RAE) displaced populations 72; URA 2 30
Krasniqi, G. 72
Kummrow, L. 66, 74, 75

labour, migrations in socialist Yugoslavia 70
Le Pen, Jean-Marie 40
Le Pen, Marine 40
legal aid withdrawal, front-line workers in UK 89
Lévi-Strauss, Claude 44
liberal interventionism 22
Lille 58, 59
liminal legality 67, 68
Ludford, Sarah 42, 44

Maastricht Treaty 20
Macedonia 40, 66, 70, 72, 76; asylum applications in Germany 74
Madrid 99, 100, 101, 102
Maroni, Roberto 42
marriage 104–105
Marseille 58
matter-without-place 52
McNevin, A. 45
media: A2 migrants 'moral panic' 86; anti-Gypsy rhetoric 38; French evacuation memo 43–44; Italian emergency legislation 41; post-Yugoslav Roma 66; stereotypes in 88
meritocracy 46
Mezzadra, S. 18, 27
migrant crisis 25–26, 52

migrant statuses 65–77; diverse in EU 76
migrants: borders between 'normal' and 'abnormal' 36–37; narratives of irregularity 37
migration, cultural characteristic of Roma 36
minimum wage 10, 28
minor mothers 104–105
'mobility' 9–13
Montenegro 55, 70, 74
Movimento Sociale Italiano 40
Mujić, Nazif 66, 76
multi-agency meetings (UK) 83, 86, 87, 89

Nacu, A. 10, 11, 35, 37, 39, 40, 43
'nation in excess' 4
nation-states, important role in contemporary Europe 50–51
National Alliance 40
nationalism 4–5; 'backdoor' in Hungary and Poland 39; methodological 50 *see also* populism
Neilson, B. 27
neoliberalism 35–47, 96–108; anti-Gypsyism 46–47; development and 19, 22, 24, 25; EU enlargement and 37–39; individualization 106; politics of EU 37–39; privatization of social services 101; securitization 39–44; unequal gender and racial relations 46
NGOs 28, 69, 72, 76, 96–106
NINo (National Insurance Number) 81, 82, 83, 87, 88, 89–90, 91
Nomad Emergency Decree 42
nomadism 5, 11, 12, 36, 87
non-refoulement 52, 60
Northern League *(Lega Nord)* 40

Open Society Institute (OSI) 23, 24
Organization for Security and Co-operation in Europe (OSCE) 20–21, 23, 40, 41

'pan-European racism' 11
Picker, G. 10, 35, 40
Pogge, T. 19
Poland 38, 39
police, deportations in France 43–44
political liberalism 35
populism 38–39; in France 40; in Italy 40
poverty 18–34; breaking the poverty circle 24; IGOs approach through development 18; racialization of 19
problematization 20, 26, 29, 31n1
Prodi, Romano 41
public-private partnerships (UK) 84

race 6–9; racial profiling 75
Reding, Viviane 44
refugees: staus in Germany 73, 74, 75; treatment by EU countries 51–52; war-refugee status lost 54 *see also* asylum

Reggaini, Giovanni 41
religious belief/faith 90–92
residency rights, uncertainty in UK 81–95
rhizome, *Xomá* presence as 59–61
Roma: 'culture' 8; 'European minority' classification 20; 'nation in excess' 4; problematization of 20
Roma church *(Khangheri)* 87, 90–91
Roma/Gypsies, problematic categories 51
Roma Korturare 57
romanes 83, 86, 89, 94n5
Romania/Romanian: bilateral agreement with France 30; expulsion of Romani migrants from France 40; Italian emergency legislation 40–42; 'Romanian Roma' 86–88; transitional restrictions in UK 81–82; two categories in Spain 101
Rome, *Xomá* in 50–64
ROMED initiative 24
rumour publics 84–86

Sarkozy, Nicolas 40, 43, 44
Saull, R. 39
Schengen 52, 68; German deportees 74; Treaty 25; visa liberalization 67, 74, 76
security/securitization: contained mobilty 25–30; development-security nexus 18–34; French deportations 43–44; irregularization and 37; Italian emergency legislation 40–42; post-1989 security agenda 20–21; reproblematizing 21–25; securitization of Roma mobility 38
self-reliance, development programs 24, 27, 28, 31
Serbia 40, 55, 66, 70, 72, 74, 76; asylum applications in Germany 74; deportees from Germany 74
Shire, G. 37
Shiva, V. 46
Sigona, N. 2, 3, 4, 12, 35, 36, 37, 38, 39, 40, 41, 44, 45, 52, 54, 66, 67, 68, 71, 73
Skopje 70
Slovakia 28, 38, 42, 69
social interventions, Roma women in Spain 96–108
social workers: cultural competences 97; discretionary powers 101; street level bureaucrats 97; surveillance and control by 104–105; women as target group 102
Spain 96–108; privatization of Social Services 101; state custody of children 105
state of exception (Agamben) 38, 42, 45, 46
stereotyping: Maroni's speech 42; Roma in UK media 88; *Xomá* in Rome 53–54
Stewart, M. 3, 36, 38–39, 51, 69
surveillance and control, Roma women in Spain 104–105
Šuto Orizari 70

third-country nationals, post-Yugoslav migrants 66, 68, 76
Third World 18–19, 22
tolerated status *see* 'Duldung' status
Topaana 70
transitional restrictions (UK qualifying status) 81–95
transnational agencies 23–24

UK Independence Party (UKIP) 6
United Kingdom, previous experiences understanding legal status in UK 90
United Nations 23; Sarkozy discriminatory policies in France 43; UNDP 24
URA 2 (Kosovo Return Project) 30

van Baar, H. 2, 3, 5, 7, 9, 10, 11, 12, 19, 20, 21, 23, 24, 25, 26, 27, 28, 29, 30, 36, 37, 38, 39, 46, 66
Vermeersch, P. 3, 4, 10, 38, 39, 97
Vincle Association 103–104; state custody of children 104
Vrăbiescu, I. 2, 3, 4, 8, 10, 11, 12, 98, 104
Vullnetari, J. 67, 68
vulnerability, migrant women in Spain 96–108

Waters, T. 5, 21
welfare state actors: residency rights in UK 81–95; women migrants in Spain 96–108
Willems, W. 7
women: 'dangerous black men' 41; identified by dress 86; poor migrants in Spain 96–108; *Xomá* extended family 55
Woodcock, S. 41
World Bank 23, 24
Worth, O. 39

Xarxa ROMEST 101
Xomá 50–62; arrival in Italy 55; extension of linkages 59–61; *familja* 57; homeland 59–60; labelled as immigrants 54; mobility and dispersion 56–57; patri-virilocality 55; response to biopolitical regime 60; transnationality 57–59
Xoraxané 53, 55, 57

Yugoslavia 21, 22, 30, 55, 57, 66; bilateral agreement with Germany 71; cross-border mobility under socialist 71; managing labour migration in socialist 69–72; post-war flight of Roma to Italy 40; Roma status after disintegration 72
Yuval-Davis, N. 84, 92, 97

Zemmour, Éric 5–6